A Journey Just Begun

Editor: Laura Harris
Design: Courtney Horner
Printer: Marquis

Library and Archives Canada Cataloguing in Publication

A journey just begun : the story of an Anglican sisterhood / the
Sisterhood of St. John the Divine.

Includes index.
Issued in print and electronic formats.
ISBN 978-1-4597-2369-6

1. Sisterhood of St. John the Divine--History. 2. Sisterhood of
St. John the Divine--Biography. 3. Anglican monasticism and
religious orders--Ontario--Toronto--History. I. Sisterhood of St. John
the Divine, author

BX5185.S58J69 2014   271'.98309713541   C2014-907095-0
                                              C2014-907096-9

1   2   3   4   5   19   18   17   16   15

   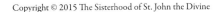

We acknowledge the support of the **Canada Council for the Arts** and the **Ontario Arts Council** for our publishing program. We also acknowledge the financial support of the **Government of Canada** through the **Canada Book Fund** and **Livres Canada Books**, and the **Government of Ontario** through the **Ontario Book Publishing Tax Credit** and the **Ontario Media Development Corporation**.

Care has been taken to trace the ownership of copyright material used in this book. The author and the publisher welcome any information enabling them to rectify any references or credits in subsequent editions.
J. Kirk Howard, President

All quotations from the Bible except the Psalms are from the *New Revised Standard Version Bible*, copyright © 1989 by the Division of Christian Education of the National Council of the Churches of Christ in the U.S, and are used by permission. All rights reserved.

Quotations from the Psalms are from the *Inclusive Language Psalter*, copyright © 2003 by the Sisterhood of St. John the Divine.

Unless otherwise noted, all photos are owned by the Sisterhood of St. John the Divine.
Title page photo: Michael Hudson

The publisher is not responsible for websites or their content unless they are owned by the publisher.

Printed and bound in Canada.

VISIT US AT
Dundurn.com | @dundurnpress | Facebook.com/dundurnpress | Pinterest.com/Dundurnpress

Dundurn
3 Church Street, Suite 500
Toronto, Ontario, Canada
M5E 1M2

THE SISTERHOOD OF ST. JOHN THE DIVINE

A Journey Just Begun

The Story of an Anglican Sisterhood

DUNDURN
TORONTO

To the memory of
SSJD Archivists extraordinaire:
Sister Thelma-Anne, SSJD,
Sister Margaret Mary, SSJD,
and Noreen Spencer-Nimmons
(Associate of SSJD and great-great niece of the Mother Foundress)

Contents

FOREWORD

My earliest recollection of the Sisters of St. John the Divine is of Sister Constance Murphy, who lived to be 109 years old. She had been invited by Bishop Leonard Hatfield, who had a great heart for the Sisters, to offer the meditations at a Church synod in the early 1980s. It was one of the earliest at which I was present as a young priest of the Diocese of Nova Scotia and Prince Edward Island. I was struck by her energy, enthusiasm, prayerfulness, and wisdom.

Years later, after I had become a bishop, I connected with the sisters in search of a quiet place for sabbath rest, reading, and prayer. I found that at St. John's House in St. Lambert in the Diocese of Montreal. How I enjoyed the train ride there and the warmth of the sisters' welcome and kind hospitality during my stay. It was in that house that I was admitted as an associate on March 17, 2000, along with my dear friend Barry Clarke, who would in time become the Bishop of Montreal. I cherish this association with SSJD, and am grateful for the sisters' care and prayer for me and my ministry.

These days, I have the privilege, from time to time, of presiding and preaching at the convent in Toronto. I enjoy an annual gathering with the sisters in their common room, chatting about what matters and ought to matter in the life and work of the Church "in and for the world."

My wife, Lynne, also has a very close relationship with the sisters. When we moved to Toronto she volunteered in their guest house and currently works in their fundraising department. Affectionately Lynne speaks of "her" sisters and in so doing has found herself called to be an oblate.

Our Church is so blessed by the work of this monastic community. Daily they lift the life of the world and the labours of the Church heavenward.

While prayer has always been their first and foremost work, the sisters have given themselves to numerous other ministries including nursing, tending the elderly, teaching, and working with the poor. They continue to provide pastoral care at St. John's Rehab, now part of Sunnybrook Health Sciences Centre.

The sisters travel to many places across the country to lead quiet days, retreats, and parish missions. Within the convent itself, they exercise a ministry of gracious hospitality and spiritual direction. In the quiet peacefulness of their house, one can withdraw from the noise and frenzied pace of the world and be still long enough to hear once again, or perhaps for the very first time, that still small voice of calm — the calm of God speaking to the heart of a pilgrim soul.

Archbishop Justin Welby, Archbishop of Canterbury, in conversation with Archbishop Fred Hiltz, Primate of the Anglican Church of Canada, at St. John's Convent in 2014.

Through the Sisterhood's annual "Women at a Crossroads" program, many women have discerned the nature of ministry to which God is calling them.

The sisters have a wide circle of associates, both women and men, and a growing number of oblates. More recently they have welcomed "alongsiders" — women who live with the sisters for a limited time and experience the daily round of prayer, community life, and good works in the convent and in the community.

In their 130 years, the Sisters of St. John the Divine have served the Church with great devotion and we in the Anglican Church of Canada and beyond have much for which to be grateful.

As the sisters keep this special anniversary, they are being very intentional in discerning their ministries for the future — in and out of the convent, for and through the Church in the service of God's mission in the world. In this hard work, in this holy task, they are of course trusting in the leading of the Holy Spirit. The wondrous ways in which She moves are perhaps best grasped, in so far as we are able, in the beautiful words of the hymn by Gordon Light:

> She comes sailing on the wind,
> her wings flashing in the sun,
> on a journey just begun, she flies on.
> And in the passage of her flight,
> her song rings out through the night;
> full of laughter, full of light, she flies on.[1]

The Most Reverend Fred Hiltz

PRIMATE, THE ANGLICAN CHURCH OF CANADA

PREFACE
Who Is St. John?

One of the most frequent questions asked of the sisters of St. John the Divine is: "Who is St. John the Divine?" It's helpful to know that the adjective *divine* does not signify divinity in this context; it is used to describe a theologian, and in the Orthodox Church, John the Divine is known as John the Theologian.

Our founder, Mother Hannah, chose the name St. John the Divine for the Sisterhood because she had worshipped in the London parish church of St. John the Divine in Kennington, when she and her husband lived in England. The church helped to form her spirituality, which in turn was passed to the Sisterhood.

In determining which John of the many Johns in the Bible is the Sisterhood's patron, we need to dig into current biblical scholarship. The gospel that we attribute to St. John was written well after the other three synoptic gospels of Matthew, Mark, and Luke. You can see plenty of similarities in those three gospel accounts, which use some common source materials. The gospel according to John is a more theological and mystical presentation of the good news of Jesus Christ, and presents many parables and stories unique to this gospel. But it probably was not written by John the Apostle as has traditionally been assumed.

Around the year 90 CE, there was a community of devout followers of "The Way," as Christians were known, who were expelled from the synagogues where they worshipped. These Christians had a connection to John the Apostle, one of the disciples listed in each of the other gospels, and their community came to be known as the Johannine community. Their understanding of Jesus' life and ministry as passed on to them by the Apostle John led several of them to write their own account of The Way. And that is the book we know as the gospel according to John. It was probably written about sixty years following the crucifixion.

The gospel presents a new creation; indeed the opening words of the gospel echo the first words of Genesis, revealing Jesus the Messiah as the light of the world:

> In the beginning was the Word, and the Word was with God, and the Word was God. He was in the beginning with God. All things came into being through him, and without him not one thing came into being. What has come into being in him was life, and the life was the light of all people. The light shines in the darkness, and the darkness did not overcome it. (John 1.1–5)

The gospel as a whole presents John the Apostle as a man who followed in Jesus' footsteps and learned the way of Jesus' prayer. And this is true also for the author of the letters of John. We read in the first letter of John:

> We declare to you what was from the beginning, what we have heard, what we have seen with our eyes, what we have looked at and touched with our hands, concerning the word of life.... This is the message we have heard from him and proclaim to you, that God is light and in him there is no darkness at all. (1 John 1:1, 5–6)

Whoever wrote the gospel and the letters of John certainly followed the tradition and theology of John the Apostle.

According to one tradition of the early Church, the "beloved disciple," often identified as the Apostle John and the one who reclined next to Jesus at the Last Supper, was the same John who went into exile on the island of Patmos, and authored the Book of Revelation. However, this identification is unlikely. The Revelation presents an apocalyptic vision of the end times and follows in the tradition of the Book of Daniel from the Hebrew scriptures. The author writes about the twelve apostles in the Revelation but does not include himself as one of them. His knowledge of the rites in the temple in Jerusalem and in-depth knowledge of the Hebrew scriptures has led scholars to speculate that he may have been a Palestinian Christian — and an entirely different John from the John who inspired the Johannine community.

What we do know is that John the Apostle was the brother of James; the two brothers left their father Zebedee's fishing business and followed Jesus with their whole heart. They were given the nickname *Boanerges*, meaning "Sons of Thunder," for their stormy temperaments, signalling their passionate love and zeal for Christ as they left everything to follow him and worked to proclaim the good news of Jesus Christ.

For Mother Hannah, however, following the scholarship of her time, there was one John who wrote the gospel, the three letters, and the Revelation. She embraced the spirituality of the gospel and the letters with their emphasis on God as light, and the intimate and mystical relationship to which God calls us; and she was also influenced by the vision of heaven and the new creation in the Book of Revelation. All of this she would have experienced in the parish church in Kennington where the John of the gospel and letters was understood to be the same as the John of Revelation. The sisters of today, while they have the benefit of modern biblical scholarship, nevertheless embrace the spirituality of the Johns and the Johannine community.

The heart of John's gospel and Johannine spirituality is expressed in the well-loved verse from John 3:16 — "God so loved the world that he gave his only Son, so that everyone who believes in him may not perish but may have eternal life." (John 3:16). This love is passionate, open, and inviting for the whole world, with no exclusions. The life of John the Apostle exemplifies this love. As we remember him standing at the foot of the cross, watching his best friend and beloved teacher die, we are invited to delve deeply into the mystery of Jesus' death and resurrection through our own life of prayer to find the ultimate message of God's love for the world.

The sisters' sense of mission and service springs from that mystery and from that moment at the foot of the cross when Jesus tells John to take his mother Mary as his own mother and into his home:

> When Jesus saw his mother and the disciple whom he loved standing beside her, he said to his mother, "Woman, here is your son." Then he said to the disciple, "Here is your mother."

And from that hour the disciple took her into his own home.
(John 19:26–27)

In the Lady Chapel at St. John's Convent you will see a beautiful stained glass window that depicts this scene of John taking Mary to his home (see image on page 232). It is an image that has become an inspiration of hospitality and healing to the Sisterhood, and of the sisters' love in action through service to others.

Another important theme in John's gospel is the emphasis on obedience to God's will. From the miracle of the water made into wine at the wedding feast in Cana — one of the stories unique to John's gospel — the Sisterhood draws its motto, "Do whatever he tells you" (John 2:5). Another work of art, a large icon of St. John the Divine in the convent lobby, centres on this motto and embraces in its symbolism the writings of the gospel, the letters, and the Revelation (see image on page 148).

In the sisters' commitment to a life of love, prayer, and service, we strive to emulate the passion and zeal of John the Apostle; to build the community of love described in the letters of John; and to respond to the joy and challenge of the vision of the end times and the new creation in the Revelation of John. This we have done for the last 130 years, and this we will continue to do as we read, study, and pray with the writings attributed to John. But we have only just begun.

Sr. Elizabeth Ann Eckert
REVEREND MOTHER, THE SISTERHOOD OF ST. JOHN THE DIVINE

Part I
Sacred Time

INTRODUCTION

In 1509, Henry VIII of England came to the throne and nothing was ever the same again in the Church of England. Before Henry, the Celtic and Roman Christian traditions were held in a creative tension and the average worshipper was totally unaware of the political conflict between the government of England and the powerful hierarchy in Rome. The average worshipper would also have been ignorant of the radical ideas brewing on the continent with Luther in Germany and Zwingli and Calvin in Switzerland, who were calling for a new emphasis on the theology of God's free grace, for translations of the Bible into the local languages so that ordinary people could read it, for worship in the language of the people rather than in Latin, and for more autonomy in the leadership of the Church in their countries.

In the meantime, Henry fought with the Pope over the issue of divorce — a personal issue for him, but one that brought the conflict with Rome to a head. Ultimately, it led to a declaration of independence for the Church in England, and in 1534 an Act of Parliament transferred the authority for the English Church to the king.

It was the beginning of a complete revolution, both good and bad. Among the good was the publication of the first Book of Common Prayer in 1549, allowing the English people to worship in their own language. Several English translations of the Bible culminated in the King James Version in 1611, one of the great monuments to the English language.

The most tragic outcome of the English Reformation was the dissolution of the monasteries. Between 1534 and 1536 Henry confiscated all the property belonging to the monasteries in England, where the consecrated members had followed a life of prayer, served the poor, and preserved British and European civilization in dark times. The monasteries had been the libraries, schools, hospitals, food banks, and shelters of their day. Without an appreciation of their significance, Henry managed to expel all the monks and nuns in England, Wales, Ireland, and Scotland, compelling them either to flee to France as religious refugees or to wander the roads of England begging. There was nothing left for them in the British Isles, and for the next three hundred years there were few guest houses or orphanages or hostels for the poor. Most of what we regard today as the social safety net was gone, along with the daily round of prayer that had sustained ordinary citizens throughout Britain.

By the middle of the nineteenth century, a group of theologians at Oxford University wanted to recover some of the catholic traditions of the English Church that had been lost at the time of the Reformation in England. They also wanted to provide help for the desperately poor in England's industrial cities. Out of these concerns arose the Oxford Movement. The theologians, clergy, and lay people who formed this powerful movement helped to re-establish religious orders in the Church of England — a benefit to both the Church and society at large with their service to the poor, their learning, their art and their music.

The Anglican sisterhoods that developed out of this movement were the immediate predecessors of the Sisterhood of St. John the Divine. There is a common belief that women joined these new orders because they wanted to lead a contemplative life of prayer. But in fact the motivation for the earliest sisterhoods was very different. The Oxford Movement provided the theological justification for sisterhoods: Jesus himself had lived a celibate life of service to the poor, in common with a band of friends. The Christians of the first century had shared their property and cared for the poor among them. Now in late-nineteenth-century England women who did not want to be tied down to the confined role of the Victorian wife or daughter were drawn to a new vision made possible by the sisterhoods: caring for the poor, living in a community of friends and co-workers, and using their gifts in a bigger arena than the family home. Of all these motivations, one of the strongest was service to the poor. As Susan Mumm, a sociologist and historian of the earliest sisterhoods says:

There is evidence that for many first-generation sisters the impetus to join was an urgent desire to cease being collaborators with social and economic injustice; they were no longer "content smilingly to lie on a bed of roses while they know that thousands around them sleep on thorns." The single-minded search for personal sanctity sometimes imagined by outsiders was a rarity in the early days of sisterhoods. In all the successful early Anglican communities, the desire to do good weighed more heavily than any devotional impulse.[1]

By the second generation of sisterhoods in England, that priority was starting to shift. As Mumm points out, the new communities that were formed in the last quarter of the nineteenth century, and the newer members of already-established communities, were focused on a life of prayer first, and social work (or teaching or hospital work, depending on the sisterhood) second: "By this time, as the embryonic welfare state was being discussed with increasing seriousness, and as opportunities for women's employment grew ... [women] were now much more concerned with the development of the inner life than had been earlier recruits."[2]

Into this shakeup of Victorian values stepped Mother Hannah. In 1884, the newly founded Sisterhood of St. John the Divine was clearly in the second generation of sisterhoods. Mother Hannah and others associated with the early days of the Sisterhood of St. John the Divine talked often about the importance of prayer and community life coming first, and about how the sisters' active ministry must be secondary, however important it was. The frequency with which Mother Hannah and others reminded the sisters of this priority, however, is an indicator that not every sister agreed, and many came with a powerful motivation for a life of service. Throughout the story of the Sisterhood, over the past 130 years, the community has held the values of prayer and service in a creative tension. As the sisters look to the future, that tension will probably always exist if the community is to grow (spiritually and numerically) and remain healthy. Like the Anglican Church that grew out of the English Reformation, the community strives to follow the *via media*, not sitting on the fence, but balancing the life of prayer and service, the best of traditional music and contemporary music, holding to basic Christian beliefs while open to new understandings. They have also had powerful models to follow in the Roman Catholic communities in Quebec and Ontario, which were opening schools and hospitals in the mid-nineteenth century, and in Roman Catholic monastic communities.

Above all, the sisters' values and style of life are rooted in the *Rule of St. Benedict* — a guide for monks and nuns written in the sixth century. Although St. Benedict called it "a little rule for beginners," it has had a big impact on religious communities in the centuries since. Mother Hannah based the sisters' first *Rule of Life* on Benedict's Rule, and it has also been embraced in recent years by lay people who find its emphasis on a balanced life — prayer, service, community, and hospitality — helps shape and support their own lives. Benedictine values are gospel values lived out in community. And the sisters' history is the story of how they have tried to be faithful to those values.

Join us now as we journey through the history and the future of the Sisterhood of St. John the Divine. In Part One we view the sisters' lives through the historical and social lens of each of the Reverend Mothers who led the community through vastly different periods. In Part Two we tour the Sisterhood's convent and learn how the values of monasticism shape the architecture of a religious home. It is a journey that began 130 years ago and yet, in another sense, a journey just begun.

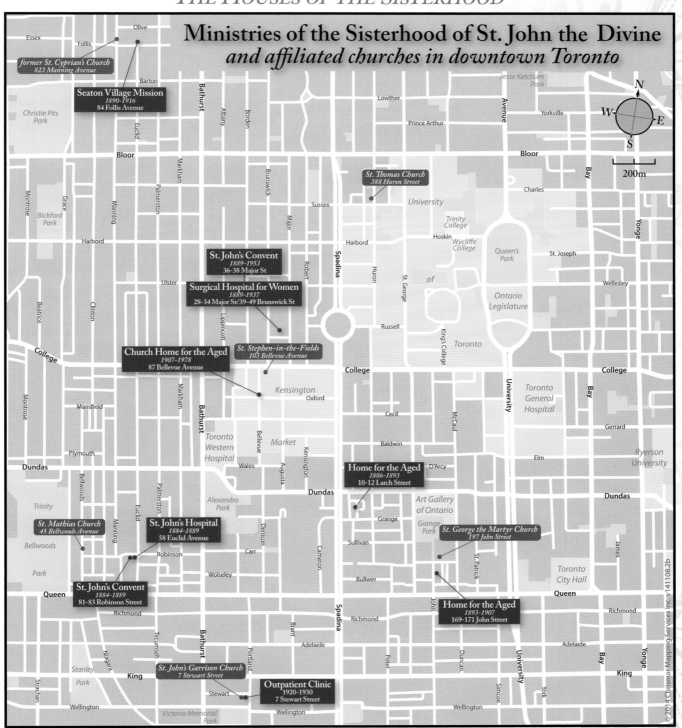

The Houses of the Sisterhood

Ministries of the Sisterhood of St. John the Divine
and affiliated churches in downtown Toronto

former St. Cyprian's Church
823 Manning Avenue

Seaton Village Mission
1890–1916
84 Follis Avenue

St. Thomas Church
388 Huron Street

St. John's Convent
1889–1953
36–38 Major St

Surgical Hospital for Women
1889–1937
28–34 Major St/39–49 Brunswick St

Church Home for the Aged
1907–1978
87 Bellevue Avenue

St. Stephen-in-the-Fields
103 Bellevue Avenue

Home for the Aged
1886–1893
10–12 Larch Street

St. Mathias Church
45 Bellwoods Avenue

St. John's Hospital
1884–1889
58 Euclid Avenue

St. George the Martyr Church
197 John Street

St. John's Convent
1884–1889
81–83 Robinson Street

Home for the Aged
1893–1907
169–171 John Street

St. John's Garrison Church
7 Stewart Street

Outpatient Clinic
1920–1930
7 Stewart Street

© 2014 Chrismar Mapping Services Inc. v141108.2b

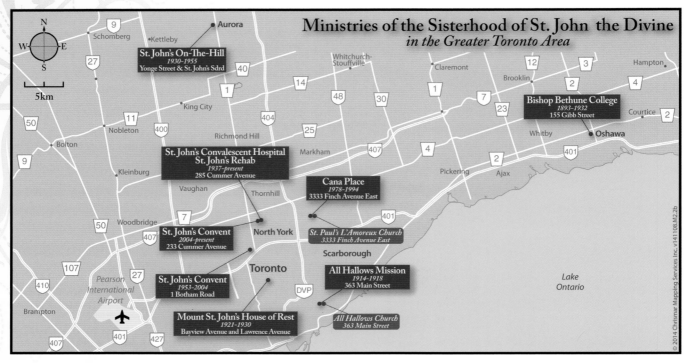

Ministries of the Sisterhood of St. John the Divine
in the Greater Toronto Area

5km

St. John's On-The-Hill
1930-1955
Yonge Street & St. John's Sdrd

Bishop Bethune College
1893-1932
155 Gibb Street

St. John's Convalescent Hospital
St. John's Rehab
1937-present
285 Cummer Avenue

Cana Place
1978-1994
3333 Finch Avenue East

St. John's Convent
2004-present
233 Cummer Avenue

St. Paul's L'Amoreux Church
3333 Finch Avenue East

St. John's Convent
1953-2004
1 Botham Road

All Hallows Mission
1914-1918
363 Main Street

Mount St. John's House of Rest
1921-1930
Bayview Avenue and Lawrence Avenue

All Hallows Church
363 Main Street

Lake Ontario

Schomberg · Aurora · Kettleby · Whitchurch-Stouffville · Claremont · Brooklin · Hampton · King City · Nobleton · Bolton · Richmond Hill · Kleinburg · Vaughan · Thornhill · Markham · Pickering · Ajax · Whitby · Oshawa · Courtice · Woodbridge · North York · Scarborough · Toronto · Brampton

Pearson International Airport

DVP

© 2014 Chrismar Mapping Services Inc. v141108.M2.2b

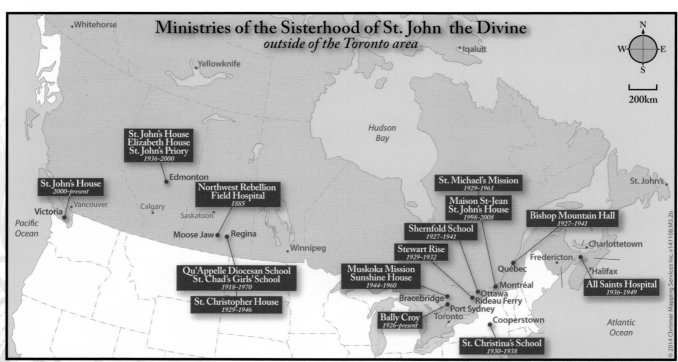

Ministries of the Sisterhood of St. John the Divine
outside of the Toronto area

200km

Whitehorse · Iqaluit · Yellowknife · St. John's

St. John's House
Elizabeth House
St. John's Priory
1936-2000

St. John's House
2000-present

Northwest Rebellion
Field Hospital
1885

St. Michael's Mission
1929-1961

Maison St-Jean
St. John's House
1998-2008

Bishop Mountain Hall
1927-1941

Shernfold School
1927-1941

Stewart Rise
1929-1932

Qu'Appelle Diocesan School
St. Chad's Girls' School
1918-1970

Muskoka Mission
Sunshine House
1944-1960

All Saints Hospital
1936-1949

St. Christopher House
1929-1946

Bally Croy
1926-present

St. Christina's School
1930-1938

Edmonton · Calgary · Saskatoon · Moose Jaw · Regina · Winnipeg · Victoria · Vancouver · Pacific Ocean · Hudson Bay · Québec · Montréal · Ottawa · Rideau Ferry · Bracebridge · Port Sydney · Toronto · Cooperstown · Fredericton · Charlottetown · Halifax · Atlantic Ocean

© 2014 Chrismar Mapping Services Inc. v141108.M3.2b

OF SEEDS AND GROWTH, 1884–1916
Mother Foundress Hannah

1

Most religious communities begin with an individual's resolute belief that they have been singularly called by God to establish one. Such was not the case with the Sisterhood of St. John the Divine: Canada's first Anglican community of sisters sprang to life when a church committee cornered a reluctant widow who was trying to leave the country.

Of course, there was much more to it than that. The Sisterhood's beginning is the story of a great need being answered by a woman whose experience and circumstances ultimately led her to respond unselfishly. It is a story that illustrates how the mission of the community was shaped, and it is a story that mirrors the experience of many of the community's members, who were as reticent and as surprised as their foundress to be called to the convent.

The sixth child and third daughter of John Grier and Eliza Lilias Geddes, Sarah Hannah Roberta Grier was born October 28, 1837, at Carrying Place, Ontario, part of a former portage route between the Bay of Quinte and Lake Ontario. By the time Hannah was in her teens, the family had moved to the larger and more bustling town of Belleville, where her father served as rector of St. Thomas' Church.

John Grier was an Irish-born, Scottish Presbyterian graduate of Glasgow University. He joined the Anglican missionary organization known as the Society for the Propagation of the Gospel and was dispatched to Canada in 1823 where he was ordained deacon, then priest, and posted to Carrying Place, considered at that time to be the Ontario outback. He married Eliza Geddes, an army surgeon's daughter, in 1827.

The Griers were a large, boisterous family brimming with fun and Irish humour. A blind woman who worked in the Grier household remarked aloud one day: "I was

working at the Griers' on Monday, and they are such a wild, noisy lot of young ones — boys and girls laughing and rushing up and down stairs, chasing one another about the house. I thought that when their pa came in surely now there would be some peace and quietness — but no! he was as bad as any of them and there was more racket than ever." The blind woman realized too late that she had made her remarks to the Griers themselves. That she was able to keep her job says something about her employers' easy-going nature and mischievous sense of humour. One can imagine the Griers bursting to share the anecdote with family and friends.

It is not surprising, then, that Hannah was naturally predisposed to practical jokes and possessed a quick wit. She most certainly was not the type of girl who showed signs of early saintliness, nor was she pegged by local busybodies as having a great future in the church. One Sunday, at the age of six, Hannah begged to be excused from attending church, pleading an imaginary headache. She and her brother then proceeded to spend their time cutting up pillows from a spare bedroom so

Mother Hannah.

that Hannah could use the feathers to decorate her dolls' bonnets. As was expected in Victorian times, the children were punished, but one gets the sense that their parents appreciated the frivolity of the event. In later years, Hannah valued the lessons learned from loving parents who could delight in children's creative behaviour while also instilling values of truth and obedience.

Hannah's father was busy in the parish and her mother worked to raise awareness and funds for various charitable ventures. This service-focused upbringing informed Hannah's character and her life's calling. Even as a young woman she was drawn to helping the poor and the sick in her father's parish.

The Griers' rectory became a popular spot for the young Englishmen who were employed to build the Grand Trunk Railway between Belleville and Kingston. Between intervals of work they congregated at the Grier home to dance, play croquet, and generally enjoy the company of the young women of the neighbouring towns. It was during this time that Hannah caught the eye of one of the young men, Charles Horace Coome, a talented British engineer who had apprenticed on the construction of London's Crystal Palace. Hannah and Charles became engaged when she was nineteen, and they married two years later, on July 23, 1859. The newlyweds made their home in Kingston for several years before Charles was recalled to London, England.

It was a good marriage. The couple was well off and well liked, and their unstuffy, fun-loving nature endeared them to everyone. But their happiness was marred by the miscarriage of their only child, and it plunged Hannah into a long and painful convalescence and depression, exacerbated. The couple's devastation at learning that they would never be able to have children.

When Hannah regained her health, she found herself drawn to the community of St. Mary the Virgin, Wantage, which ran a mission for the poor not far from the southeast London district of Kennington where the Coomes resided. Hannah threw herself into parish work, helping those on the fringes of society who needed both care and an advocate. She made friends with the sisters and forged what would be a lifelong bond with them.

In the early 1870s, Charles and Hannah moved from London to Wrexham, in north Wales, where they indulged their love of nature by hiking the undulating trails of the Welsh countryside and coastline. Around this time, Charles' health began to fail and although he continued to work and accept commissions, his lack of energy was worryingly noticeable. On a business trip back to southern Ontario in 1877, Charles became so ill that he and Hannah diverted their journey and headed immediately to the Chicago home of Charles' relatives. There, he was diagnosed with advanced cancer.

In Chicago, Hannah nursed her husband, and during the interludes of care she resolved that after his death she would return to England and commit her energy and talent to God's service with the community of St. Mary the Virgin, Wantage. Back in their London days, Charles had often joked that Hannah spent so much time with the sisters that he fully expected to arrive home from work one day to find that she had joined the community. At the age of forty-one, as she faced the prospect of her husband's death, the religious life became a viable alternative to widowhood.

When Charles died, Hannah did not return to England immediately but stayed on with his relatives in Chicago. She made friends among that city's artistic and ecclesiastical circles and put her formidable talent for church embroidery to use at the city's cathedral, where she made altar frontals and hangings. The quality of her work was so impressive that she was offered (but politely declined) the job of director at the Chicago School of Decorative Art.

Hannah was, in fact, rather accomplished in a number of areas besides embroidery. She would have learned about the Bible, church history, theology, and the devotional life from her father, as well as the practicalities of mission work in the parish. From her mother she would have learned a great deal about household management. Like other accomplished women in Victorian times, she knew the sisterhoods were a place where women's talents and training could be well used. By 1881, Hannah was ready to return to England. The sisters at St. Mary, Wantage, had accepted her request to join their community and she was eager to start her life with them. En route to England, she stopped off in Toronto to say goodbye to her family. It was a side trip that would alter the course of her life.

During these same years, a cauldron of change was bubbling in the Church of England in response to the Oxford Movement of the 1830s, which had revived public interest in monasticism. What began as a reaction against the British government's proposal to restructure the Church's hierarchy and make changes to the leasing of Church land had turned into a mobilized group decrying the watering down of Church tradition. The disappearance of rich medieval practices and pageantry and the loss of monasteries, convents, friaries, and priories during

Henry VIII's Reformation began to trouble the Victorian psyche. There were calls for a return to some of the Catholic traditions, leading to a rise in Anglo-Catholicism, and the founding of religious orders for men and women in the Church of England. Its charismatic leader was John Henry Newman, an Oxford priest, but at the height of the movement — and to the stunned amazement of all — Newman left the Church of England and was received into the Roman Catholic Church (he was beatified by Pope Benedict XVI in 2010). The torch of the Oxford Movement passed to fellow Oxfordite Edward Pusey, a priest and an academic.

In addition to to the renewed interest in liturgy and religious orders, many followers of the Oxford Movement were deeply concerned for and involved in works of social justice. Revitalizing the Church meant, for many, following more closely in the footsteps of Jesus of Nazareth, with his love for the poor and the needy.

By the late-nineteenth century, the Oxford Movement had reached Canada, where the idea of reviving some of the ancient church practices and traditions began to percolate in the minds of Canadian Anglicans. Many saw the spiritual and practical benefits that religious communities could provide in a growing country like Canada.

By the 1880s, a committee of Toronto Anglicans had spent the better part of the previous decade in search of a British or American professed sister who could establish an order of Anglican sisters in Canada. Unfortunately, they could not find a suitable candidate.

This was the environment into which Hannah arrived when she returned to Toronto in September of 1881. She was looking forward to spending a bit of time with her sister Rose Grier, who was headmistress of Bishop Strachan School, a girls' boarding school established for the daughters of Anglican clergy. Rose Grier also happened to be a member of the committee working to establish a sisterhood in Canada. When she knew Hannah was going to be in Toronto, she organized a garden party. It is not known whether Rose had an ulterior motive in mind or whether it was all sheer coincidence, but when the committee members were introduced to Hannah at the garden party they immediately saw in her the answer to their prayers.

Hannah, however, wasn't so sure. She was preparing to enter an established community with built-in companionship, ready-made buildings and chapel, music, routines, traditions, mission, and *Rule of Life*. Furthermore, she wasn't even a sister; and yet here she was being courted to start a religious order. From scratch!

Hannah consulted her friends and spiritual advisors on both sides of the Atlantic. All agreed that this was a distinct calling — a vocation within a vocation — that she should not pass up. They also urged her to undertake her religious training in the United States rather than in England because the religious and social conventions in the United States were more like those in Canada.

So, the unlikely widow with plans to slip quietly into religious life in England with the community of St. Mary the Virgin, found herself the following June in Peekskill, New York, with a different community of Saint Mary, accepted into its novitiate for two years of training in the spiritual and practical life of a religious.

In the meantime, the committee of clergy and lay Church leaders who had enticed Hannah to take on this challenging vocation began meeting in earnest, to gain support for the project and most importantly to raise funds. Sister Eleanora, the author of *Hannah Grier Coome: A Memoir*, which chronicles the early days of the Sisterhood, tells of this committee's interesting work. A seminal meeting was held of 250 supporters from Toronto and distant cities such as Hamilton and Kingston at St. George's Schoolhouse[1] on April 17, 1882. Many leaders of the Church, both in Canada and in the United States (where women's religious communities had already been established), spoke passionately in favour of the project.

The Reverend J.D. Cayley, rector of St. George's Church, spoke convincingly in favour of women's communities and the importance not only of the work they could do, but the quality of a life of prayer and what that could mean for the Church: "There is one branch of work which in this Diocese and Country has not yet received a proper share of attention. I mean the association of women, not only in the outward work of the church, but in the Life of Devotion, the aiding, strengthening, and sanctifying of that work."[2]

At the same meeting, the Reverend Provost Body spoke even more powerfully on behalf of women's leadership in the Church:

> I think that on the whole, we may congratulate ourselves on *one* characteristic of the times we live in, namely, that the work of women in every department of life is coming to the fore. In these days we hear a great deal about the higher education of women and of the influence which they are to wield in the political and social world, and I think we need to be reminded, and

it makes one ashamed to remember, that in such an old-fashioned book as the New Testament, we find the work of women set forth as one of the foremost means of strength in the first days of the Church. We need to be reminded that the modern movement, for winning back for woman the place that rightly belongs to her, is only restoring to us what we, in our Branch of the Catholic Church have, in a great measure, lost, namely the peculiar and distinctive work of women. We do not need to be reminded of the women who ministered to Our Lord, or of the Deaconesses, a distinctive Order in the Primitive Church.[3]

At another meeting, as recounted later by Sister Eleanora, Mrs. Georgina Broughall, got straight to the point about

the great help sisters would give by their work in this place; [she] spoke of the work and continuance of bands of devoted women from the days of the early church until the Reformation ... [and] concluded by urging that as women just devoting themselves to work give up all for Christ, they are entitled to the support afforded by a small endowment fund which it is needful to raise, namely $25,000."[4]

That day forty-five people agreed to serve on a fundraising committee, most from Toronto, some from other places in southern Ontario, and one from Michigan.

With the support of this remarkable group of dedicated men and women, Hannah could confidently pursue her training for her unique vocation as the foundress of the first sisterhood in Canada.

She took to religious life as if she had been born to it. Upon her arrival at St. Mary's in June 1882, she was dismayed to discover that she was being put in charge of all the housekeeping while the sister responsible was temporarily away — an overwhelming task for a newcomer — but she soldiered on. She honed her skills in needlework, served as sacristan and housemistress, worked with delinquent girls, and received professional nurse's training. She didn't lose any of her spirited personality and was apparently a unique and rare specimen prompting her Novice Mistress to wonder "why she was sent to me to be trained." A fellow novice recalled that "our beloved Novice Mistress held her up to us as an example many times" and "wondered what training could she need for she was a model of recollection and dignity ... charity and sweetness ... a soul living in the remembrance of the indwelling Christ."[5]

Sister Eleanora noted:

> the Novice Mistress was a remarkably saintly and spiritual woman, but without the keen sense of humour which marked both the Reverend Mother at Peekskill and our own Mother, so that the witty sayings of the latter were not always appreciated, and her buoyant spirit was thought to need some discipline. This seems to have been the only fault to find, however, and her laborious Novitiate was a remarkably happy one, and all too short.[6]

Two years later, on September 8, 1884, Hannah made her profession vows at Peekskill in the presence of the Bishop of Toronto. She earned the distinction of being one of the few women in history to be professed as a sister and simultaneously become the Mother Superior of a community.

Mother Hannah was very clear about the ideals for her community:

> The Life of Prayer and Devotion must come first, or the community will soon sink down into a society of persons living together for the work they can do, instead of a Society gathered together in the Church to live in loving devotion to Almighty God, irrespective of the work each member may accomplish. From this side of the Sister's life she draws her courage, and her inspiration for her Active Works of Charity: teaching, nursing, ministering to the fallen, the aged, and the poor. But these works, admirable as they are, rank second in importance; for she who does them does them because she is a Sister. These very things are being done every day by devoted women who are not called to a Sister's life; to do them does not constitute a Sister. The distinctive feature in a Sister is this, that she has chosen a State of Life.[7]

Striking a balance between prayer and work became a constant theme in the early days of the Sisterhood (a tension that continues to this day), as the sisters were constantly called upon to address the needs of the poor, the elderly, the ill, and the injured. But Mother Hannah was uncompromising in her strong belief that the sisters had chosen "a state of life" and not a job or career. This principle would keep the sisters grounded for the next 130 years — particularly as the temptation to do "good works" at the expense of prayer was always present.

The newly minted Mother Hannah returned to Toronto with the only other sister in her new community, Novice Aimée. They lived at Bishop Strachan School with Mother Hannah's biological sister, Rose, while the dedicated band of women who were to become the Sisterhood's first associates raised money to purchase a semi-detached house on Robinson Street and prepared it for its new owners. A few months later, on December 27, the Feast of St. John the Evangelist, the Sisterhood of St. John the Divine was officially declared established by the Bishop of Toronto. The community's name came from the church that Mother Hannah had attended in the London parish of Kennington where she had received so much spiritual sustenance during her years in England. Now, as she stood alongside the bishop and Novice Aimée, she could certainly be forgiven for wondering how this was all going to work out.

Thankfully, she had the Reverend Ogden Pulteney Ford to lean on. Ford was raised outside of Toronto, in Brockville, not far from where Mother Hannah grew up. A priest at Holy Trinity, St. Matthias, and St. Luke's churches in Toronto, all in the "high church" tradition, he was considered a brilliant scholar as well as a man of

The first convent on Robinson Street as the building is today.

31

wisdom and thoughtfulness. He had a guiding influence on the establishment and development of the Sisterhood, and in the Sisterhood's early years he was both confidante and spiritual director for Mother Hannah. She was in need of both.

In those days, religious communities were not greeted with open arms by everyone; there was a streak of hostility aimed at them, especially those set up for women. Horror stories of Roman Catholic orders kidnapping unwilling candidates were relayed to the nodding heads of those who were convinced that no good ever came out of religious communities.

The Evangelical Churchman included a fascinating article cautiously acknowledging the benefits of sisterhoods:

> An effort is being made to establish a sisterhood in the City of Toronto. That ladies, without home ties or relative duties, should devote themselves to ministries of love among the poor, the sick and the ignorant, should receive special training for these duties, and should live together in a home whose appointments are marked by regularity and sanctified by the Word of God and by prayer, is in all respects unexceptionable and worthy of praise. The deaconesses and trained nurses both of Germany and of England have and are doing noble work. Protestant churches might well emulate the wisdom of Rome in this matter and learn how to use to greater advantage, the gifts with which the gentler sex have been endowed, in works of philanthropy.[8]

But great concern was expressed as well. A report from the Rochester Conference in England was quoted in *The Evangelical Churchman* the following year:

> There are two very strong objections to such an institution ... the one is the proposal to bind the sisters by vows to a celibate and conventual life; the other is to the whole system of so-called religious seclusion. We have not a word to say against the association of women of suitable age and under suitable circumstances, in order to be able the better to undertake some work in which all are interested, but such associations ought to be voluntary

and not cemented with artificial ties, and kept together by the bond of a vow laid on the conscience of each member.[9]

Mother Hannah experienced first-hand this backlash as the associates looked for a suitable convent. It seemed only the parish of St. Matthias — the one where Ogden Ford worked — would accept them.

As she and Novice Aimée made their rounds wearing long black habits, passersby sometimes taunted them. The habit was not that different from what secu-

The Reverend Ogden P. Ford.

lar women were wearing in those days, but the sight of women attired in religious uniforms stirred unholy sentiments. Assuming the women were Roman Catholic, hecklers called them "papists." (Toronto was an "Orange" city in those days.[10])

Still, there were many who supported the sisters; some of those who were skeptical to begin with came to appreciate the extraordinary sacrifice of these compassionate and capable women as they went about the city caring for the poor and dispossessed. Even the Orangemen — who were initially so vehemently opposed to the sisters' living and working in St. Matthias parish that they threatened to burn down their house — later became their supporters. At their annual meeting a few months after the sisters moved in, the Orangemen "voted the offering taken at their Religious Service to be given for the work of the sisters of St. John the Divine; some of their friends and acquaintances having received the ministrations of the sisters in the meantime."[11]

The sisters' reputation spread quickly far beyond Toronto, and ironically the outbreak of social and political unrest in western Canada enhanced their reputation for responding to human need compassionately and efficiently. The North-West Rebellion had started, and troops and supplies were being rushed to Saskatchewan to restore order. An urgent call went out for nurses and medical services.

The Minister of Militia, the Honorable A.P. Caron, was asked by Bishop Arthur Sweatman of Toronto if he would accept the services of volunteer nurses for the base hospital to be set up in Moose Jaw, Saskatchewan. The reply was "No volunteer nurses. If you can send an organized body under an organized head, they will be welcome."[12] At that, the diocesan synod asked sisters to take on the challenge, and they agreed, in return for safe passage and rations.

In May 1885, Mother Hannah, Novice Aimée, two postulants, and three nursing graduates left Toronto and set off by train and boat for Moose Jaw. While crossing Lake Superior, Mother Hannah took the scissors to her long dark hair, dropping it overboard. It was as much a matter of practicalities as it was a gesture of sacrifice. It may also have been a personal statement, definitively signaling her break from her past life for this new, adventurous one.

Sisters, nurses, and patients in front of the soldiers' hospital in Moose Jaw.

When the sisters and nurses arrived in Moose Jaw, a small ceremony was held to welcome them, and with a little flourish they were handed the keys to a large, tar-papered building. Opening the door, they discovered it was completely empty. The sisters were expected to create hospital facilities from scratch. Starting from scratch was becoming a frequent theme for Mother Hannah.

Soon forty beds were installed, and just as quickly all forty were filled with sick and wounded soldiers. Outside the makeshift hospital a marquee was erected, and tables and chairs were set up as a recreation tent. The wounded were helped outside at every opportunity to enjoy the fresh air. This homey arrangement was pure Mother Hannah. Among the "vital" supplies she had brought from Toronto were magazines, newspapers, snack food, chessboards and cribbage boards, books, and pipes and tobacco, for she knew that it takes more than medication and surgical tools to heal people; it takes compassion and certain little comforts to make the sick feel valued and to speed their recovery. Mother Hannah believed in looking after the "whole soldier," not just his injuries. This revolutionary concept set the Sisterhood apart from other health care practitioners of the time, and it became a hallmark of the sisters' holistic approach to medicine.

Eventually, word got out about this hardy and independent-thinking band of Anglican sisters from Toronto who were nursing the soldiers involved in quashing the Rebellion, and women from across the country and from all religious denominations chipped in, sending supplies, fruit, fresh eggs, and cake.

It was a short uprising — only three months — but it was a pivotal experience for the Sisterhood: it established the community's raison d'etre, and gave it a national profile. As a gesture of thanks for the Sisterhood's work in the field, Mother Hannah was presented with a medal from the Government of Canada, a token that remains a priceless memento among the Sisterhood's collection of honours. An article in the St. Matthias magazine of July 1885 reflected the increased acceptance of the sisters:

> We are glad to announce the return of the sisters and nurses from the North-West. Their work was greatly appreciated by all parties, from the General-in-Command to the humblest private in the Hospital Ward. Certainly, the practical work they have done there is but another evidence of what organized women's work can accomplish, and ought to go far to break down the unreasoning prejudice which people have to the existence of Sisterhoods within the English Church, and to win for it a pecuniary support sufficient to place it on a sure and stable foundation. The sisters come back to increased work.[13]

It was this increased work that concerned Ogden Ford. Sister Eleanora said he worried that "before long they would have no Sisterhood, because too much was being demanded of them. He said this seriously, because it should be remembered that their number was small (six to be exact) at the time, and they could not do everything at once. He concluded an earnest address by dwelling on the fact that the motive of the whole work was *love to Christ.*"[14]

The tension between prayer and active work continued. The sisters followed a *"Rule of Life"*[15] that Mother Hannah had adapted from the Peekskill community, which called for hard work on the part of all; it also called for the equally demanding work of prayer — altogether, eight services a day in the chapel.

While the sisters in Moose Jaw had been ministering to the war wounded, three other sisters who had stayed behind in Toronto had carried on the neighbourhood mission work, and the sisters' associates had acquired a house around the corner from the sisters' convent, on Euclid Avenue, for the first St. John's Hospital. As predicted by Ford, once the sisters returned from the West, they barely had time to catch their collective breath from the frontlines when they faced the numerous demands of a growing city.

Mother Hannah decided to put into practice the pioneering care the Sisterhood had developed in the field. Although the sisters' patients had all been men, Mother Hannah decided that her first hospital would specialize in the care of women. The Moose Jaw experience had convinced her that holistic care had to be the cornerstone of the community's nursing mission. Emotional and physical healing went hand-in-hand: she had witnessed its benefits in the field hospital, and she had drawn on the experience of her own slow recovery from her miscarriage years earlier, a recovery that could have been quicker had she received the type of care the sisters had provided to the soldiers.

With the help of her loyal associates, the little community pulled that first hospital together. Many patients were cared for in those first years before a new hospital was built in 1889. The facilities were rudimentary at best: the refectory table did double duty as an operating table, and the acquisition of surgical equipment was dependent upon donations and fundraising conducted by the associates.

In the meantime, other needs claimed the sisters' attention too. "Perhaps there is nothing which so exercises the patience, and which is so needed these days; places where men and women in their declining years may, in quiet religious surroundings, prepare for the summons for the life beyond the veil,"[16] Mother Hannah wrote in the first *Rule of Life*, and to that end she made elder care another ministry pillar for the Sisterhood.

In 1886, the parish of St. George the Martyr purchased a house for the care of the elderly on Larch Street, close to Spadina Avenue, in the area now known as Trinity Bellwoods, and asked the sisters to take on the work. It served those from all walks of life who were unable to cope with looking after themselves. Aside from Mother Hannah, no sisters had yet been professed. One of the first novices, Sister Margaret, at the age of thirty-five and brand new to the religious life, showed exemplary leadership. Along with one other novice and a couple of not-very-efficient staff, they cared for twelve men and women. She was to become instrumental in starting many other works of the Sisterhood.

The need was so great that after seven years on Larch Street the home was moved to a building on John Street, which provided more space for the growing ministry. The building, however, was older and not as convenient as the one on Larch Street, and the sisters discovered it was infested with bugs. Nevertheless, they persevered and stayed in that building for thirteen years, until the community's founder of associates, Georgina Broughall, prevailed upon her husband, the Reverend Abraham James Broughall, rector of St. Stephen's Church in Kensington Market, to hunt for a suitable building. In 1906, he found one at 87 Bellevue Avenue, at the corner of Oxford Street, and it became the Church Home for the Aged. The following year, an addi-

The former Church Home for the Aged as the building is today.

tion was built, known as the Gwynneth Osler Memorial Wing, which provided accommodation at a lower rate. The Church Home flourished in Kensington until 1978, when the sisters' work with the elderly moved to Scarborough.

Georgina Broughall was a powerhouse of energy and enthusiasm, and without associates like her the Sisterhood would never have gotten off the ground. Indeed, the community's earliest associates were in place before the Sisterhood itself was formally established. These were lay women and male priests who saw themselves as sharing in a common life

Georgina Broughall.

with the sisters and helping to provide for the sisters' needs. They took up an annual collection for both the maintenance and the endowment of the Sisterhood. The first reception of associates took place in a little chapel on Robinson Street in June 1885, with five women admitted, including the mover and shaker Georgina Broughall, Hannah's mother, and her sister Rose. By the 1890s the associates had grown to seventy-five; by 1930 to five hundred; and today there are more than eight hundred.

Mother Hannah understood the valuable role the associates would play in the Sisterhood's existence and sustainability. During those times when the workload and the expenses kept her awake at night, she knew that it was the associates — the tireless and dedicated group outside the convent walls — that she could count on. They were a fount of ideas for the community, and it was the associates who suggested the sisters produce a newsletter that would publicize both their work and their needs. This publication, known as *St. John's Messenger* (later superseded by *The Eagle*), began in 1891.

Within three years of opening St. John's Hospital, more than 450 patients had been cared for, and larger facilities were urgently required. Again, the associates sprang into fundraising mode, and on June 1, 1888, the foundation stone was laid for the new and considerably expanded St. John's Hospital on Major Street, a few blocks north of the first hospital. According to Sister Eleanora writing in the *Memoir* of 1933,[17] eleven members of the community were present at the ceremonies: Mother Hannah, Sister Helen, and Sister Margaret; novices Aimee, Sophia, Sarah, Mary Alice, and Eleanora herself; and postulants Mary and Kate.[18]

Looming over that auspicious day was the serious illness of the Sisterhood's warden, Ogden Ford. He asked to see each sister and novice, and gave them his blessing and final words of counsel. His death barely three weeks later was an enormous blow to Mother Hannah and to the rest of the community, which had nursed him through his cancer and had read and prayed diligently at his bedside. On the day of his death, Mother Hannah returned to the convent in time to say Vespers, her face showing the strain of the day. During the last prayer she broke down, and the sisters knew that their beloved warden was now with God.

Dr. Alexander Bethune, headmaster of Trinity College School in Port Hope, Ontario, and a long-time friend of Mother Hannah, agreed to be the community's next warden.

The following year, in March, the new hospital was ready for its first patients. It was an imposing, handsome brick building on a large lot with 140 feet of frontage, with peaked rooflines, tall, rounded windows, and slim chimneys.

St. John's Hospital on Major Street.

Sprawling verandahs on the upper and lower storeys overlooked lush gardens and mature trees. Before the first patients were admitted, the sisters moved in and fashioned a bright interior with gauzy curtains and homey furnishings such as hooked rugs and rag rugs on the floor, comfortable chairs covered in cheerful chintz, and crocheted doilies on side tables. Behind the new convent and hospital building they designed and planted gardens, harvested crops to feed the patients, and collected fruit from the garden to make preserves. It was most likely the first "healing garden" established in Canada.

The hospital's verandahs and porches enabled the patients to be brought outside for fresh air, whether on crutches, in wheelchairs, or on rolling beds. The sisters did all the nursing, day and night, and they followed Mother Hannah's lead by not merely treating illness and injury but treating the whole person. Their grateful patients, inspired by the expertise of the sisters' care, became the hospital's advertising agents.

There was no shortage of projects for this fledgling religious community to undertake. As more novices joined, they accompanied the other sisters in teaching Sunday school, nursing and visiting the poor and the aged, and providing twice-weekly dinners to invalids and convalescents.

In the same year, 1889, the Sisterhood was incorporated. On May 2 that year, the first chapter was called, by-laws were enacted, and a council established to be comprised of the Mother, Assistant, Novice Mistress, and four elected members.[19]

In 1890, the Reverend John Charles Roper, Rector of St. Thomas parish, (and later Bishop of Ottawa) suggested that the sisters establish a mission in the parish of St. Cyprian's for the poor and unemployed. It was a rather big challenge for the Sisterhood: the community was barely six years old, and running a bustling hospital was an enormous task. Still, Mother Hannah agreed. A small house at the corner of what is now Mission House Lane (one block east of Euclid Avenue) and Follis Avenue became Seaton Village Mission. Mother Hannah described the mission building as "small, wooden, and exceedingly airy (not to say drafty!)." Money for its operation came from money brought into the community by two sisters and subscriptions.

This was the parish of St. Cyprian's, but a church had yet to be built, and with no other church nearby the sisters invited residents to join them for worship in their small convent chapel. The first St. Cyprian's church was built in 1892, some blocks away at Christie and Dupont. When the second St. Cyprian's church was built across the street from the mission house in 1907, the sisters moved the mission into the new church hall. They distributed clothing and groceries, served dinners, ran a dispensary, conducted mothers' meetings and a children's sewing circle — everything that was needed in an impoverished community. The chapel was a centre of activity as well, with the sisters running a sanctuary guild, the Guild of Holy Faith, a needlework guild, a mission band, and the girls' auxiliary (established in 1894).

Back on Major Street, there was a need for a larger chapel than the one in the sisters' convent, as well as a need for more guest space. In 1892, a beautiful and imposing gothic chapel was built within a building that also held meeting and office space, guest rooms, and in the basement a laundry. It was designed by Frank Darling with his partner at the time, S. George Curry. Darling, the premier architect in Canada in this period, had designed the original Major Street building as well as many churches and civic buildings in Toronto and was the architect to Trinity College. The son of the Reverend William S. Darling, Anglican rector of Holy Trinity Church and an influential member of the committee that had supported the founding of the Sisterhood, Frank Darling understood the sisters' Anglo-Catholic style of worship and their desire for a chapel that was both beautiful and serviceable. In spite of this, there was some disagreement between him and Mother Hannah. The architect believed that beams would be necessary to support the beautiful red cedar roof, while she believed there should be nothing to obscure the vista from the chapel entrance to the altar. The Mother Superior convinced the architect, and the high rounded arches of the ceiling were a testament to her vision and his engineering.[20]

A description of the laying of the cornerstone for this building captures the excitement the sisters must have felt:

The chapel of the convent on Major Street (1892).

The corner-stone was laid by the Bishop of Toronto on October 5th, 1892, amidst the rejoicing of associates and friends.... After the hymn, 'We love the place, O God" ... the stone was placed with prayers, and as it was being fixed in place there was said, "In the faith of Jesus Christ we place this head stone in the foundation in the name of our Lord Jesus Christ."[21]

The sisters' work at the new convent and hospital on Major Street continued to grow. As the need arose, additional houses along adjacent Brunswick Street were purchased, and in time the backyards formed an inner-city compound for the sisters, both workplace and home, for the next sixty-four years.

A cornerstone of Benedictine monasticism is hospitality, and the extra space enabled the sisters to welcome guests — students and working women, as well as visitors to the city. The seeds of the Sisterhood's retreat ministry were planted. All the rooms were rented: there was an obvious need for such accommodation by women who didn't want to live in a traditional boarding house. One such woman was Annie Woods, the hospital's laundress, who is buried with the sisters in St. James Cemetery. Several other Brunswick Houses were combined and made into residences or guest houses, including two for the Sisterhood's new nursing school when it was founded in 1900.

It was during this period that a theme developed, one that has continued to the present: the sisters' concern about being crowded out by the hospital (in terms of both space and the demands of the ministry itself). One of the houses on Brunswick Avenue had been used as a guest house. As Sister Eleanora wrote in 1933, looking back on the year 1912:

> The growing claims and extension of the Hospital, however, caused this work to be given up, and the Guest House and seven others on Brunswick Avenue are now used as Medical Building, Offices, Training School, Nurses' Residence, etc. There is danger of the Convent as well being submerged by the rising tide of Hospital claims, and if we do not soon find a safe refuge above high-water mark we shall be obliged to

live in tents, on whatever small space of lawn the Hospital and its many adjacent buildings may vouchsafe us![22]

Many hands were needed to keep the Sisterhood's various ministries in operation. The production of altar bread was initially for in-house use only, but it did not take long for production to expand. Like the guest facilities, the making of altar bread provided a modest stream of income for the sisters, and soon communion wafers were being produced for a number of churches in Toronto and around the province, and eventually across the country.

Sewing and embroidery, particular passions of Mother Hannah, were important creative activities for the Sisterhood, and when her convent was set up she made certain it contained adequate space for a workroom to make habits, stoles, and chasubles. The less intricate but equally important white work — altar cloths, purificators, lavabo towels, and credence cloths — was also undertaken by the sisters for local churches initially. But like the sewing and embroidery work, and in fact everything the Sisterhood put its hands to, it eventually acquired commissions from churches throughout North America.

If the impression conveyed here is of a little convent in Toronto turning into a powerhouse, then that impression is correct. The Sisterhood was a veritable hive of activity, groaning under the weight of diverse and necessary ministries, all of them requiring a great sacrifice of time. As nursing became one of the Sisterhood's chief ministries, the sisters often were pressed to set aside the religious duties they were committed to in their *Rule of Life* to attend to the responsibility of handling the surgical, medical, and rehabilitation needs of those in their care. At one point, they even gave up the convent's chapel in order to add beds. The increased work made it necessary to hire outside help, so the sisters opened a School of Nursing, which graduated its first nurses in 1903.

The around- the-clock staffing required at the hospital made it impossible for all the sisters to be present for the offices (worship times) held eight times a day. One can imagine a raised eyebrow and tight-lipped disapproval on the face of the Reverend Mother of the community of St. Mary in Peekskill where Mother Hannah had trained when she came for a visit. It could not be helped. No doubt the sisters' spiritual life deepened despite this challenge, or they would not have been able to sustain their common life, their active ministry, and pastoral and practical care of so many people.

The Sisterhood's ministry did not end at the Toronto city limits. In 1892, the community was asked to take over Bishop Bethune College, an Anglican boarding school for girls in Oshawa.

Thanks to Robert Samuel McLaughlin, Sr., whose McLaughlin Carriage Company was about to merge with General Motors to create General Motors of Canada, Oshawa was on the verge of becoming the automotive hub of Canada. Puffed with pride at its sudden wave of fortune, Oshawa began to vie with Toronto not just on economic matters but on social and religious ones. As civic competition intensified, Oshawa Anglicans were aware of potential competition from Roman Catholics should they open a girls' school (another example of the unfortunate rivalry between Protestants and Catholics at the time). A charter was procured to open an Anglican girls' school and the former residence of T.N. Gibbs was purchased. As the school in Toronto was named after the *first* Bishop of Toronto, Oshawa would name its school after the *second* Bishop of Toronto, and so Bishop Bethune College opened in 1889.

Within three years, the college had spiralled into debt and had few students, and Roman Catholics were interested in purchasing it. The board appealed for help from the church. It was at this time that the sisters, whose reputation for organization and frugality made it the go-to institution to turn things around, were asked to step in.

Mother Hannah was understandably cautious about proceeding. She didn't want the Sisterhood to end up with a white elephant on its hands. She worked out a financial guarantee with the board, stipulating that if the school closed the sisters would not be held financially liable; if it thrived the college would belong to the Sisterhood.

"The house is handsome, and the Chapel accommodation sufficient for at least forty-five pupils," wrote Mother Hannah following her initial inspection of

Bishop Bethune College.

Bishop Bethune College, Oshawa, Ont., Canada

the college. "The girls' sitting-room [is] cosy and homelike. The dormitories are divided into cubicles, securing the very desirable privacy of the pupils."

One other stipulation Mother Hannah made to the board was that Sister Margaret be installed as headmistress of the college. She had set up the Church Home for the Aged as a novice and had become Mother Hannah's right hand. Capable and of sound sense, she added a measure of refinement and gentleness to all her projects.

Under Sister Margaret, Bishop Bethune College blossomed. From the three timid students who showed up on February 9, 1893, (greeted by three equally quaking-on-the-inside sisters), enrolment shot up so that by the beginning of the school year that September the dormitories were full. The college bubbled with the excitable and contented chatter of teenage girls while outside the grounds there were murmurs of ignorant distrust. Sister Eleanora recalls:

> We had a lugubrious-looking manservant, of strong Protestant tendencies, whose favourite work was going for the mail twice daily, when he met kindred spirits with abundant leisure, and answered questions concerning "them Protestant nuns and their Popish ways." These gentlemen threatened to remove "that Cross which had no business on a Protestant building" but evidently the undertaking was too much like work, or they decided that discretion was the better part of valour for the Cross still stands on the highest gable of the "Protestant Building."[23]

Students of the college in the 1920s.

Given the extraordinary breadth of work that occupied the sisters, and the countless duties and responsibilities that fell to Mother Hannah herself, it is astonishing that she could fit anything else into her day. She saw the importance of keeping the associates and friends of the Sisterhood updated, and used *St. John's Messenger* to keep communication lines open between those inside the convent and those outside it. This was a community of religious sisters with no intention of cloistering itself from the rest of the world; indeed, out of the sisters' prayer grew a strong desire to be at home with those in the secular world, regardless of religious affiliation, to spot the gaps in social welfare and health care, and to apply their abilities, talents, and advocacy skills to those in need.

As word spread of the Sisterhood's openness to people of all faiths and beliefs, and its love and readiness to help, people who were once antagonistic toward the sisters began to soften and the formerly wary neighbourhood around Kensington Market warmed to them.

Internally, doubts continued about the viability of a religious community. Novice Aimée left, having decided that religious life was not for her. Vocations to the religious life had slowed down. However, patience and a belief in the power of prayer were Mother Hannah's strong gifts, though even she had many moments when her confidence in the Sisterhood's future was tested. She could rely on the Sisterhood's associates but even their powers of persuasion among the wider community were limited. As she wrote to Georgina Broughall in 1896:

> It has been very difficult to manage this year. There have been so many calls upon our resources, and yet, through no fault of our collectors, who faithfully went from house to house, the result was so much below the usual sum provided for us, that in every possible way we have tried to do without things which appear to be necessary. And where at all times economy rules, it is difficult to cut down expenses. I trust no one will think that we complain — we are only bearing our share of the general depression and poverty which we try to lighten for others — but as you have asked me, dear Mrs. Broughall, to write, I must write quite simply and truthfully what you ask for.[24]

Mother Hannah had suffered from sciatica and other health difficulties for many years as a result of her miscarriage as well as stress and overwork. She made several trips to England and one to friends in Charlottetown, partly for rest and recuperation but also to consult with advisors and develop the Sisterhood's

Rule of Life. In 1909, her departure reminded the sisters that more of them were getting older, and plans were made to equip the building with an elevator, which they did later that year. It was justified as a health expenditure, and made it easier for the sisters to get up and down to the refectory, which was on the top floor (the kitchen and living rooms were on the ground floor). Sister Eleanora wrote a fascinating, tongue-in-cheek description of the elevator installation process:

> The elevator was installed at once, a great comfort and convenience, especially to those of us who boast no Highland ancestry and have no taste for climbing. Some have though, and enjoy the walk uphill provided by several flights of stairs, in this flat country. Now and then, when the power goes off, and both elevator and lift from the kitchen retire from duty, our younger members taste some of the delights of the golden past. On the day the elevator came into use, Mother and a select party boarded it triumphantly for its virgin flight, just as the supper bell rang. It refused, however, to carry them more than half-way up the shaft, and there they stuck, tantalized by the pleasant sounds and odours from the refectory, until someone heard their despairing knocks and cries; and after about half an hour's suspension in mid-air, they were released by the electrician. This happened several times at first, and we felt tempted to supply ourselves with food and books on entering, to alleviate a possible term of confinement in the cage. One nervous person used to fear the possibility of the capricious thing shooting through the roof one day, but it has long been our faithful friend, and the antics of its youth are a thing of the past.[25]

In spite of challenges faced by the sisters due to health and finances, they continued to respond to outside requests for their help. At a special chapter in 1914, the sisters agreed to start a new mission in the All Hallows district of the parish of St. Saviour's (shortly after that, All Hallows became its own parish). With donations from the ever-faithful associates and friends, they built a new mission house, which opened in September 1914, and carried on work similar to Seaton Village.

In 1916, Mother Hannah turned seventy-nine. She had been the head of the community for more than thirty years. During that period more than seventy women had joined the community to "test their vocations" and forty-five had stayed through to Life Profession. The number of sisters had increased to thirty (a number had left and some others had pre-deceased Mother Hannah.) The community was poised to grow in numbers, in works, and most of all in the life of prayer on behalf of the Church and the world.

Society was changing and the work of the sisters was evolving. Even the old neighbourhood was diversifying: the extreme poverty of the immigrants that had necessitated the founding of Seaton Village Mission had declined; there were more jobs and more social infrastructure available to them in Toronto, and so the sisters decided to close the mission. The altar, chapel accessories, and vestments from the sisters' chapel at Seaton Village were transferred to All Hallows' Mission.

The construction of the new St. Cyprian's Church in 1907 meant the old building could be used as a parish hall and for continuation of the mission work which the sisters had founded. The sisters' residence became the church rectory, for which the sisters received a financial return.

The sisters remained connected with St. Cyprian's for many years. Sister Doreen remembers putting on a Halloween party with Sister Alison in the 1960s for one hundred children. (The church building has since become a Russian Orthodox church.)

Frail health continued to plague Mother Hannah, and she realized it was time to retire. She sought the advice of the community's warden, the Reverend Arthur Jenks, and asked him to inform the sisters and arrange for her successor to be elected.

The decision took the sisters by surprise, but they duly conducted an election, voting in as their second Mother Superior Sister Dora Grier, Mother Hannah's niece.

Rooms were prepared for Mother Hannah. The sisters could not help but continue referring to her as "Mother," and they frequently dropped in to visit her. Her own sister, Rose, long since retired from Bishop Strachan School, now lived full-time at the convent.

Rose's death on October 28, 1920, was a blow to Mother Hannah. The two had been devoted to one another, and she felt the loss of companionship acutely.

The following February 9, on Ash Wednesday, Mother Hannah died, with her sisters gathered around her. Her funeral was held at St. Thomas Church, where the sisters typically attended the Sunday services. The church was packed with the sisters, associates, friends, clergy, and many of Mother Hannah's family. The Bishop of Toronto officiated at the committal when her body was buried in the sisters' plot at St. James Cemetery. Her life's work was summed up in an address given by the president of the associates:

> Just forty years ago, a little group of Church people in and near the City of Toronto were praying for the revival of the Religious Life for women in Canada, and hoping for the foundation of a Canadian Order of Sisters. Today they look back, members of that group who remain, and a great company who have joined them since, and offer heartfelt thanks to God for prayers answered and hopes fulfilled in the life of Mother Hannah, who entered into rest on Ash Wednesday morning. Those who knew her in the day of small things and anxious tentative beginnings, and have watched the growth of the Community and of its activities, realize how much has been due to the Mother's own gifts and character, to her deep apprehension and personal care for the Community to which she devoted all her great gifts and energies, and her experience of the dedicated life. For many years in the fullness of her powers she watched loyally and lovingly over the inner life of the Community, eager that the spirit of those who wait constantly upon the Lord should be the spirit in which all outward works of mercy and service should be offered to Him.[26]

Mother Hannah had accepted the loss of her husband and transformed her grief into a new adventure and challenge. She built a religious community from the ground up, and shaped the focus of this made-in-Canada sisterhood. Her love and sacrifice, however, were not kept behind the cloister walls. Far from it: her legacy of compassion and care spilled over into the secular world in numerous ways — pioneering in rehabilitation health, homes for the aged, and the education of children; caring for those with developmental disabilities, ministering to those living in poverty, offering spiritual guidance and instruction in prayer. It was Mother Hannah who planted those seeds, who recognized how the soul and body both benefit from the touch of God.

2 INTO THE BREACH, 1916–1945
Mother Dora

One could be forgiven for thinking that genetics had a hand in matters when Sister Dora was elected Mother Hannah's successor in 1916 (she was, after all, the Mother Foundress' niece), but such speculation would be dismissed the moment Mother Dora sailed into view. Tall, angular, unfailingly cheerful, and friendly, there was never any question that she was destined to be at the helm of the Sisterhood of St. John the Divine. Like Mother Hannah, she possessed an innately balanced blend of organizational skill and pastoral sensitivity.

Born January 31, 1874, to Robert and Rosetta Grier in Wisconsin, Dora Lilias Grier was just ten years old when the Sisterhood was founded, and could hardly have imagined the profound impact that it would have on her life. She was educated at Saint Agnes' School in Chicago, and later at Bishop Strachan School in Toronto (where her aunt Rose was headmistress). Robert was the older brother of Mother Hannah, and the one with whom Hannah and Horace had stayed during Horace's final illness. Robert and Rosetta were devout Christians, which was no guarantee that their offspring would follow suit, but Dora appears to have slipped into religious life as easily as into a well-loved glove.

In 1900, at the age of twenty-six, she offered herself to the Sisterhood as a postulant and was professed two years later. Her upward trajectory was like a direct missile, serving as Sister-in-Charge at Bishop Bethune College, then as Novice Mistress, and later Assistant Superior. She was exactly the type of leader the Sisterhood needed at that time — maintaining the high standards and ideals set by Mother Hannah while steering the community into the modern age.

Mother Dora was very much her own woman, and was not shy about voicing her opinions or corralling people to assist in various ventures. Such forthright people can be equal parts inspiring and intimidating, but Mother Dora's personality was tempered by her down-to-earth approach: she was neither imperious nor given to a holier-than-thou attitude. She loved being surrounded by people, especially young people, and they in turn gravitated to her.

Mother Dora.

Mother Dora had an imposing physical presence in her prime. People were drawn to her as much by the graceful way she wore her black habit as by her natural friendliness and curiosity. Sister Nora once said, "When you saw Mother Dora you were never in any doubt about who was the leader. It was her grace and eagerness that people both inside and outside the convent found so attractive."

Former governor general Vincent Massey was certainly smitten. In his 1963 memoir *What's Past is Prologue*, Massey recalled Mother Dora approaching him to chair a committee that would raise funds for St. John's Convalescent Hospital. When he met her in person he said he knew immediately what his answer had to be: "She had all the compelling force of a medieval abbess," he wrote.

For the nearly thirty years that Sister Dora served as Mother Superior, she would certainly need to exercise all the "compelling force" she could muster.

Her term bookended two world wars, and the intervening years saw extraordinary advances in society and in the sciences: women won the right to vote in Canada, Britain, and the United States; the Milky Way was discovered and astronomical

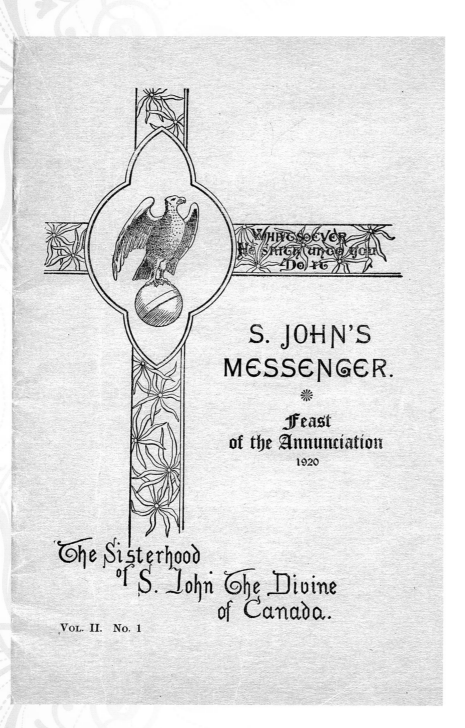

S. JOHN'S MESSENGER.

Feast of the Annunciation

1920

The Sisterhood of S. John The Divine of Canada.

Vol. II. No. 1

interest soared among ordinary people; penicillin and insulin helped usher in modern medicine, and the artificial heart was invented. It was a heady era with growth spurts among the world economies. In popular culture, the introduction of "talking" motion pictures and the growing Hollywood celebrity cult helped to keep the general population distracted during a period of intense flux.

Under Mother Dora, changes were occurring within the Sisterhood, too. A year after her installation in 1917, a pipe organ was built in the Major Street chapel, allowing the sisters to give full voice to Christian worship and explore religious music in greater depth. Previously, their worship had focused on plainchant, sung without accompaniment and not always in tune! Rose Grier, who had come to live at the convent after her retirement from Bishop Strachan School, was an organist and may have had an influence on the building of the organ. By 1919, the sisters had purchased copies of *The English Hymnal* for the chapel and were well on their way to developing a strong tradition of accompanied

St. John's Messenger, 1920.

hymns. On a visit to England in 1924, Mother Dora obtained from the sisters of St. Mary the Virgin, Wantage, reams of sheet music for voice and accompaniment. The sisters never looked back: music became a central part of their worship, and this was expressed in singing as well as in composing and performing.

The ranks of associates also rose — by 1923, there were 250 of them. They continued to be an essential resource for the Sisterhood, and the sisters were now taking more responsibility for them. After a hiatus of several years, *St. John's Messenger* was resurrected to keep associates better informed. A general reorganization of the associates was undertaken with Sister Winifred being made the first warden of associates (a role previously held by the Mother Foundress). Spiritual rigour and purpose were re-emphasized; new associates were now required to pass a three-month probationary period and all associates were to report annually to the warden on their keeping of the associates' *Rule of Life* — different from the sisters' rule and designed for busy people living in "the world." This new arrangement was successful: by 1939 the number of associates was seven hundred. They were reminded that "the power of each associate's prayers, her helpful service and quiet joy, would attract others," and yet that "Quality of life, rather than numbers, is our ideal."[1]

Within the community, the lay sister category was discontinued in 1919. The Sisterhood was founded during the Victorian era, when class distinctions in England were normal, and when religious communities in North America maintained some of the customs of English society, even though outside of the convents, social life in North America was less class-oriented. Like their counterparts in England, the sisters had both "choir" sisters and "lay" sisters. The choir sisters attended all the chapel services, had a fairly rigorous program of study (including music and theology), and often held the leadership positions in the community. The "lay" sisters were not required to come to all the chapel offices; they did more of the manual work, and had less study. In 1919, the Sisterhood discontinued this inequality and the lay sisters were given their rightful place in the community.

Ironically, the rise of female emancipation in the Western world was taking place just as religious life was experiencing a boom. Canadian women won the right to vote in 1919, and a veritable stampede of postulants, 136 of them, sought admission to the Sisterhood from 1920 to 1950, of whom more than half (seventy-four) stayed through to Life Profession. This rich influx necessitated the opening in Toronto of St. Agnes House on Washington Avenue, just a block from St. Thomas Church, to handle the overflow. It also enabled the Sisterhood to expand its work in Toronto and across the country.

Mother Dora wanted to establish a permanent presence for the Sisterhood in western Canada, and the opportunity arrived in the form of a request from the Diocese of Qu'Appelle (centered in Regina, Saskatchewan). In 1911, under Bishop Malcolm McAdam Harding, the diocese had purchased a large piece of land near the centre of Regina for its diocesan headquarters. Bishop Harding envisioned a generous campus that would include a boys' school, girls' school, theological college, and a cathedral. His dream would never be completely realized, but St. Chad's theological college, which had opened in 1907, was eventually moved to the campus, and his idea for a girls' boarding school — specifically one for the daughters of clergy — caught the attention of Aylmer Bosanquet, a fearless missionary from England and an associate of the Sisterhood. She threw her support behind Harding's idea, and urged him on, insisting that the best women to operate such a school were the sisters. When Bosanquet added ballast to her conviction with a generous donation to Harding's cause, Harding got in touch with Mother Dora.

Qu'Appelle Diocesan School.

The Sisterhood agreed to take up the task, and four sisters were dispatched in 1918 to start the Qu'Appelle Diocesan School (QDS), later to be re-named St. Chad's Girls' School.

In retrospect, it may appear reckless that women in long black habits ventured into what was then pioneer territory — and an intensely impoverished one at that — with nothing but the clothes on their backs. But this willingness to risk was undergirded by an abiding faith and a determination to respond to God's bidding, even when the odds were stacked against them.

When the sisters arrived to start the school in 1918, the severe economic depression that devastated the Prairies, together with the polio epidemic and other hardships, were the least of their challenges. The school itself was completely independent of government funding, which immediately prompted suspicion from the Saskatchewan Board of Education. The school applied for official inspection and followed the board curriculum, but this did little to win them favour.

The general population in fact was wary of habit-wearing women teaching their children — "Are they Roman Catholics in disguise?" — and famine and drought had all but obliterated the resources and the interest of lower-income families in having their daughters educated for university. A steady stream of academic-minded sister-headmistresses — Sisters Katherine, Francesca, Constance, Margaret Ann, and Beryl — gently persevered. Teachers with higher qualifications were hired, academic rigour was imposed, and generally standards were raised to prepare young women not only for life on the Prairies but for colleges and universities.

Sister Francesca had started out as a teacher at Bishop Strachan School in Toronto and from there joined the Sisterhood. She later taught at QDS, and Sister Beryl, a young student at the time, remembers an end-of-term talk when Sister Francesca remarked that school was meant to impart a spiritual experience. She said it should help students become lovers, in the sense that to love meant to suffer, which would make girls stronger and better qualified to take up their vocation in life. It planted the question in young Beryl's mind: "What does God want me to do?" After achieving her degree in education and teaching in India, she joined the Sisterhood.

Around that time, another western ministry was being launched: Sunday School by Post. Aylmer Bosanquet hatched this idea, too, but when illness prevented her from undertaking it herself, she shared it with an acquaintance named Eva Hasell. Like Bosanquet, Hasell was a wealthy Englishwoman eager to save Canadian farm children from Christian illiteracy. She had a sleeper caravan custom built, and during the sweltering and unforgiving summer months she delivered bibles and Sunday school lessons to children living in rural isolation who had never attended Sunday school.[2] By 1928, the tenacious Hasell had nine vans on the road, all operated by women, all dispatched to far-flung regions of the Prairies. These travelling teachers would read Bible stories to the children and leave them homework, which they would complete under the supervision of their mothers, and then mail it back to be marked.

Teaching Sunday school was as familiar as breathing to the sisters, and they were enthusiastic about helping Hasell. She, on the other hand, felt the sisters' black and austere habits would frighten the children and lead people to think that Sunday School by Post was a Roman Catholic enterprise, so she sometimes kept the sisters behind the scenes to develop the curriculum and mark the lessons.

The vans were only part of the Sunday School by Post program, which went on all year through the mail. It was especially successful in the Diocese of Qu'Appelle a southern, rural diocese in Saskatchewan, where it began in 1926 and continued until 1951. This was the first area where the Sisters of St. John the Divine were involved. Sister Ellen was a distributor of materials at the Sunday School School by Post head office, housed at St. Christopher House in Regina (a few blocks from the Qu'Appelle Diocesan School). She would send out materials and then correct them and make helpful comments when they were returned to her. She would then send the corrected materials back to the children, often putting supportive letters and colourful cards in with them.

Sunday School by Post and the summer van ministry were also successful in the Algoma diocese in northern Ontario. For several years it also operated in the central Ontario region around Bracebridge. In 1937, at its peak, ninety vans roamed the remote regions of Canada. At the first sniff of winter, Eva Hasell would return to England to fundraise tirelessly for the venture while sisters and others who worked with Sunday School by Post continued their contact with children through the mail.

The Sunday School by Post vans.

Sisters Margaret, Mary, and Katherine were all involved in the beginnings of this ministry, and much later, the current Sister Elizabeth (then in her twenties) worked with a van ministry around the Diocese of Saskatoon during the summer of 1966. Sister Beryl, who grew up in Saskatchewan, remembers the Sunday School by Post van arriving at her parents' farm, and bringing the latest installment of the program to her and her brother. They would obediently complete the assignments left for

TOP: *Sister Dorothea hosts a birthday party at Shernfold School.*
MIDDLE: *Sister Ella offers a student guidance in prayer.*
BOTTOM: *Sister Cora teaches bed-making.*

them and mail them in to be marked. When her brother developed a serious ear infection and had to be flown to Regina for emergency medical attention, the sisters were able to start visiting him immediately because they knew the family from the Sunday School by Post program.

During the 1920s, the sisters built on their work in western Canada, while another group of sisters planted seeds in eastern Canada. It was a memorable time of steady growth for the Sisterhood of St. John the Divine.

In Ottawa, the sisters were prevailed upon by the city's then-mayor Charlotte Whitten, a friend of Mother Dora's, to care for mentally and physically disabled girls, specifically those with birth injuries. It was felt that the sisters had the necessary training, patience, and tenderness to care for such fragile souls, sixteen in all, at Shernfold School. From 1927, when they began this work, the sisters taught the girls basic skills such as how to make beds and set the table. During the summers, they would take them on summer vacations to Christie Lake, outside of Ottawa. It was extremely rewarding work for the sisters and lifelong friendships were forged with some of the children. One of these was with Joan Trowles, who, when the sisters left the school, came to live at the convent and became a close friend of the sisters as well as an associate. Later in life she moved to Cana Place and then to Belmont House. She remained a member of the sisters' extended family into her old age. When she died in 2012, her funeral in the convent chapel was attended by many associates and friends of the community.

Bishop Mountain Hall.

In Quebec City, the sisters took over an orphanage. Based on early photographs, it would be difficult to describe the Protestant Female Orphan Asylum as hospitable. Even the name makes one shudder. Gloomily gothic, the building was given an immediate overhaul when the sisters took it over. In 1927, they opened the orphanage and school under the name Bishop Mountain Hall, named after George Jehoshaphat Mountain, the third and much-loved bishop of the Diocese of Quebec. They cared for and taught the orphaned children, and they also took in teenage boarders from the surrounding countryside whose parents had sent them to Quebec City to be schooled. It was a bucolic life for the nearly thirty children who lived there. They played in the property's gardens, and each child had his or her own flower plot. Records indicate a happy family atmosphere that was supported by kind and generous friends of the sisters, among them Lord and Lady Tweedsmuir, who provided the necessities as well as treats in the form of stays at summer camps.

When the number of orphans fell to five in 1941, the sisters decided to withdraw for practical reasons so they could be deployed elsewhere. The children were placed in the capable hands of a Miss Machin, who had worked with the sisters on the Sunday School by Post program in Regina, and was doing similar work in the Quebec diocese. Although the sisters' work at Bishop Mountain Hall lasted only fourteen years, they had the joy of watching an entire generation pass through their gentle hands, and many of their charges were gainfully employed — one of them as a teacher — by the time the sisters left. In 1997, the sisters' work at Bishop Mountain Hall was recognized by the Quebec government when a monument was erected to commemorate religious orders that had run schools in the province — the Sisterhood of St. John the Divine being the only non-Roman Catholic order.

Children at Bishop Mountain Hall.

In 1929, Sisters Lucina, Lily, and Louise started St. Michael's Mission on Dorchester Street in the Montreal parish of St. John the Evangelist to provide spiritual strength and compassion to the destitute. The mission offered Sunday school, evening services, mothers' meetings, and clubs for boys and girls. The sisters distributed food and clothing, visited homes, and taught courses on cooking and infant care in conjunction with the Social Services Department of the Montreal General Hospital. They held picnics for mothers and tots, created a reading room for children, raised money for camp fees, grew a vegetable garden, and formed

a children's choir and a Junior Auxiliary. It was a greatly needed and busy mission, especially during the Depression years. Sister Beryl recalls a family that collected the cinders from the mission's furnace to bring home for heat. Thousands of desperate families were fed and clothed by the sisters.

In 1930, the sisters took on the challenge of running St. Christina's School in Cooperstown, New York. It was the community's only foray outside Canada's borders.

The original Cooperstown School had been founded in 1870 by Susan Fenimore Cooper, who was interested in rehabilitating the poor and needy children in the Susquehanna River valley of the Catskill Mountains. St. Christina's School was subsequently founded in 1918 and was run by the sisters of the Community of the Holy Child Jesus. In 1930, however, that community left, unable to continue the work. The Sisterhood of St. John the Divine was asked to step in, which they agreed to do. After all, the sisters had lots of expertise in teaching and administration, especially in dealing with vulnerable children. But it quickly became apparent to Sister Miriam, who was put in charge of the school, that these were not just disadvantaged children — they were children who had suffered appalling abuse in their own homes. For the next eight years the sisters helped children from primary school through high school and tried to give them the confidence to pursue professions and manage a home, but the children needed help and training that the sisters didn't have. The sisters had the wisdom to acknowledge this, and in 1938 handed the school over to the State of New York. Sister Miriam, who had worked hard to make the school a success, left the community not long after.

In 1936, three sisters travelled to Springhill, Nova Scotia, at the request of the area bishop to take charge of All Saints' Hospital. The fifty-bed general hospital served the mining and farming communities, as well as several lumber camps and two fishing ports. At the end of the Second World War, the building required extensive repairs and fire protection upgrades,

Sister Veronica says grace with the Sunday school children at St. Michael's Mission.

which the diocese could not afford, and so the decision was reluctantly made to hand it over to the municipality.

Back in western Canada, a much more positive venture was taking shape in Edmonton. In 1936, the sisters were invited by Bishop Arthur Burgett to take charge of a house on diocesan property and open a shelter for young women — particularly unwed mothers. Sisters Isabel, Lilias, and Aquila were the first to take on this work, which required a compassionate and non-judgmental heart — a glaring contrast to the prevailing social attitudes of the day. The home looked like any modest family home behind a white picket fence, and the young women who arrived under unhappy circumstances were buoyed by the sisters' humour and gentleness. Such was the need for this type of ministry that it became the sisters' chief work in Edmonton for many years. There were few social mechanisms in place in those days to keep disenfranchised women fed and sheltered, and much of this responsibility fell to religious orders like the Sisterhood and their Roman Catholic counterparts.

In the Toronto area, the Sisterhood's workload continued to soar.

Enrolment at Bishop Bethune College in Oshawa continued to rise, and the school underwent expansion to accommodate this growth. It had operated for about thirty-five years and its future looked bright. Mother Hannah had indeed been wise to appoint Sister Margaret as headmistress, and Mother Dora was happy to have her continue. The school endeared itself to its students and the community at large, and the respect was mutual. A beautiful angel window, donated panel by panel by the Old Girls of the Bishop Bethune College, graced its chapel. At the end of the 1920s, the college was blessed with such robust numbers that the

Top: All Saints' Hospital.
Bottom: Nurses' graduation at All Saints' Hospital.

sisters began talking about building a junior school. At this point, the winds suddenly changed. There was considerable debate among the sisters and staff about this new venture, and the issue became so heated that some staff and students left the college and founded a rival school — Hadfield Hall — nearby. An attractive prospectus of the college was produced in 1931, endorsed by both the Bishop of Toronto (James Sweeny) and the Bishop of Ottawa (John Charles Roper), but it could not stem the exodus. The arrival of the Great Depression added an extra burden to cash-strapped families, and the school was forced to close in 1932. It caused great sadness and disappointment to the Sisterhood and to those who valued their work at the school.

Sister Margaret gracefully accepted the circumstances, returned to the convent, and applied her considerable talents elsewhere. She was responsible for the Church Workroom, and focused her attention on church embroidery. She inspired the sisters to reach for a perfection of artistry and devotion to beauty in all their needlework. Sister Margaret was one of the great women of the Sisterhood, and a plaque to her memory can be found in the chapel of St. John's Rehab, along with the beautiful series of angel windows from the former Bishop Bethune College, and many of the furnishings from the school's chapel, such as the altar, choir seats, and canopies.

These were uncertain times, whether one was inside a convent or outside it. The church tried to be a stabilizing force in an increasingly secularized world. Forays into ecumenical dialogue were made, earning a Nobel Peace Prize for Nathan Söderblom, the Bishop of Uppsala, Sweden, in 1930. New ecumenical expressions of religious community were manifesting themselves in the form of the Iona community in Scotland (1938) and the Taizé community in France (1940). Through it all, a Lutheran pastor named Dietrich Bonhoeffer put the spiritual fortitude of Christians to the test when he modelled a powerful opposition to the Nazi regime. Revolution in varying degrees and guises was reconfiguring the social, cultural, political, scientific, and religious landscape. It was also the advent of air travel, and of international communications. The Canadian Broadcasting Corporation was established, and the telephone was commonplace in homes.

This communications *zeitgeist* would have found favour with Mother Dora, a master networker. Outgoing and enthusiastic, she forged connections with people from all walks of life and all denominations. She opened the lines of communication with overseas communities in England and Korea. Her can-do attitude was infectious, and her advice was sought by Anglican clergy at all levels across the country.

As we have seen, the sisters always responded immediately to requests for help and gamely stepped into the breach where they were needed. But this approach was beginning to take a toll. They were quite simply run off their feet, and they needed a place of respite. Doctor friends of the sisters from St. John's Hospital recommended they get away from the city for the summer.

In the early 1920s, the sisters rented a house in Port Sydney, a village tucked around the southern shore of Mary Lake, south of Huntsville, in the Muskoka region of Ontario. In 1926, the property came up for sale and the Sisterhood purchased seven lots and five hundred feet of waterfront on a sandy beach. They named the property Bally Croy — Welsh for "beautiful hill" — and it became a lakeside retreat for exhausted sisters who were working around the clock in the heart of the city.

The scent of soaring pines, the sound of the gentle *thwap* of the cottage's screen door, the music of lapping waves against the shoreline, and the brilliant stars at night (nearly invisible in the over-lit cities where most of the sisters lived and worked) provided soothing relief. According to *St. John's Messenger*, Bally Croy was a real asset in building up the physical and spiritual health of the sisters.

Bally Croy gave the sisters a place to get away from it all, but it also gave them an extra place of worship and a place of true contemplation where they could indulge their creative gifts such as painting and poetry. Sister Jean, for example, hauled out her paint brushes and palette and captured the serenity of Bally Croy in watercolour paintings, many of which now hang throughout the convent and guest house. A skilled carpenter, Sister Jean designed and built the tabernacle, credence table, and altar that furnishes Bally Croy's chapel.

Another place of rest, this one for convalescent patients, was established in 1920 on Bayview Avenue, south of Lawrence, on six acres of property donated by the Kilgour family.[3] It came to be known as Mount St. John, and it followed the sisters' values of caring for the whole patient.

Bally Croy, the original house used by the sisters.

The House of Rest at Mount St. John was formally dedicated on a brilliantly sunny May 19, 1923. More than two hundred friends of the Sisterhood made the journey to attend the festivities. Led by J.F. Sweeny, Lord Bishop of Toronto, the crowd sang Psalm 128 and processed through the house, room by room, as prayers and versicles were recited.

In the subsequent issue of the *Messenger*, the following paragraph appeared describing the House to those unable to attend the opening:

> The wide doors from the verandah open into a large reception room, the width of the house, with large, easy chairs, pretty chintz curtains, books, flowers, and all that is needed to make a room comfortable and attractive. On the south side of the House there is a large sunroom with beds for five patients. From the reception room there is a passage with rooms on either side, bedrooms, a dressing room for visitors, the sisters' Common Room and Refectory, a bathroom and pantry. The kitchen is downstairs. On the upper floor there are four rooms for sisters and helpers, and the Chapel. There in the Chapel, with its lamp burning before the Altar "in token that the House is always watching under God," its Altar with its Whitsun hangings and vases of red tulips radiant in the sunlight which streamed through the window above, its atmosphere of reverence and peace, one felt that this was no ordinary Convalescent Home but very truly a House of Rest.[4]

Some of the sisters enjoy an excursion on Mary Lake.

In the meantime, Mrs. Alice Kilgour (who had donated the original six aces of property for the House of Rest), expressed her strong views that the sisters were too crowded in the convent on Major Street, because the hospital had taken over so many of their buildings, and she also felt the neighbourhood was no longer appropriate for a sisters' residence. There had been talk for some time about the possibility of establishing a new convent and also a convalescent hospital outside the city or in the suburbs, and Mrs. Kilgour donated twenty-five thousand dollars to the sisters, suggesting they build a convent elsewhere and leave just a few sisters on Major Street until a decision was made about a convalescent hospital. Discussions went on for several years about the location of both convent and a new convalescent hospital, and one site that was considered was the Bayview property.

However, an advisory committee to the Mother Superior stated in a report to the Sisterhood that they "felt that the Bayview site would be unsuitable [for either convent or hospital]. First, because it is a valuable site and could bring in a sum which would add substantially to the building fund. Secondly, because the acreage would not be sufficient to meet fresh growth and future development of the community."[5]

The Advisory Board recommended purchase of a new piece of property that was found in Aurora, north of Toronto — nearly a hundred acres of farmland. With the donation from Mrs. Kilgour and the proceeds of the sale of the Bayview property, the sisters paid for the Aurora property and also added to their building fund. In the end the House of Rest on Bayview closed, and neither that property nor the Aurora property was used for either convent or hospital. However, a significant ministry developed on the Aurora property.

Four sisters went to live at the farm in Aurora. Along with two men who were hired to do the heavy work, the sisters kept eight cows; enough hens to provide eggs for themselves, the convent, and St. John's Hospital on Major Street; three hundred chickens; eight young pigs; two calves; and six geese. They grew wheat, mixed grain, and hay, and also harvested fruit and vegetables from their gardens.

A year later, those four hardy sisters started to take in paying guests, and in the summer of 1932 they began receiving a number of convalescent patients. Sister Emily, a professional masseuse, had her equipment installed to provide therapy treatment. Around that time the property became known as St. John's on the Hill, or simply "the farm."

The farm became home to seven intellectually disabled children in the autumn of 1935. For twenty years, the children lived with the sisters in a family atmosphere. Each child was given a daily task and one hour a day of handiwork; some learned to read and write; those with musical talents were encouraged. The animals on the farm were a great source of enjoyment, therapy, and education.

In 1941, a wing was added to the original farmhouse, and it housed three invalid sisters as well as two sisters from the community of St. Peter in Kilburn, England. By this time, there were fourteen children in residence.

While Mother Dora did not mind expanding the Sisterhood's work where it was needed (a dispensary was opened in 1921 in the Garrison Church on Portland Street, staffed by sisters and St. John's Hospital staff), her practical side did not allow nostalgia to keep open ministries that were no longer useful, such as the Major Street Nursing School, which was discontinued in 1930.

Gerontology was considered a priority — Mother Dora ensured it remained so. The sisters continued to pioneer in this area at the Church Home for the Aged on Bellevue Avenue. It earned the appreciation of medical professionals, though it would be some years before they would grasp the importance of this emerging field of study and care.

The field of convalescent care, however, was gaining ground as the Sisterhood persevered to have it formally recognized and accepted by the medical establishment. The sheer number of convalescent patients the sisters were treating in their surgical hospital could no longer be regarded as a blip on the health care chart. A number of First World War veterans received convalescent care at the old hospital, though it was not funded by the government. What Sister Beatrice and the other sisters wanted to do was to secure funding for convalescent care in a publicly funded hospital.

Mother Dora asked a group of prominent Torontonians to form a Board of Trustees to raise funds for the construction of a convalescent hospital. The Honorable Vincent Massey was appointed board chair. With approval from the Government of Canada and the Province of Ontario, and the support of the general hospitals in Toronto, convalescent care was finally recognized and established as a necessary health service.

A parcel of more than thirty acres of land was purchased on Cummer Avenue in Willowdale, just north of Toronto's city limits. On December 7, 1933, in the presence of the Archbishop of Toronto and Mr. Massey, the cornerstone was laid and construction commenced. Four years later, on May 22, 1937, St. John's Convalescent Hospital (now St. John's Rehab division of Sunnybrook Health Sciences Centre) was officially opened by Lord Tweedsmuir, the governor general. Fittingly, its dedication was made by the Archbishop of Ottawa John Charles Roper, who had been chaplain of the Sisterhood since its earliest days and its Warden since 1920.

The new building accommodated sixty-four patients, in addition to the sisters who had living quarters on the top floor, and several staff members on the main level. There was more than enough land for the hospital, and so between 1936 and 1949, the sisters rented out the acreage for farming. Eventually they planted trees, created gardens, and turned the land around the hospital into a beautiful place of healing. The Auxiliary had a metered walkway laid around the hospital and encouraged patients to get outdoors and enjoy the therapeutic properties of the gardens.

The hospital's location might have been beyond Toronto's city limits but it quickly gained a reputation among the medical and health care establishments as a premiere facility. From the moment it opened, it was filled to capacity, and once the war had ended plans were in motion for its expansion.

Sister Beatrice was the hospital's first administrator, a position she held until her retirement in 1954. She had been the director of nursing at the Major Street hospital, and was a strong proponent for the idea that the Sisterhood's work in health care needed to be in the field of convalescence and rehabilitation. She knew that the Sisterhood would never have been able to compete with the major acute care hospitals, and she believed that rehabilitation treatment and care was a distinct discipline, one that needed its own hospital.

The philosophy, ethics, and ethos of the hospital solidified under Sister Beatrice as

TOP: *St. John's Convalescent Hospital from the front (1937).*
BOTTOM: *St. John's Convalescent Hospital from the back, showing the verandahs.*

she ensured it was grounded in the Sisterhood's values of care for the whole person. She also leaned less heavily on the sisters for staffing the hospital. In the early days of the hospital, the Sisterhood's novices were all trained in nursing. However, Sister Beatrice realized that it was too much to expect them to do two kinds of training at once: they needed dedicated time to be trained and formed in the religious life before they got involved in professional training.

Downtown, the Major Street hospital was in the process of closing and the sisters were considering various uses for the buildings. Some of the empty wards were transformed into bedrooms for guests and visiting religious, further expanding yet another of the Sisterhood's ministries — hospitality.

Alongside all this creative activity, a more destructive picture was materializing in the secular world: another world war loomed. Two world leaders had emerged from the wreckage of the First World War and their personalities could not be more opposite: Mohandas Gandhi and Adolph Hitler — the peacemaker and the destroyer — personified the extremes of fear and love. The sisters stepped up their prayers for world peace and continued to do what they could to relieve the suffering of the sick and the poor locally.

When Mother Dora learned that a British boarding school run by the sisters of the Order of the Holy Paraclete (OHP) was being evacuated to Canada until the end of the war, she immediately offered the Sisterhood's help in settling the students and teachers at St. Hilda's College on the University of Toronto Campus, close to the convent. The Sisterhood organized supplies and various comforts for the evacuees, and provided hospitality to the OHP sisters for their retreats and holiday time. It marked the beginning of a relationship between these two Anglican religious communities, situated on opposite sides of the Atlantic, that endures to this day.

In 1944, the Society of St. John the Evangelist asked the Sisterhood to take over the mission work from the Society of St. Margaret in Bracebridge, Ontario, at the time a poor farming community. As Mother Dora was quoted in *St. John's Messenger*, "We must again pioneer even as we have done in the past sixty years and do our utmost to meet this pressing need." She set up a jubilee fund to support the work.

The Sisters of St. Margaret left their convent and much of their equipment to the Sisterhood. The Bracebridge convent had rooms for sisters and guests who came on retreat, and the novices were housed there for a short time. There was even a plan to move the convent to Bracebridge, although that plan was reversed.

In addition to the host of ministries already mentioned, numerous others continued or developed in Mother Dora's era: the listening ear, the ecclesiastical embroidery and linens supplied to churches across North America, the baking of communion bread, the leading of retreats, the provision of spiritual direction, and the cleaning and maintenance of the convent and its branch houses without the support of paid staff.

It was once said of William Morris, the founder of the Arts and Crafts movement in England, that he died simply from being William Morris, "having done more work than most ten men." The same could be said of Mother Dora. In 1945, heart specialists counselled her to relinquish her many responsibilities. She took their advice and retired later that year. In 1948, she moved to St. John's on the Hill in Aurora and stayed there for several years, returning to the convent in Willowdale where she lived until her death in 1966 at the age of ninety-three. During Mother Dora's time in office, an unprecedented number of women had tested their vocation in the community. The community was poised to take on the challenges of the post-war era.

3 WINDS OF CHANGE, 1945–1970
Mother Aquila

In 1945, the Sisterhood elected Sister Aquila as its new Mother Superior. Even this heralded a change, for she was the community's first leader who wasn't from the Coome-Grier fold.

Born Kathleen Marion Goodman on June 10, 1902, in Chiswick, England, she had graduated from the College of the Ascension, a training college for missionaries at Selly Oak, a suburb of Birmingham. The same year, she was sent to Edmonton as a missionary by the Society for the Propagation of the Gospel. There, she became acquainted with the sisters, and subsequently joined the community, adopting the appropriate if exotic-sounding name of Aquila (Latin for "eagle").

Tall and thin, with piercing brown eyes and a warm smile, she possessed an infectious faith. "She had intense eyes," recalls Sister Wilma, "but they were not intense in a forceful way. They were the eyes of someone who listened intently while carefully assessing a situation. She also had a wonderful sense of humour and could laugh at herself."

Like the Aquila who was a companion of St. Paul, she understood the ways in which God drew people through a loving heart; like the eagle that represents St. John, she kept the sisters focused on their call to pray first and to allow their ministry to flow from their prayer. In all her teaching, she reinforced Mother Hannah's belief that a religious community could not survive and thrive unless prayer was its first priority.

If Mother Dora's term was defined by expansion, Mother Aquila's was about drawing the community in and stabilizing it amid a shifting world. She had served under Mother Dora as Novice Mistress, but her quiet, contemplative nature contrasted with Mother Dora's extroverted style. In spite of the feverish political and social change in those heady post-war years, Mother Aquila was not the type to be easily swayed, and she kept her hands firmly on the wheel, resisting change for change's sake while steering the community toward those opportunities that helped to further the Sisterhood's mission.

Outside the cloister walls, world events infused the religious realm with renewed vigor. Mere months before the end of the Second World War, the German Lutheran pastor and theologian Dietrich Bonhoeffer was executed by the Nazis: his martyrdom lit a fire of social activism that united the religious and the secular worlds, and this was further fanned as the hidden horrors of the war were subsequently revealed during the Nuremberg Trials.

Progressive change took root in the church throughout Mother Aquila's time in office: in Hong Kong, Florence Li Tim-Oi had been ordained a priest in 1944 for reasons of wartime necessity, but it kick-started what would become a lengthy and controversial movement for women to be priested; the World Council of Churches was founded in 1948; Billy Graham's nascent evangelical ministry coincided with the advent of television, and its phenomenal success catapulted him to celebrity status in

Mother Aquila.

1949; Canadian Anglicans received new autonomy with a name change, in 1955, from the Church of England in Canada to the Anglican Church of Canada; and the 1963 Anglican Congress was held in Toronto in the midst of the worldwide attention on the new spirit coming out of Vatican II.

Mother Aquila's strength was not in administration, but she was clever enough to know this and wasn't shy about delegating. She had a knack for choosing the right person for the right position to support her. Consequently, much of the administrative work fell to Sister Nora, who served as Mother Aquila's secretary for most of her time in office, handling much of the administrative work of the community. She also served, under both Sister Aquila and later Sister Frances Joyce, variably as assistant administrator at the hospital, as Assistant Superior for the Sisterhood, and as bursar at the Convent. Sister Nora was a woman with a unique blend of financial and administrative gifts, and an engaging way of relating to people both inside and outside the community.

Mother Aquila paid attention to world events but didn't allow them to distract her. She relied on prayer and a thoughtful assessment of the realities of a situation to guide her decisions. A quiet, reflective teacher in the ways of prayer, Mother Aquila encouraged the spiritual growth of each sister, and the conferences she gave on various aspects of the religious life, and especially the vows, encouraged the same values that Mother Hannah had insisted on — that the life of prayer must come first if the sisters' active work was to be meaningful.

She was a shrewd judge of character, weighing the capabilities of the sisters against the possibilities of a given opportunity, and not afraid to encourage the sisters to make controversial or difficult decisions — such as closing a branch house or focusing on a new ministry — if the situation called for it. Although she tended, herself, to be traditionally minded, she kept an open mind to give the sisters a chance to explore their calling through new forms of worship and through all the changes that were naturally happening in society and therefore also in the community.

During Mother Aquila's early years with the Sisterhood, before her time as Mother Superior, she had helped establish St. John's House in the northwest quadrant of Edmonton, where the sisters cared for unwed mothers. She felt a natural bond with that city, and wanted to build on the Sisterhood's work there. The sisters agreed, and in 1946 they opened Elizabeth House as a home for elderly women. The building was just behind St. John's House on the adjacent block, and a chapel was built between them.

In Toronto, too, the sisters provided more space for short-term retreat and longer-term residence where people could find quiet and renewal. The sisters' ministry of hospitality provided eight guest rooms within the convent and a number of residences on Brunswick Avenue, with a garden between them and the Major Street buildings. One of the Brunswick Avenue buildings was known as the Terrace; it was where Sisters Rosemary Anne, Philippa, and Margaret Ann lived before entering the community. Their time living at the Terrace no doubt greatly influenced their sense of vocation to enter the community. Sister Rosemary Anne was a deacon working at Little Trinity Church on King Street East, while Sisters Philippa and Margaret Ann were completing their education at the University of Toronto. Once they joined the community, they occasionally regaled the sisters at recreation with stories about their activities and antics, which would be supplemented by Sister Faith, who was in charge of the Terrace at that time.

Another goal of the sisters was to grow the novitiate, a challenging one given the post-war era's changing attitudes to women in the workplace and to female equality in general. Women had been integral to the war effort. They had learned new skills and found new confidence in their ability to make a significant contribution outside the home. When the war ended, men returned to their jobs and women were steered back to their domestic duties and traditional roles: But that wasn't going to last for long. If they could fill in for men in factories, farms, and on the assembly lines while the men were off fighting, then why couldn't they do the same in peace time?

As the sisters had hoped, just when women were pressing for equal rights there was a growth spurt in new vocations. Thomas Merton's *The Seven Storey Mountain*, which chronicled the monk's life and conversion, was published in 1948, and it triggered everywhere a flow of traffic to monasteries and convents that continued until the mid 1960s. At the Sisterhood of St. John the Divine, eighty-five women tested their vocation during that period, and thirty-one stayed to Life Profession (36 percent — a fairly typical percentage for religious communities of the day).

Mother Aquila was certainly on the lookout for novices, but she wasn't so eager that she allowed them to bypass their education before they entered. The three women mentioned above are good examples of her individual guidance. Margaret Ann Macfarlane who had studied at McGill University and was now working on a social work degree at the University of Toronto, felt called to religious life, but Mother Aquila insisted that she complete her degree before making a decision about entering the Sisterhood, and she was admitted in 1950 after she had graduated. She was to be influential in the community both as headmistress of QDS / St. Chad's School, and then for twenty-five years as Novice Mistress, helping to shape the future of the community through the new women who were trained under her as novices.

On the other hand, Rosemary Anne Benwell was working as a deacon while she lived at the Terrace, and she recalled Mother Aquila checking in with her every so often to see if she was truly happy in her job. "I was happy in my work," Sister Rosemary Anne related, "but it had crossed my mind a few times about joining the Sisterhood, and then one day when I was sitting reading in the garden, Mother Aquila passed by and — she had a way of wording things, sort of hinting — said, 'I expect you've been doing a lot of thinking lately.' I was!"[1] Sister Rosemary Anne would become one of the first women to be ordained to the priesthood in Canada in 1977, the sister in charge of the Priory in Edmonton for many years, guest mistress on Botham Road, spiritual director to many clergy, and director of western associates.

Dorothy Watson (later known as Sister Philippa) was completing a degree in library science at the University of Toronto and then was encouraged to enter the community. She was life professed as a sister only a few days before the move to Botham Road. After spending the first few months setting up the sisters' library at the new convent, she was assigned to St. John's Convalescent Hospital, where she spent almost the whole of her life in the Sisterhood.

Mother Aquila's discernment about the vocation of each of these sisters, and the respective ministries they had in the community, shows her ability to assess individual needs and to recognize the timing appropriate for each.

One of the looming challenges facing Mother Aquila concerned the convent and former hospital buildings on Major Street and Brunswick Avenue. The community had outgrown them, in terms of both size and practicality. Since the opening of St. John's Convalescent Hospital in 1937, the former hospital buildings had been used for guest houses and residences and they were falling into disrepair; some had been condemned by the City of Toronto. The convent buildings that the sisters themselves occupied needed extensive repairs and costly renovations, and it was decided that it would be cheaper to move than to stay downtown. A search committee was struck, and the hunt began for a suitable property.

In fairly short order (1952), one was found just outside the Toronto city limits. The area around York Mills Avenue and Yonge Street was considered suburbia in those days, and the property the sisters had their eye on was just north of there in Willowdale, a block above Highway 401. It was closer to the new St. John's Hospital on Cummer Avenue, but it was also a more serene location than the sisters' downtown location. Perched on the edge of one of the beautiful ravines that crisscross Toronto's Don River system, and bordering a golf course, it was quiet, peaceful, and green, an idyllic place of colourful gardens, soaring trees, stone pathways, and privacy. Spread over twenty acres of lawns and ravine and anchored by a handsome stucco home, it offered plenty of potential for the active sisters as well as for those who were elderly and infirm, and it offered the scope to expand as the need arose. What's more, proximity to the recently constructed Highway 401 offered quick access to other parts of the southern Ontario region. (At the time, no one imagined that the four-lane highway would, in less than forty years, morph into a massively intricate gridlocked eighteen-lane expressway.)

The Botham Road location was deemed perfect. The sisters had raised many donations for the building fund through appeals in the *Messenger* since the 1940s. And so they immediately started to build a three-story addition to the original house for sisters' bedrooms and work space for their various ministries. In June 1953, the sisters moved in to their new home, having quickly sold the Major Street property to doctors who subsequently opened The Doctor's Hospital.

Despite the gracious and pastoral new home, it wasn't an easy transition. Moving from downtown Toronto to the outer limits of the city was not unanimously welcomed by all the sisters. Many missed the old neighbourhood and their community's historic attachment to an area that had become synonymous with the Sisterhood since its inception in 1884. It was their patch; they knew every laneway, every person they met on the streets. Their connections were with the inner city, and now every vestige of familiarity was altered. They didn't like change. And yet it was inevitable, even necessary. Poor building conditions aside, the Sisterhood and its various missions were expanding, and more space was needed to accommodate its family of seventy-five sisters.

The convent on Botham Road showing the old house and part of the bedroom wing.

A temporary chapel was set up in what would later become the Mother Superior's office. It was a tight squeeze — the chapel had space for the sisters living at the convent and a handful of guests. There were only three bedrooms available for guests. Administrative offices were housed in the original house, and space was renovated to provide a workroom for church linens, a sewing room, and a music room. The altar bread department and library were on the ground floor of the sisters' residence wing. Every inch of space was used.

Over the next ten years, a series of renovations and additions took place to increase space and functionality at Botham Road. In 1954, barely a year after the sisters moved in, another fundraising appeal was launched to expand the convent. A generous legacy from Eila Gibson made possible the construction of a guest wing, community room, and infirmary as well as the convent's crowning centerpiece, the chapel, which was consecrated by the Archbishop of Toronto, W.L. Wright, on September 1, 1956. Eight years later, two other legacies, this time from the Gerald Larkin Estate and the Estate of Ethel Wilson (a Montreal associate and Sister Lois' sister), enabled construction of a new kitchen, refectory, an expanded infirmary, and an expanded guest wing (bringing the total number of guest rooms to twenty-four). A divided cloister for guests and sisters connecting the chapel to the refectory created a beautiful enclosed garden. Funds had also been raised through the sale of approximately eight acres of frontage on Yonge Street, and the entrance to the convent property was re-routed to an adjacent street.

Beyond the convent, mission work outside of Toronto expanded and contracted as the need arose. A few yards from the sisters' branch house in Bracebridge, Ontario, the Sunshine House mission was opened two days a week to provide practical support, clothing, and meals to needy

Mother Aquila with a model of the convent, chapel, bedroom wing, infirmary, and guest house.

residents in the area. A few years later, when the happy discovery was made that food and clothing were no longer critically needed, the decision was made to withdraw from the work.

In 1955, the sisters decided reluctantly to withdraw from work with the intellectually disabled at St. John's on the Hill in Aurora. The property was sold to the Diocese of Toronto, which turned it into the Aurora Conference Centre. (Some decades later the diocese sold the property when the buildings were no longer safe and required too much money to renovate.)

The Sixties opened an era of excitement and seismic shifts in social morality. North America had turned its back on the austerity of the war years, and was speeding toward a more modern and materialistic lifestyle, steamrolling over traditions and values. Religious authority was hanging on by a thread, but questions about the existence of God and the validity of organized religion were very much alive. A revival in the works of the nineteenth-century father of nihilism, Friedrich Nietzsche, spawned debate and launched radical attitudes. Nietzsche's aphorism "God is dead" was a frequently quoted slogan, and entering the conversation, the English Bishop John Robinson wrote a book called *Honest to God,* which set in place a lively theological debate.

A group of children in procession in Bracebridge.

But God was definitely not dead, and strong evidence of that was seen in two events that had a profound impact on the Sisterhood: the Anglican Congress which took place in Toronto in 1963, and the Second Vatican Council in Rome between 1962 and 1965.

The Anglican Congress represented the coming of age of the Anglican Communion. The theme of the Congress was "Mutual Responsibility and Interdependence in the Body of Christ." It called for churches in developed countries to do more than offer financial aid to churches in developing countries, but to understand mission as something that demanded personal involvement. It launched a global conversation about unity in the midst of diversity. No church or religious community was untouched by it, and the commitment to deeper conversation with each other and deeper involvement in the Church as a whole was shared by the Sisterhood. It brought into light in a new way how much we need each other.

The Second Vatican Council, even though Roman Catholic, had an equally strong influence on all the Anglican communities. Under the leadership of Pope John XXIII and with the invited presence of Christians from denominations all over the world, a fresh wind of the Spirit moved through the Church. When the council closed in 1965, its decisions created ripples and sometimes waves far beyond the Roman Catholic Church. Everything seemed to change: the Church's liturgy, the role of the laity in the life of the Church, and the role of religious orders. Above all, it was clear that the Roman Catholic Church was eager to engage with the modern world. Catholics were encouraged to pray with other Christian denominations and to interact with non-Christian faiths. Latin was no longer the language of the mass, and vernacular interpretations in many forms — new prayers, new hymns, new music — made their appearances at the Sunday services. Gregorian chant was replaced by six-string guitars and casually dressed choirs. Religious orders were directed to go back to their founding visions and reassess their ministries in the light of their founding values.

The changes that came out of Vatican II for religious communities were not immediately embraced by everyone. What was a breath of fresh air to some was a traumatic reckoning to others. Many who had given themselves to religious life felt spiritually injured; they feared for the survival of religious life as they knew it, and feared for their own survival within it. To them the old traditions were being jettisoned merely for the sake of modernity, and they could not reconcile this seemingly quixotic (for the Church) change in posture with the reliable and simple routine they had followed and that had drawn them to religious life in the first place.

Anglican communities were not untouched by these changes, and most sisters in most communities found the changes empowering.

Though she was in many ways a traditionalist, Mother Aquila oversaw the dramatic change of moving the community from the rhythm of seven daily times of worship (common to all monastic communities) to a simpler pattern of corporate prayer, and she allowed experimentation with new forms of worship.

The minutes of the sisters' chapter meetings from those years in the late 1960s indicate the sisters wanted their worship to align more closely with the Church as a whole, and the new Canadian *Book of Common Prayer*, published in 1962, made this possible with a four-fold daily office of Morning Prayer, Noon Office, Evening Prayer, and Compline (night prayer).

This in itself was not without controversy. To some of the older sisters, this change would have amounted to a revolutionary deviation from the millennium-old Benedictine pattern of seven times of worship each day. And yet, practicalities had to be acknowledged and realities faced. The Sisterhood of St. John the Divine was a community that blended the active with the contemplative. Running a convent had become more complex and busier, and while Mother Aquila recalled the sisters to Mother Hannah's strong belief that prayer had to come first, she was also realistic enough to understand that the four-fold office made that more possible. Worship was central to the community, and it could only be effective when its sisters were both physically and mentally present. Both at QDS and the hospital, the schedule was arranged so the sisters could be present in chapel for worship together — one of the advantages of sisters running their own institutions.

An experimental revision of the Sisterhood's *Rule of Life* was also undertaken at this time to catch up with the realities of the day. For example, the Sisterhood's Rule discouraged sisters from going out alone, and yet, there were sisters who were travelling alone all the time, all over Canada, to do mission work, to lead quiet days, or to give talks on the religious life. Some were away for weeks at a time.

In the late 1960s, the habit was simplified, and washable material became available, much to the comfort and delight of the sisters. Optional colours of blue or beige were also introduced at this time and mixed with the traditional black habits and the white ones of the sisters at the hospital.

Sisters no longer moved directly from the novitiate to life vows — instead they took "first vows" for three years in order to allow a longer period of formation before they made their Life Profession.

Doreen McGuff, who entered the Sisterhood when she finished university at the age of twenty-two, strode through the psychedelic social upheaval of the Swinging Sixties to test her vocation post–Vatican II:

There were seven of us who came in around the same time. And I would say that of the seven, probably five of us were typical products of the Sixties. It was a time of great change in community as much as in society. The community was experimenting with modern liturgies, free-standing altars, and guitars. In fact, when Sister Allison and I were clothed as novices — May 5, 1966 — guitars, the experimental Qu'Appelle liturgy, and a temporary altar were used.

Furthermore, changes were made to the Customary — the guidelines for community living and rules of decorum among the sisters. Sister Thelma-Anne recalled this period:

> Of course in the 1960s, when all this started to happen, change was in the air, everywhere, one thing after another. I can remember, for example, that we used always to curtsey to one another when we passed each other, and that was to recognize the presence of God in each one, but I remember someone saying, "Wouldn't it be alright to smile at the person instead of curtsey — a more human touch?" We also used to have silence in the early afternoon. That went by the board because we felt, at that stage, we needed to begin relating more to one another, to talk to one another more and do things together; go for a walk and chat with one another, which coincided with our rest time and things like that. As well, the separation between guests, or externs as we used to call them, and the sisters, began to lessen. As late as 1964 a folding divider was used in the refectory to keep us apart from guests.

By the late 1960s the divider was used only on the sisters' monthly retreat days, to give them privacy. Sunday "talking suppers" with guests were now a regular event, and men were admitted as overnight guests in the guesthouse and ate with the sisters in the refectory.

Even the name of the community's newsletter wasn't immune to change: *St. John's Messenger* was renamed *The Eagle* in 1961. This subtle form of rebranding reflected the community's link with St. John in naming it after the symbol associated with him and with the Resurrection: it also reflected the community's desire to be seen as upwardly soaring and undeniably alive within an ethos of contemplative prayer.

It mirrored its leader in that, despite the busyness and changes inside and outside the convent, Mother Aquila remained committed to a contemplative life and presence. Rooted and grounded in their daily round of prayer, the Sisterhood's mission work continued to evolve.

In Montreal, the widening of Dorchester Street in 1963 meant that the building housing St. Michael's Mission had to come down, and so the sisters moved their work to the Church of St. John the Evangelist on what is now President Kennedy Avenue. The sisters lived temporarily with the sisters of St. Margaret at St. Margaret's Home while the parish hall at St. John the Evangelist was renovated for the mission, and space for a sisters' residence was prepared on the top floor of the parish hall. As late as 1961, the number of homeless men seeking clothing and a bed numbered more than three hundred a month. The sisters also provided Sunday breakfasts for more than two thousand people a year, taught Sunday school to countless children, and made numerous home visits to fill emotional and spiritual needs: one sister is reported to have made six hundred home visits in a single year.

As the government gradually provided more social services, the sisters withdrew from the work at St. Michael's mission in 1964. The parish of St. John the Evangelist, however, continued the mission and it grew and accommodated the new needs of a modern city in Montreal's urban core. Today it serves young unemployed men, former psychiatric patients, alcoholics, drug addicts, and former prison inmates. The mission continues to be grounded in the Sisterhood's core belief that we are all made in the image of God and are therefore all called to support one another in love.

With telecommunications opening up access to all parts of the country, the sisters also ended their work with Sunday School by Post, though Eva Hasell, the program's founder, would faithfully continue it well into the late 1970s. And the sisters' commitment to Sunday school in various parishes also continued.

In 1964, another donation from the Larkin Estate allowed the sisters to rebuild their cottage, Bally Croy, in Port Sydney, Ontario. It retained the warm and homey feel of the original cottage, though it was considerably larger with twelve bedrooms, a large sitting room with a wood-burning fireplace, a dining area that could comfortably seat fourteen people, an open kitchen, a number of bathrooms, a small reading room, and a laundry room. It also has a simple but beautiful chapel that continues to be used for the sisters' worship while on holiday.

Changing social attitudes directly affected the sisters' work in Edmonton. A more sexually permissive society no longer viewed unwed mothers as "fallen women," and the arrival of "the Pill" and its widespread use lessened the incidence of unwanted pregnancies.

"It was the good girls who got in trouble," recalled Sister Doreen, who ministered at St. John's House in Edmonton during the late 1960s. "They were scared; they had made a mistake. Most of the babies were given up for adoption, and the girls returned to their homes, most of them on farms. While they were with us it was important to give them a safe, caring place and to let them know that they were good, and that they could go forward with their lives. We all loved the babies; it was a warm, family home."

The sisters withdrew from their work at St. John's House and Elizabeth House in 1967, but they were back in Edmonton the following year. The Diocesan Bishop Gerald Burch, in extending his invitation to the sisters, said it was the presence and prayer life of the sisters that was valued more than any specific work. Given Mother Aquila's fondness for the Prairies and her eagerness to maintain a foothold in the city, it is easy to understand her delight at receiving the bishop's request. A group of sisters moved back into the Elizabeth House building, renovated and redecorated it, and re-opened it as St. John's Priory where they provided hospitality for associates and other guests.

Sister Doreen recalls a sense of adventure and discernment during that time, a chance to try new things. Several generations of standard poodles even became a regular part of life at the priory.

Not everything was seen as an "adventure" though, particularly by those sisters who were engaged in institutional work at the Church Home, Qu'Appelle

The new Bally Croy in 1964.

Diocesan School, and St. John's Hospital. Tensions arose within the Sisterhood about their direction as more sisters began to gravitate toward the idea of leading retreats, quiet days, going out to preach, and doing inner-city work. But Mother Aquila helped the sisters maintain a creative balance, and all three of the Sisterhood's institutional ministries continued to flourish.

In Regina, at QDS/St. Chad's School, the school continued its evolution. Enrollment shot up to the point that the Diocesan bishop recommended (and personally collected the funds for) an urgently needed new gymnasium. Sister Margaret Ann was the well-loved headmistress from 1958 to 1968, and the school continued to achieve and surpass its academic goals. Thanks to the work of its teachers, both sisters and lay, more and more of its graduates were winning city-wide medals for academic excellence, and being awarded scholarships and university placements.

A series of much-needed renovations was completed in 1967, thanks to a large loan from the diocese, and the school was transformed. Its beautiful interior, its bountiful library — considered one of the best high-school libraries in Saskatchewan — improved its standing in the community. Sister Beryl, who had been both a student and teacher at St. Chad's before joining the Sisterhood, returned as a sister in 1968 to became headmistress when Sister Margaret Ann returned to the convent to become Novice Mistress.

TOP: *Sister Margaret Ann, headmistress of Qu'Appelle Diocesan School.*
BOTTOM: *A group of students at the Qu'Appelle Diocesan School.*

Sister Audrey was a teacher there for twenty-nine years and her influence was considerable. She taught art, literature, and scripture, and helped build up the school's library. The drama club grew out of the literature classes, and the Christmas and Easter tableaux out of her scripture classes. The "little people" in the kindergarten were her pride and joy, and many generations of these came under her loving care.

Expansion and change was also the order of the decade at St. John's Convalescent Hospital. In 1951, the Goodwin Gibson Wing opened to provide more than a hundred ward beds, and the original building was remodelled to allow for additional private and semi-private rooms. In 1953, a beautiful chapel was added to the main hospital building, with stained glass windows and furnishings from the chapel at Bishop Bethune College (which had closed in 1932). It provided a place for the sisters who lived and worked at the hospital to pray the four-fold daily office and celebrate the Eucharist, as well as conduct services for patients and provide a welcoming space for patients and staff to pray and meditate.

Sister Audrey with students in the library.

That same year, 1953, the hospital board acquired eight acres of land that were annexed to the hospital property. A graceful and functional L-shaped residence was built — one wing providing a private residence for the sisters who worked at the hospital (they had previously been housed on the third floor of the hospital) and the other for hospital staff and medical, nursing, and physical therapy students. In 1961, a new rehab wing was added to the hospital building, providing a gym, treatment areas, two therapy pools with electric hoists, facilities to accommodate exercises centred on daily living activities and rehabilitation, and rooms for speech and remedial therapy. The concept of rehabilitation therapy had grown exponentially and before the end of the 1960s, negotiations had begun with the Ministry of Health to expand and modernize the hospital further.

Sister Vera, who succeeded Sister Beatrice as administrator in 1954, was involved in the planning and execution of all the additions and expansions of the original building right up until her retirement in 1969, after thirty-two years of service. She was succeeded by Sister Philippa, who carried on the planning with Mathers and Haldenby, the original architects of the hospital.

Sisters Vera and Philippa were members of the American College of Hospital Executives and, along with Sisters Merle and Patricia, were founding members of the Canadian College of Health Services Executives. All had specialized training in hospital management through the Canadian Hospital Association and were influential in the Ontario Hospital Association and the Toronto District Health Council. These dedicated, accomplished women maintained the values of patient care established more than a century earlier by the community's foundress while integrating the many policies and procedures mandated by provincial and professional health care bodies. Hospital administration is meticulous and onerous work and requires the patience of a saint. Yet the sisters never forgot the basic needs of the patients and never sacrificed quality of care to satisfy the demands of record keeping.

The 1970s opened on a sober note for the Sisterhood as its school in Regina was forced to close for financial reasons. The diocese had been carry-

The chapel at St. John's Convalescent Hospital.

ing a debt caused by necessary renovations to the building. The school was paying its way but was unable to help the diocese clear the debt. It was an enormous disappointment to the sisters. St. Chad's had been one of the Sisterhood's greatest achievements; it was beloved by its graduates.

The school had been a model of the Sisterhood's ability to transform lacklustre institutions into centres of academic excellence. St. Chad's had also been a place where First Nations girls

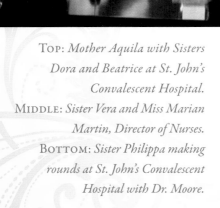

TOP: *Mother Aquila with Sisters Dora and Beatrice at St. John's Convalescent Hospital.*
MIDDLE: *Sister Vera and Miss Marian Martin, Director of Nurses.*
BOTTOM: *Sister Philippa making rounds at St. John's Convalescent Hospital with Dr. Moore.*

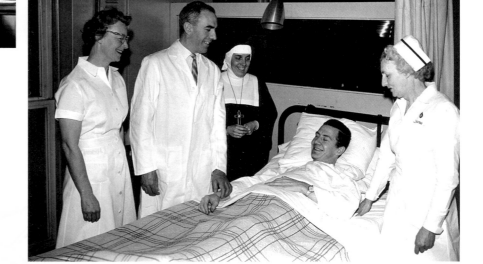

were completing high school. After fifty-two years, many people were sorry that the school had closed.

It was around this time, following twenty-five years of loyal service, that Mother Aquila retired as Superior. She joined the chaplaincy staff at St. John's Convalescent Hospital, and focused on pastoral ministry where she devoted her time to what she loved most: ministering to patients and their families. As the community's leader, Mother Aquila had made a major contribution to the life of the wider Church. She conducted Schools of Prayer and led retreats both in Canada and the U.S. She was appointed by the Primate to the Board of Women's Work of the national Church, she chaired the Board of the Church Home, she was a member of the hospital board, and a founding member of the Council on the Religious Life (CORL) for the Anglican and Episcopal religious orders in North America.

After a short illness, Sister Aquila died at the age of ninety-four on August 19, 1996. Sister Constance Joanna remembers being with her, along with the Sisterhood's long-time friend and chaplain Bishop Henry Hill, at North York General Hospital in Toronto the night she died. They were given a private room, and Sister Constance Joanna and Bishop Hill sang all her favourite Ascension hymns until she quietly slipped away to be with the Lord she had loved and served all her life.

Sister Doreen describes Mother Aquila's leadership throughout a tumultuous time in the history of the church, the world, and the Sisterhood as "quiet and contemplative, realistic and courageous, risk-taking and peacemaking. She was courageous and adventuresome — someone who believed that God was always in charge making things new!"

4 EMBRACING RELIGIOUS UNITY, 1970–1994
Mother Frances Joyce

Frances Joyce Grazier (known as Joyce to her family) had her heart set on being a missionary nurse in India. She was certainly qualified for it, but as so often happens in life, God steers us to the place where we are truly needed, and in this case God needed Joyce in Canada.

Born on February 4, 1924, into a clergy family in Strasburg, Saskatchewan, Joyce took a business course and worked at a bank in Yorkton before moving into nursing and training at the Regina General Hospital. Quiet and observant, she excelled in nursing, and when she graduated in 1948 she received the Florence Nightingale Award for devotion to duty, an apt indicator of her personality.

After graduation, she began her career at Moose Jaw General Hospital, and then moved to Winnipeg where she became the superintendent of the Church Home for Girls, a residence for unwed mothers run jointly by the Anglican and United churches.

When her brother's wife died during the polio epidemic of 1952, Joyce moved back to Yorkton to look after him and his two young children. A few years later he remarried, by which time she had decided to move to Toronto and join the Sisterhood of St. John the Divine where her younger sister Wilma was already a novice.

When she first entered the community, there was already a Sister Frances and a Sister Joyce, and so in keeping with the custom at the time, she was given another name in community — Felicity — although before her Life Profession she was given permission to return to her birth name of Frances Joyce.

Sister Frances Joyce made an indelible impression in the community with her exceptional nursing skills and her commitment to patient care, making her an obvious choice to run the Sisterhood's infirmary. She was a nurse's nurse: firm, capable, and compassionate. She had a sixth sense of knowing exactly what was needed to make a patient comfortable. Her nursing skills were utilized not only at the convent but also at St. John's Convalescent Hospital and at St. Michael's Mission in Montreal. Five years after her Life Profession, Sister Frances Joyce spent a year with the Society of St. John the Divine in Pietermaritzburg, South Africa, in response to that community's request for help in developing and establishing its own nursing practices and infirmary.

Not long after her return from South Africa, she became Assistant Superior to Mother Aquila in 1967, and in 1970, the community elected her its fourth Mother Superior.

Mother Frances Joyce was not an "ideas" person, but, like Mother Aquila, she had a knack for gathering around her sisters who complemented her own strengths. She also had the gift of listening, and encouraged the sisters to share their ideas and develop them for the benefit of the community.

Hard-working, diligent, and modest, she had a sense of humour

Mother Frances Joyce after she received her honorary Doctor of Divinity degree from the College of Emmanuel and St. Chad in 1989.

and could laugh at herself, which was a good thing since she was said to be on the slow side when it came to catching on to jokes. She took the subsequent ribbing from her fellow sisters in stride. She had a spirited style of conversation, and whether she had returned from an overseas trip or from a visit to a branch house she would regale the sisters with details and anecdotes.

Her calm countenance and spirited conversation were much in need. The community was still grieving the closing of St. Chad's, and it was not the only ministry that would be coming to an end. Mother Frances Joyce had been encouraging the sisters to review the community's many ventures with an eye to the future. With the median age of the sisters increasing and fewer young women entering the novitiate, some ministries simply could not be sustained.

Coloured embroidery work on chasubles, copes, and altar cloths had been stitched by the sisters since the community's inception, earning the sisters a deserved reputation as gifted and skilled practitioners of the art. But while a large and denominationally diverse clientele kept the workroom busy, there was only one sister remaining who had the gift for that kind of artistry. Sister Joanna had learned from Sister Eva, who had been in charge of the workroom from 1915 to 1935, a period of exceptional craftsmanship that had not been seen since the pre-Reformation era. Sister Eva had passed her knowledge and training to Sister Joanna, who was

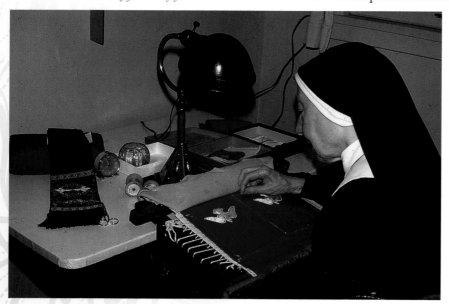

Sister Joanna did fine coloured embroidery for many years.

a true artist, and even in her later years she continued making beautiful stoles, her last being a design for the ordination of Carol Adamson (the niece of Sisters Wilma and Frances Joyce). The design featured a prairie crocus, and when asked if she had a pattern, Sister Joanna replied, "No, I just made one."

As Sister Joanna herself was now advancing in years, she had no one to train as her successor. This intense, highly specialized art requires many pairs of skilled hands and eyes and there was simply no one to carry it on at that time (though recent years have seen a revival of interest in the art among at least one younger sister). When Sister Joanna's weary eyes could no longer handle the strain of the work, she asked to be relieved of her duties. It was disappointing but inevitable: This was a creative ministry that had begun with Mother Hannah, and while the Sisterhood's reputation was legendary, church embroidery was quickly going out of fashion as modern tastes in ecclesiastical garments began leaning toward inexpensive and easily produced appliqué designs.

White work (altar cloths, fair veils, lavabo towels, and purificators) had also been part of the Sisterhood's ministry since the earliest days of the community, and while it, too, required nimble and creative fingers, there were more hands who could manage this work.

Altar bread was another ministry that was discontinued during Mother Frances Joyce's time. The department had been prolific, producing about two million discs of bread per year; but after seventy years of baking, cutting, scoring, counting, and packing by hand, more efficient production methods were being employed elsewhere, and in 1976 the bake room closed.

As these ministries concluded, opportunities opened for other ministries to evolve.

The Church Home had long been a priority of the Sisterhood. Over the years, the sisters' pioneering approach to holistic care for the elderly, ranging from preserving independence to providing total care, continued to develop. The Church Home for the Aged comprised two wings: Bellevue House and the Gwynneth Osler Memorial Wing, the latter originally caring for women who were not able to pay for their care. The distinction had been abandoned some years earlier, but an interesting reminder that it once existed was related by Sister Wilma. When she was sent to work at the Church Home in the 1970s, she noticed that there were still two sets of silverware: the plainer one had originally been used in the Osler wing, the fancier one in the Bellevue wing. This two-tiered attitude seems unfair to us now, but in the culture of the time, charitable institutions provided for residents (and hospital patients) and if you were a paying resident or patient you got the good silver; if you were being subsidized, you got the plainer tableware.

By the early 1970s, it had become apparent that the structure and age of the building at 87 Bellevue was no longer suitable to any of its residents. Its location was problematic, too. Across the road was a factory whose production had shifted into an all-night operation. It wasn't just the noise from the factory that jarred, it was the smell, and one day it all became too much for feisty and diminutive Sister Constance. She marched over and asked the nature of their business. They explained that they made plaques and monuments. Sister Constance succeeded in convincing the factory's manager to minimize the noise and the odour, and for a little while things were peaceful. But then the racket resumed, disturbing the tranquillity the sisters sought for their elderly clients. When Sister Wilma took over managing the Church Home in 1972, she joined forces with the neighbourhood residents' council and the representatives of St. Stephen's Community Centre next door to see if their combined efforts would make inroads with the factory, but it had little effect.

However, in spite of some annoyances in the environment, most of the sisters who worked at the Church Home thrived in the location. Sister Wilma relates:

> We loved the carnival atmosphere with nearby Kensington Market, the lively Portuguese neighbourhood, St. Stephen's Church, involvement with the Parkdale Deanery, the inner city, the historic closeness to the foundation of the Sisterhood on Robinson Street, Major Street, and Brunswick Avenue, and our friends at the firehall across the street. Delicious memories, never to be forgotten and never to be repeated.

Around that time, the Bishop of Toronto, the Right Reverend George Snell, was creating an organization called Anglican Houses that would bring several diocesan houses for troubled youth and homeless men and women under one organizational umbrella. A similar arrangement was envisioned for diocesan homes that cared for the elderly: Strachan Houses (a residence for the elderly run by the Women's Auxiliary of the diocese) was not far from the Church Home for the Aged, and at the bishop's suggestion the two amalgamated and were brought under the management of Anglican Houses.

A new site for this venture was found in the Scarborough parish of St. Paul's L'Amoreaux, where its priest wanted to build a new St. Paul's Church that would integrate the needs of its growing congregation and provide accommodation for its senior citizens. Cana Place became part of this complex and it opened in 1978. The name was suggested by a long-time, beloved friend and associate of the Sisterhood, the Reverend Brian Freeland, a priest at St. Thomas' Anglican Church, and a CBC TV personality who started popular television programs such as *Hymn Sing* and *Man Alive*. He suggested "Cana" because when Jesus worked his first miracle (as recorded in St. John's gospel), he turned the water into wine at a wedding in Cana of Galilee, and the people were surprised that the host had "saved the best wine for the last." The word "Place" was suggested by Miss Ethel Stevens, a ninety-year-old resident, because it was contemporary and because of its scriptural connection: "I go and prepare a place for you" (John 14:3). Both aspects of the name Cana Place reflected the strong value the sisters have always placed on creating a home environment for the people they have worked among, and their strong belief that the last years of a person's life should be the best.

Cana Place accommodated forty-six residents within an active, Christian, family-like atmosphere. Sisters Wilma and Doreen, who at different times served as administrator of Cana Place, worked with other dedicated sisters and staff to provide residents with round-the-clock professional yet home-like care.

The Sisterhood never shied away from experimentation, and Mother Frances Joyce encouraged forward-thinking ideas among her sisters. Sister Constance's work with the elderly, for instance, was a passion of hers since joining SSJD in the 1930s although she was equally passionate about education for the young. She had been a strong and successful headmistress of the Qu'Appelle Diocesan School before she came back to Toronto to take charge of the old Church Home for the Aged. When she left the Church Home in 1972, she continued tirelessly

The patio at Cana Place.

to campaign for more awareness of seniors' needs, before the discipline of gerontology had even been coined. Sister Constance was encouraged by the community to continue her studies and her work with the elderly. In addition to her front-line work with the elderly in several nursing homes and homes for the aged, she attended conferences as a delegate, chaired committees, wrote papers, presented academic studies, and helped found the Canadian Institute of Religion and Gerontology in 1974. The following year she went back to school at the University of Michigan at Ann Arbor. (There were as yet no graduate programs

in gerontology in Ontario.) She studied hard while enjoying campus life, riding her bicycle, and eating peanut butter sandwiches for lunch. She earned her Master's degree in Education and Gerontology in 1977 at the age of seventy-three.

Sr. Constance's work with the elderly as well as with children was honoured many times through her life, including honourary doctorates from the College of Emmanuel and St. Chad, Saskatoon, and Trinity College, Toronto, and the Commemorative Medal for the 125th Anniversary of Confederation. She was an international observer several times at the White House Conference on Aging, and she put her own life on the front lines by participating for decades in the Baltimore Longitudinal Study on Aging at Johns Hopkins University. She died in 2013 at the age of 109 ½, leaving behind a treasured autobiography published in 1997, *Other Little Ships*.

Another major event in the 1970s was the further expansion of St. John's Convalescent Hospital. The Gibson Wing was demolished in

Sister Constance used to ride her bicycle to visit the elderly.

1975 to make way for a five-storey addition, named the Agnew Wing after the doctor who had so much influence in developing rehabilitation medicine, Dr. Harvey Agnew. The foundation bricks of the former Gibson Wing remained in place and became the border of a beautiful garden adjacent to the Agnew Wing. At the same time, the original 1937 building was remodelled and named the Scadding Wing after Dr. H. Crawford Scadding, the first president of the hospital medical staff.

As the 1970s drew to a close, there was much discussion and considerable divided opinion among the sisters about whether to continue doing institutional work (at the hospital and at Cana Place). At its 1980 general chapter, the community voted to give St. John's Priory in Edmonton a new mandate for work in the inner city, the result of a long-held desire of many sisters to work among the poor as they had done years earlier in Toronto and Montreal. Four sisters went to the priory to start the new work. While keeping the house as a place of hospitality for many who needed support and a safe haven, the sisters also worked in shelters and prison chaplaincy, in a shelter for women in the inner city, and in an adult literacy program that continues to this day at the Boyle Street Community Services.

Meanwhile, the secular world had continued to change and evolve, and Mother Frances Joyce believed that the monastic world needed to keep pace. The first astronauts had landed on the moon in 1969, a few months before she was installed as Mother Superior, and during much of her time in office people around the world were fascinated by the vision of space travel and the potential for international co-operation. And there were positive signs: the Berlin Wall came down and Nelson Mandela was released from prison. But there was much conflict and violence too, especially with the outbreak of the Vietnam War. In the world at large, the twenty-four years of Mother Frances Joyce's time in office was a see-saw of hope and despair, conflict, and cooperation.

The sisters at St. John's Priory: Sisters Nora, Rosemary Anne, Patricia, and Sarah Jean with their dog Caspian.

This fractious period inspired Mother Frances Joyce to focus on an issue close to her heart: unity, especially among the churches. A few years before she took office, in 1966, a joint working group had been established between the World Council of Churches and the Roman Catholic Church, and in 1971 the Anglican Church of Canada voted to participate in the "Plan of Union" with the United Church. As the lofty ecumenical ideals of church union gave way to a more modest goal of churches working together for mutual understanding and common mission, Christians in and out of the cloister started experiments in co-operation. Many ecumenical advocacy groups were founded and grew during Mother Frances Joyce's time. One close to the heart of the sisters was the Task Force on the Churches and Corporate Responsibility, which involved the sisters in social justice advocacy for several decades.

The community recognized the importance of forging local links and networks and eliminating barriers as a means of opening up dialogue and exchanging ideas. As the world marched toward globalization and the walls around the status quo began to crumble, it no doubt spurred in the sisters the confidence to move toward the same vision of openness. Mother Frances Joyce encouraged ecumenical friendships with local Roman Catholic and Orthodox communities, inviting them to gatherings at the convent so that they could worship together, learn from each other, and share common interests. Annual ecumenical evenings were held during the Week of Prayer for Christian Unity.

Bishop Henry Hill was an associate of the Sisterhood, and its warden in the 1980s (the title later changed to senior chaplain). He shared Mother Frances Joyce's views on ecumenism, and in 1981, he was appointed by the then-Archbishop of Canterbury, Robert Runcie, as co-chair of the Anglican Orthodox Joint Doctrinal Commission, a post in which he travelled widely among the Eastern and Oriental Orthodox churches. As a soul-friend to the sisters in the 1980s and 1990s, Bishop Hill broadened their international and ecumenical vision, and brought to the convent friends from many faith traditions. The sisters discovered the riches of Orthodox iconography and chant as well as the writings of the Orthodox spiritual tradition. It was through Bishop Hill's influence that the leaders of two large Romanian Orthodox monasteries for women came to spend several months with the sisters in the summer of 1979. Mother Nazaria and Mother Lucia had a lasting effect on the Sisterhood, creating friendships across the barriers of culture, language, and religion. It was a creative time for all the sisters who had the opportunity to meet and get to know them. At their suggestion, Patriarch Justin of the Romanian Orthodox Church invited the Sisterhood to send two sisters on a reciprocal visit. And so in August and September of the following year, Sister Thelma-Anne and Sister Andrea received the generous hospitality of the Romanian people, and they spent time at both Mother Nazaria's monastery in Pasaea and Mother Lucia's monastery in Moldavia. Sister Thelma-Anne summed up their experience in an article in *The Eagle* (Christmas 1980):

> To share the life of Christians of other traditions and to come
> to know and love them as persons puts theological discussion
> in perspective and also provides an incentive to work and pray
> for greater understanding and unity.

The sisters' interaction with Orthodox groups, especially the Oriental Orthodox (Coptic, Ethiopian, Armenian, and Syrian), increased when Bishop Hill came to live at the convent in an apartment hermitage that he had built on the side of the convent in 1984. Soon, bearded clerics in their cassocks and exotic headdress mixing with sisters in blue habits became a familiar sight. The clerics came to visit Bishop Hill in his role as emissary, and by extension these religious visitors became friends of the sisters as well. It eventually led to the Sisterhood hosting in 1990 the International Anglican-Orthodox Dialogue.

Relationships continued to develop with other Anglican communities as well.

In 1989, supported by a generous trust from a mutual friend of the two communities, Carol Bunker, the Sisterhood began an annual exchange program with the Order of the Holy Paraclete in Whitby, England, the

The International Commission for the Anglican-Orthodox theological dialogue in Dublin in 1984 — Bishop Henry Hill is in the centre of the front row.

same religious community whose students and teachers the community had billeted during the Second World War. A joint venture of both communities that began at this time was the knitting of teddy bears to raise money for Amnesty International. It is a liaison that continues to this day, enriching the friendships and the prayer life of both.

In 1984, another ecumenical venture began that built deep friendships between the sisters and a male Roman Catholic Cistercian community. Sister Margaret Ann had come to know Father Lawrence, at that time Novice Master and later Abbot of Mount St. Joseph Abbey in Roscrea, Ireland. They had met at an ecumenical gathering of novice directors, and in 1984 he came back to Canada for another conference, and visited Toronto. A decision was made to start a "twin" relationship between Mount St. Joseph Abbey and the Sisterhood. Various sisters became pen pals of some of the brothers, often matching their roles in the community (as Sister Margaret Ann and Father Lawrence were both novice directors). A sister who worked in the kitchen became friends with a brother who ran the bakery at Roscrea. A sister who loved to garden developed a creative relationship with a brother responsible for the gardens in Roscrea. And eventually there were some personal visits. Sister Jessica spent a week at Roscrea in the autumn of 1989; Sister Constance Joanna spent a week with the brothers in 1992, and other sisters followed. The close relationships that developed across gender, cultural, and denominational lines brought increased openness to both communities. Sister Jessica reflected on her experience at Roscrea:

> My reason for feeling so strongly bonded to this marvelous group of down-to-earth holy men was because at the core of the life of both our communities is the Benedictine ethos, the Christ-centered living. Only God's loving generosity and wisdom could bring to fruition this wonderful experience of twinning between a Roman Catholic Cistercian monastery in Ireland and an Anglican sisterhood in Canada."[1]

As the sisters visited communities overseas and the community's doors opened to visitors from around the world, so, too, in reciprocal fashion, were doors opened to the sisters. Sunday talking suppers continued at the convent, which facilitated informal and spirited conversation between guests and sisters. The exchange of information and ideas invigorated the sisters, encouraging them to test different styles of worship, and add new prayers and music to their offices. In particular, music from Taizé and Orthodox churches enriched the Sisterhood's liturgy.

This climate of openness led to other forms of experimentation. In the early 1980s, the community studied the Myers Briggs Type Indicator, a psychological questionnaire designed to assess personality type and how people's preferences and perceptions affect their decision-making and interaction with others. Today, the Myers-Briggs test is widely used as a human resources tool by corporations and institutions around the world. For the sisters, it helped develop deeper understanding of themselves and each other in the context of building a strong community life.

"We found the Myers Briggs method very helpful," Sister Thelma-Anne recalled several years ago:

> We've gone through a stage where we were thinking the Jungians were very influential, so we are much more attuned to the positive side of psychology. It was a transformational time in the community. We talked a lot — did the Myers Briggs, studied the Enneagram, learned to understand ourselves and each other, and above all talk on a deeper level to one another. Chapter meetings became longer. In 1983, Dom Benedict Reid OSB from Three Rivers, Michigan, gave a retreat to the sisters that really opened things up, and as a result two Pilgrim groups were started — one for the older sisters and one for the younger ones: the former did not last long but the younger group remained together for a number of years.

The "Pilgrim" groups were what might be called faith sharing groups today, and gave sisters the opportunity to share, in an informal setting, their hopes, dreams, fears, and challenges, both personal and communal.

As the sisters conversed, they came to know each other at a deeper level and the community spent more time in meetings and discussions. The names that sisters called each other began to shift as well. In 1987, after some years of discussing names and titles off and on, the sisters agreed to drop the "Sister" title when conversing with one another inside the community (and when individuals were comfortable with that), and they also changed the titles of a number of offices in the community. The term "Superior" was dropped, as the sisters preferred a more egalitarian and family-like title, reflecting more accurately the democratic and consultative relationships within the community. Thus the title of the community leader became simply "Reverend Mother," though the form of address remained "Mother Frances Joyce." (Later, when Sister Constance Joanna became Reverend Mother, she asked the sisters to call her informally by her name, and to use "Sister" Constance Joanna rather than "Mother" as a form of address with those outside the community. That custom continued with Sister Elizabeth Ann's time in office.)

All this delighted Mother Frances Joyce as she carried the ecumenical flag beyond her community's doors. She sat on the Superior's Council of the Conference on the Religious Life (CORL), which later evolved into the Conference of Anglican Religious Orders in the Americas (CAROA). For three years she served as its representative at ecumenical meetings in Rome, Israel, and in the United States. Her determined work earned her an honorary Doctorate of Divinity from the College of Emmanuel and St. Chad in Saskatoon.

Vocations to the community were about half those of Sister Aquila's time, as new opportunities had opened for women both in the church and in society at large, and as church membership in general declined in the latter half of the twentieth century. But women did come knocking and a trend began to emerge. The aspirants were modern, often well-educated, strong-minded, and opinionated women, and they were older on average. The Sisterhood had always attracted some women who were mature, who had perhaps been married, or who had found their vocation as a "second career." And while religious life had historically drawn many women in their early twenties, it was now attracting more "older" women, into their thirties, forties, and even fifties. Between 1970 and 1994, forty-four women tested their vocation with the community and fifteen stayed to Life Profession (about 33 percent, not much different from the percentage who stayed in Sister Aquila's time).

The women's movement continued to be a defining *zeitgeist* of this period. In 1975, the Anglican Church of Canada became one of the earliest provinces of the Anglican Communion to approve the ordination of women to the priesthood, second only to the Diocese of Hong Kong. Canadian Anglican women were now free to be ordained priests and had far more vocational opportunities within the church as well as in secular society.

The Sisterhood was very much involved in that momentous and historic achievement. In 1977, on November 18 — St. Hilda's Day — Sister Rosemary Anne Benwell became one of the first women, as well as the first sister, to be ordained in Canada.

Sister Rosemary Anne had studied at the Anglican Women's Training College (later merged into the Centre for Christian Studies) and been ordained a deaconess before entering the Sisterhood. She served in many of the community's ministries in Montreal and Edmonton as well as Toronto. She was a sister who could do almost everything: at different times she was responsible for the altar bread department, had oversight of the kitchen, served as associate director, led missions in many places in Canada, was Sunday school superintendent at St. Philip's Church on Caribou Street in Toronto, and served for five years at the convent as Assistant Superior to Mother Aquila, in addition to being a talented artist. In 1969, she had returned to Edmonton to re-open the former Elizabeth House as St. John's Priory. She served there until 1995, except for a few years in the 1970s when she returned to Toronto. She studied theology at Wycliffe College (University of Toronto) and assisted in two Toronto parishes.

Her longing to be a priest had been with her since she was a young woman, but when the opportunity finally presented itself in 1977 she worried that she was too old for ordination (she was sixty-one). With encouragement from Mother Frances Joyce, Sister Rosemary Anne received the blessing of the community, met with the Bishop of Toronto, and put her name forward as a candidate for ordination. In due course she became the Reverend Sister Rosemary Anne, and was ordained at St. Matthias Church, coincidentally the parish where the Sisterhood had begun its work in 1884 and where the rector at that time, the Reverend Gregory Lee, was a good friend of the Sisterhood.

She was ordained with the Reverend Galt Kortright by Bishop Allan Read (suffragan bishop in Toronto and later diocesan bishop of the Diocese of Ontario).

The Reverend Galt Kortright, Bishop Allan Read, and Sister Rosemary Anne following the ordination of Sister Rosemary Anne.

Doug Saunders, who was the organist at St. Matthias at the time, recalls the event, which was controversial because it was one of the first for a woman:

> The warden at St. Matthias had reluctantly agreed to have the ordination there though he boycotted it in the end. Friends filled out a large complement of servers. The parish pitched in and we had flowers everywhere and a splendid, sumptuous reception afterwards. The choir was made up of musical friends of mine. The dalmatic and tunicle [mass vestments worn by the two newly ordained priests] were from St. Matthias. A visiting priest had taken the chasuble from that set, convinced that the parish had no future. When I was serving at St. John's Convalescent Hospital one day, I saw a chasuble in the sacristy which was no longer in use, but matched the set at St. Matthias. I spoke to Sister Barbara, and she received approval to give me the chasuble for St. Matthias. This is the one that the bishop wore in the service.
>
> The priest at a neighbouring parish, who was not in agreement with the ordination of women, made a public protest to the validity of Sister Rosemary Ann's ordination, but he had conversed with the Bishop beforehand. The Chancellor was present (fully garbed) to declare that the canons had all been followed, and we would proceed. We had all known that it was coming, so it was not an emotional setback. Her contention that she had been ordained Deacon and not Deaconess many years earlier was upheld. Her title was changed from Sister to 'Reverend Sister' — a first![2]

There had been little opposition within the community to Sister Rosemary Anne's ordination, but that did not mean there was total agreement. Some of the sisters at that time disagreed on theological grounds with having women priests, although all of them came to her ordination to support her. As Sister Rosemary Anne recalled in an interview a number of years ago:

I would have needed only a simple majority for permission and over three quarters of the sisters voted in favor. One sister who was not in favor of the ordination of women said at the Chapter that she intended to vote to let me explore the possibility because if she voted no, someday God might say to her, "I called her and you stood in her way."

Sister Veronica was another sister who initially could not accept the ordination of women though she loved Sister Rosemary Anne. She had, however, a profound change of heart. Sister Helen Claire recounts the experience as told to her by Sister Rosemary Anne:

> Shortly before the ordination, Sister Veronica spent an entire retreat day praying about the matter. That night she had a vivid dream that woke her up. In her dream she was in the sisters' chapel, receiving communion from Rosemary Anne, who was enfolded by a pair of hands. Sister Veronica was sure the hands belonged to the Lord. She took her dream to be a sign that Christ approved of women's ordination and from that time on she prayed daily for Rosemary Anne and all the other women priests in Canada. Not only that, she actively encouraged young women to join the priesthood.

The community has always found ways to accommodate sisters who took a little longer to embrace new situations and adapt to change. For instance, when the sisters began distributing the chalice at communion, it was organized so that those sisters who were uncomfortable with this practice could come up first and receive both the bread and wine from the priest (and in some cases the male server); then the other sisters would come up to the communion rail and receive the bread from the priest and the wine from the sister who was chalice-bearer that week.

In addition to opportunities to celebrate the Eucharist and preach in the sisters' chapel, Sister Rosemary Anne served as a priest in the Parish of St. John the Divine in Scarborough, and later at St. Faith's Church in Edmonton, where she was also the sister in charge of St. John's Priory.

Mother Frances Joyce had steadfastly supported Sister Rosemary Anne's sense of vocation to the priesthood during this controversial and historic time in the Sisterhood's history and guided and supported the sisters who were not yet able fully to agree. She was known for her compassion and fairness, and that was evident in many other areas of the community's life. She was very supportive of convent employees, many of whom were refugees. The staff became members of the Sisterhood's extended family, and she knew all their children, prayed for their family concerns, and was deeply loved and respected by them.

Mother Frances Joyce's graciousness prevailed even when she held her ground on certain issues, as another sister recalled:

> After I was first professed, she and I disagreed about something, and it became clear pretty quickly that she was not going to give in. So I said to her very determinedly, "I will do it under obedience not because I agree." We parted without another word, striding defiantly down the twin cloisters of Botham Road toward the chapel for the Eucharist, our heads full of steam — me along the guest cloister, and Frances Joyce along the sisters' cloister. At the passing of the Peace we suddenly found ourselves facing one another. We stopped in our tracks and then both of us burst out laughing, and we gave one another a very affectionate passing of the Peace.

As the Sisterhood's centenary approached, the sisters decided to hold a number of events throughout 1984, including an outing to Carrying Place to visit Mother Hannah's home town and the church where she worshipped and where her father was rector. There was a special Eucharist at St. Thomas Church on Huron Street, where the sisters had worshipped for many years while the convent was on Major Street; and a Choral Evensong at St. James Cathedral in Toronto that featured music and hymns composed by the sisters, notably by Sisters Rosemary Anne and Thelma-Anne. A book of these hymns and chants was published that year, and *Songs for Celebration* continues to be used by the sisters in their daily worship.

What's a celebration without a little mischief thrown in? Some of the sisters who had returned from holiday at Bally Croy put on a theatrical concert for the community based on Gilbert and Sullivan operettas, substituting the lyrics to reflect community life. And so, Sister Nora, the bursar, sang "I'm called Mrs. Moneybags" to the tune of "I'm called Little Buttercup" from *The Mikado*.

By this time, most sisters were wearing blue habits, and some of them had begun wearing civvies during their vacations. The veil continued to be worn with the habit until one auspicious day in 1989. Sister Wilma recalled:

> Sister Anitra had done some research into the meaning of the veil and discovered, among other things, that its origin related to the subjugation of women as described by St. Paul. To many of us this was confirmation that the veil was no longer an acceptable symbol. That afternoon at Chapter when the motion was passed we agreed to appear at Evening Prayer as we wished, with or without our veils. Both Frances Joyce and I were among those who removed our veils immediately. I remember feeling somewhat conspicuous after 34 years of wearing a veil but only for the first time!

Work at St. John's Convalescent Hospital continued to develop as the hospital grew in reputation and demand. In 1982, it was renamed St. John's Hospital; and in 1987 it underwent yet another name change — to St. John's Rehabilitation Hospital. As the provincial government assumed greater control over health care, changes to policies and procedures were ongoing. Since the earliest days of the hospital, various sisters had served as hospital administrator, a job now overlaid with the complexity of union issues, employment standards, and involvement from various levels of government. The demands of the job were full time, and it was challenging to be a sister *and* a hospital administrator without sacrificing one's prayer and worship life.

Sister Philippa met that challenge admirably. She had entered the community with a degree in library sciences from the University of Toronto, but early in her life as a sister she was assigned to St. John's Convalescent Hospital. For sixteen years she served as assistant administrator to Sister Vera, and for a further twenty-seven years as administrator (later called president and CEO). During that time, she grew the hospital while also encouraging and upholding the sisters' prayer commitment. By the time she retired in 1996, the hospital had doubled in size and bed capacity, and the Sisterhood had survived a massive hospital restructuring by the provincial government. New rehabilitation programs had been introduced, and a new division was established to market SJRH's programs to private insurance patients and those covered under the Workplace Safety and Insurance Board. Sister Philippa earned a reputation in the Ontario Hospital Association for running a progressive, state-of-the-art hospital with an excellent medical staff and forward-thinking rehab specialties. All the major acute-care hospitals were clamouring to send their patients to SJRH.

Sister Philippa had clearly taken a page out of Mother Hannah's book when it came to livening up what could easily become a staid hospital atmosphere. She adored the bagpipes, and every time there was good news — winning three-year accreditation status, or government funding, or the approval of a new program — she had a recording of "Amazing Grace" on bagpipes played over the hospital's public address system. She ran a tight ship, but she knew when to lighten up, and she was unfailingly generous to the hospital staff. She was a sister who loved fun, and each year there was a Christmas party, a garden party that became the chief celebration in the neighbourhood, and an annual Robbie Burns party complete with Scottish highland dancers and the best "Address to the Haggis" this side of Scotland. There were also bazaars, rummage sales, and fêtes of various kinds that helped engage the local community.

Inside the residence where twelve sisters lived, Sister Constance Joanna and Sister Jessica remember Sister Philippa organizing social activities to create a real sense of community among the sisters, with parties for birthdays and anniversaries, informal movie nights, and barbeques.

Wearing her rehabilitation hat, Sister Philippa valued the gardens and grounds at SJRH, particularly the metered walkway, which was designed at her instigation by the Hospital's Auxiliary to ensure patients exercised (as well as staff, volunteers and sisters). Not surprisingly, every twenty-five metres was marked by a different Scottish tartan. You would have thought that Sister Philippa came from Scotland, but you would be wrong: she was very proud of having grown up in Winnipeg.

For a time Sister Jessica was coordinator of teen volunteers — the name having been changed from "candystripers" so that young men could join the volunteer pool, and so that the candy stripe dresses could be exchanged for modern T-shirts with the SJRH logo. (Sister Jessica adopted the new dress code after a young woman showed up at one of the garden parties wearing a candy stripe mini-skirt, black tights and boots!)

Another growing ministry of the Sisterhood at this time was the convent guest wing. Welcoming guests to the Botham Road convent and conducting retreats had become a major focus of the sisters' time and energy. It was seen as a vital and incredibly satisfying ministry for the community, enabling the Sisterhood to share the values of monasticism, to lead retreats and workshops, and also to offer spiritual direction. The guest wing quickly became a growing concern.

In 1993, the sisters held a seminal Roots Workshop with the help of a gifted facilitator, Sister Joan Atkinson, a Roman Catholic sister of St. Joseph. Sister Joan had previous experience helping Roman Catholic sisters to re-examine their communities in the light of their founding vision and contemporary realities. She helped the sisters plan for and present a week-long event, bringing together their stories, anecdotes, and collected wisdom about the community's history. The exercise helped strengthen the community's formation and direction, and allowed the sisters to reflect on what had gone before, and on what challenges lay ahead.

The result of the Roots Workshop was what the sisters came to call Vision 2000, a central plan that had eight "common threads" or questions to grapple with:

1. *Institutions:* whether to move away from ministry in institutions (St. John's Rehabilitation Hospital and Cana Place) and the financial impact of such a decision.
2. *Hospitality:* seeking ways of meeting the spiritual hunger of guests, patients, residents, staff, volunteers and others who looked to the Sisterhood to meet their own longing for God, for "something more" in their lives.
3. *Balance of Life:* ensuring that team ministry and shared responsibility made it possible for the sisters to have adequate time for both prayer and service (the contemplative and active dimensions of their lives); that everyone's gifts were used appropriately, and that new members were apprenticed to experienced sisters before they were given new responsibilities.
4. *Strong Centre:* ensuring that in the Mother House and branch houses the sisters' lives were focused on gospel values.
5. *Reaching Out:* seeking to include concern for social justice in all the sisters' ministries; considering flexible alternatives to long-term branch houses (van ministry, short-term residence in various dioceses); and ensuring financial independence.

6. *Location of the Mother House (convent):* considering the traffic, pollution, and lack of accessible space in the current house and weighing renovation versus rebuilding.
7. *Oblates and Associates*: considering how best to incorporate the current associates into the Sisterhood's life more fully, and whether to consider an order of oblates, as more and more people were longing to affiliate with religious orders who were unable to make a lifetime commitment.
8. *Ecumenical Ministry:* continuing the rich friendships that had been nurtured during Mother Frances Joyce's time in office and seeking ways to support ecumenical initiatives of the wider church.

These eight challenging questions were to guide the Sisterhood's discernment in the next Reverend Mother's term of office and they brought about a new era of change — not the least was the eventual decision to move from Botham Road and build a new convent for a new era.

In the meantime, in 1994, Mother Frances Joyce, having led the community through twenty-five years of creative change and adaptation, retired from that position and went to work at St. John's Rehabilitation Hospital as a pastoral visitor.

Sister Frances Joyce died at the age of seventy-six on March 1, 2000. Not surprisingly, her funeral had to be held outside the convent, at St. John's Anglican Church York Mills, to accommodate the large number of participants from widely diverse religious backgrounds. It was a testament to the woman who worked so tirelessly for the cause of ecumenism, and who, by forging and fostering so many relationships, shepherded her sisters toward a vision of hospitality and religious unity that were central to her heart and faith.

A Re-Visioned Community, 1994–2005
Sister Constance Joanna

5

The election in 1994 of Sister Constance Joanna as the new Reverend Mother ushered the sisters into a new era. This process began a year earlier when the sisters did some soul-searching about their past ministries and their future ones. The Roots Workshop had not only shown them where they had been in the previous 110 years, it allowed them to consider where their energies and skills could fit into the coming millennium.

It was obvious that a new map had to be drawn. The electronic age was upon them, and life was speeding up. Working faster and smarter was the motto in the workplace, and the sisters were not immune to the pressure to answer phone calls and emails instantly and to be constantly available. But monastic life has its own contemplative rhythm of life, and the sisters were challenged not to get so busy that they lost sight of their most important purpose — prayer.

With this wide open communication *zeitgeist*, the Sisterhood's new leader needed to be computer and financially literate, be able to bring together a variety of people with different ideas, have both administrative and people skills, be steady in the midst of controversy, and — most importantly — be able to keep the community focused on a healthy balance in its ministry of prayer and service. Sister Constance Joanna had these skills in abundance.

Born in 1941 in Cleveland, Ohio, to a Swedish immigrant father, Carl (a steelworker) and a first generation Swedish-American mother, Florence (a secretary), Constance Joanna was raised in a Methodist household where religion was practised quietly and debated rigorously but lovingly. In high school she majored in socializing rather than academics, and never achieved the grades that would have earned her a scholarship to university. When she did attend university (in Cleveland and later Minneapolis), she completely fell in love with literature and history, and this in turn led her to pursue studies exploring the Bible and Christian writings. Although she went on to do graduate work in literature and linguistics, and taught those subjects in university, she continued to study theology on her own and even to teach courses in the Bible as literature.

While at the University of Minnesota, Constance Joanna was confirmed in the Episcopal Church, but it was a number of years later, while teaching at Wayne State University, that she learned about Anglican religious orders when she visited the convent in Toronto with friends from St. Paul's Cathedral in Detroit. She maintained a connection with the sisters over the next decade, eventually becoming an associate, and continued to go on retreats at the convent even after she had moved to Virginia. Eventually, in 1984 (the Sisterhood's centennial year), she migrated across the 49th Parallel to join the Sisterhood. Sister Constance Joanna recalls: "I had long felt a call to service in the church, but wasn't sure if it was monastic life or ordination. It is often at mid-life that people get in touch with the shadow side of their personality, and for me at that time (I was forty-three) it meant a call to a monastic community rather than the more extraverted life of a parish priest."

Sister Constance Joanna.

When she came to the convent, she got to know Sister Rosemary Anne, and saw from her example how the monastic vocation and the ordained life of a priest could be complementary. Her sense of call to ordination remained in the background and would surface again some years later.

In the meantime, Sister Constance Joanna was Life Professed in 1992, and was assigned to a senior management position at St. John's Rehab with the assumption that she would eventually succeed Sister Philippa as CEO. However, that plan was scuttled when she was elected Reverend Mother in 1994 (and consequently, when the current CEO, Sister Philippa retired in

1996, the sisters and hospital board of directors sought a new CEO from outside the Sisterhood.)

Coming as the hinge between Vision 2000, as articulated by the sisters in 1993 near the end of Mother Frances Joyce's time in office, and the Associate Assembly which was to take place in 1995, Sister Constance Joanna's election represented a clear transition between the community's past and its future. The learnings of the past decade coalesced to shape the community for the twenty-first century.

Her leadership was to be marked by a comprehensive inclusion of associates, friends, and consultants in the sisters' planning for the future as they followed up on the issues identified in Vision 2000: discerning the balance between institutional ministries and the guest and retreat ministry; the location of the "mother house" of the community (the convent); ways to reach out while maintaining a strong centre spiritually; and the delicate balance between work and prayer.

While new leadership in the community would help to translate these issues into concrete decisions, it would be ten years later, toward the end of her second term, that the sisters would move into a new convent with an expanded space for guests.

In the meantime, Sister Constance Joanna consulted widely, not only with the sisters but with her peers in other communities and especially with SSJD associates. It was at a meeting of about thirty-five associates in Edmonton in the fall of 1994 that the suggestion first arose to call an assembly of associates from across the country. They had already had the experience of a large gathering of western associates at British Columbia's Sorrento Conference Centre in 1991, and believed a similar national gathering in Toronto would provide strength and vision to the sisters as they moved into a new era. Just as the original vision for the Sisterhood of St. John the Divine arose among men and women who became the sisters' first associates, so the associates felt that now was an important time for them to assist with the community's visioning and discernment for the future.

The suggestion that came from the Edmonton associates was put before the Toronto associates and embraced by them and the sisters. Soon a committee was set up to plan the Associate Assembly, co-chaired by Sister Beryl (director of the eastern associates) and the Reverend Janet Sidey (convener of the Toronto area associates). The committee chose Esther deWaal as a keynote speaker. Esther had published a book ten years earlier that was to have a lasting impact on the wider church: in *Seeking God* she talked of how 1,500 years earlier, when the Roman Empire was disintegrating, St. Benedict had brought stability to Europe and beyond through his Rule for monks, and how in the later years of the twentieth century, amidst similar cultural and political chaos, Benedictine values had the potential to meet the need of millions of people seeking meaning and purpose in their lives. She seemed the perfect person to galvanize sisters and associates alike as they tried to come to grips with what monastic life might look like in the twenty-first century, and indeed she did.

The excitement around the Assembly was palpable. Through an article in *The Eagle*, associates were invited to respond to a questionnaire in preparation for the Assembly, seeking input for the Assembly itself and for the topics it would address. The sisters had more than 240 responses, which helped to focus the theme, The Household of God. It was a theme that mirrored the sisters' life and ministry since its inception. The sisters had always surrounded themselves with capable and supportive friends, and now the Assembly would once again help them vision a future appropriate for the twenty-first century.

From October 12–16, 1995, one hundred associates from across Canada and the United States, together with thirty sisters, Esther deWaal, and a number of invited guests, came together as a Household of God. They prayed together, ate together, reflected together, and most importantly, they developed a renewed partnership between sisters and associates as they sought direction for the future of the Sisterhood.

One sister summed up the experience this way: "As we listened to Esther describe her vision of the Celtic and Benedictine households and the 'Monastic City,' and as we meditated on her slides of the Household of God, we became more aware not only of our alliance with each other, but also of our partnership with the church, with the whole body of Christ, in helping to bring about the Reign of God."

As the Assembly drew to a close, each of the small groups made a presentation to the whole with their suggestions for the future of the Sisterhood. These recommendations were further discussed by the sisters shortly after the Assembly, and a commitment was made to embrace twelve priorities:

- Bring associates more fully into the Household of God
- Consider oblates as another form of affiliation with the Sisterhood
- Find creative ways to share the story of SSJD
- Make it easier for people to connect (email was still new in 1995, and people were impatient with the sisters' phone answering system!)

- Consider a new branch house that would include partnership with associates
- Include space for more study in the sisters' timetable
- Explore opportunities for children's ministries
- Explore opportunities for new work with seniors
- Enhance our ministry of spiritual direction
- Explore opportunities for ministry with marginalized groups
- Explore the possibility of a Healing and Wholeness Centre in partnership with the Diocese of Toronto
- Consider outreach through music and liturgy

The sisters gradually worked through these various goals and what they meant in a time of upheaval in the church and society. There was declining church attendance, theological and social controversies within the Anglican Communion, a crisis around abuse in the residential schools, and conflict around issues of human sexuality. All these contributed to the widespread disillusionment with organized religions among people both inside and outside the churches. The sisters were convinced that they had a message of peace and unity for people who were seeking a sense of the sacred in their lives, who were looking for God without even knowing that was what they longed for. And so the Sisterhood focused ever more strongly on prayer for peace and unity among human beings. And they sought ways to help guide those who were looking for "something more" in their lives, some deeper experience that would assure them that the chaotic life of the world was not meaningless.

While new leadership in the Sisterhood did not create the upheaval that was seen in Canadian and international politics, it did alter the Sisterhood's landscape in many ways. The traditional hierarchical leadership of religious communities had already been modified by Mother Frances Joyce, and it continued to evolve into a more collegial style under Sister Constance Joanna's leadership, one that encouraged integration and sharing the load. To the sisters' dismay, it also led to many more meetings and committees than the community had previously known. Novices were more fully integrated into the fold; everyone shared the various roles in worship (officiant, cantor, reader, etc.); and the head table disappeared in the refectory.

Shortly after Sister Constance Joanna's installation, in the summer of 1994, the sisters reluctantly decided to withdraw from their work at Cana Place. Cana Place was under the umbrella organization of Anglican Houses — an organization that focuses on inner-city housing for the poor, the homeless, and those with addictions. The mission of Cana Place was quite different, as was the Sisterhood's management philosophy. Anglican Houses took on the administration of Cana Place, but the sisters made a commitment to continue their friendship with and support of the residents. Relationships continued strong until Anglican Houses finally closed Cana Place in 2001 and the residents were dispersed to other places of residence or nursing care — and even then the sisters continued to stay in touch, visit, and give what support they could to the people they had so loved and cared for over many years. (Some of them had been with the sisters from before the move from the Church Home.)

At the same time, many women applied to join the Sisterhood in the latter half of the 1990s and so there was the possibility of opening another branch house. For these reasons, and in response to the recommendations of the Associate Assembly, the sisters decided it was time for the Reverend Mother to make an intentional tour across the country as Mother Dora had done during her time in office.

And so, in 1996 Sister Constance Joanna took to the road on behalf of the community and travelled across Canada to various dioceses and provincial synods to let people know about the Sisterhood. She met with lay people, clergy, and bishops, and sought feedback on new ways that the Sisterhood could be relevant and of use. Former Archbishop of Canterbury George Carey once proclaimed that "nuns were the best-kept secret of the Anglican Communion," and the sisters did not want them to be a secret any longer. In return, they were invited to lead retreats, address synods, and lead workshops on the contemplative life from coast to coast.

When Archbishop of Canterbury George Carey had visited the Diocese of Toronto in 1994 and was interviewed by Valerie Pringle on CFTO TV, Sister Elizabeth Ann had been part of the studio audience. She asked him how the sisters could make the religious life better known and he responded with the recommendation that "we should get out and tell our stories."

And that is what the sisters did. Their print materials were updated and disseminated across Canada; a modernized logo based on the traditional eagle was designed by calligrapher Sister Sarah Jean; T-shirts and mugs with the new logo were given away as gifts and sold in the convent bookroom; prayers were said daily for new vocations; and high-profile religious leaders such as Margaret Silf and Margaret Guenther were brought in to lead retreats and workshops.

As a result of all these interactions, the sisters received six different invitations to open a branch house or start a new ministry. These were put before the sisters at their annual general chapter meetings in 1997, and in the end, the community accepted an invitation from then-Bishop of Montreal Andrew Hutchison (later Primate) to open a branch house in the Diocese of Montreal. They were led to a

TOP: *Maison St-Jean from the back.*
BOTTOM: *The Sisters at St. John's House in 1999: Sisters Helena, Elizabeth, Constance Joanna, Elizabeth Ann, and Jean.*

building ideally suited for their needs on the South Shore, in St. Lambert, next to a Roman Catholic Franciscan parish. The building had been the friary of the priests who ran the parish, and they leased it to the diocese. With a few creative renovations (including turning the garage into a chapel) the opening of the new SSJD branch house was celebrated with a picnic put on for the delegates of General Synod, which met that year in Montreal. Eventually Brother Tom de Hoope, an Anglican Franciscan who became interim priest at St. Barnabas parish in St. Lambert, came to live with the sisters for two years, and the success of that partnership led to other shared ministry in the branch houses.

During the 1990s, interest was expressed off and on about the possibility of having oblates affiliated with the Sisterhood. Two complementary influences had been at work for nearly a decade before that: a decline in new vocations to monastic communities, and an increasing thirst among lay people to fill their own spiritual longings by affiliating with monastic communities. The recommendation to consider oblates resurfaced, and the sisters decided to experiment with a program for women who felt

called to monastic life but for various reasons had to live it out "in the world."

The pilot program was started in 1999, and at chapter in 2002, the sisters agreed to make it a permanent part of the Sisterhood's extended family.

Since then the number of oblates has increased gradually as the program became known, usually with two or three new oblates being added each year. During the past ten years, the sisters have been immeasurably enriched by the presence of oblates, as have the oblates who have offered themselves to God in this partnership.

Other initiatives began in the 1990s. The Education for Ministry program (known across North America as EfM) was introduced to the sisters in 1994 as a foundation for new members, who are required to complete all four years of this program in lay theological education. EfM gave new sisters the skills to reflect theologically on their culture, their life experience, and ways in which the Christian faith may speak to the questions of the day. The program has continued to be such a success that older members of the community — including Sister Merle in her eighties — have taken the course and graduated after four years, and so have many friends, associates, and oblates of the community. It has been an invaluable source of connection between the sisters, seekers, and the Church at large.

Sister Doreen with Caroline Hamilton, our first Oblate.

In 1995, the sisters launched the Women at a Crossroads program. Held during the month of July for women wanting to share in the life of a prayerful community and learn the art of discernment at pivotal junctures of their lives, it was an extension of a summer Vocations Program the Sisterhood had held for a number of years. Women at a Crossroads was recalibrated for a broader range — women who found themselves at a crossroads in their lives and who wished to deepen their spiritual life. They have come from all over Canada, and some from the United States and Great Britain. Usually about ten are accepted for each annual program, and they have ranged in age from twenty to

Some classes during the Women at a Crossroads program:
TOP: *Class on discernment in St. Margaret's Chapel.*
MIDDLE: *Class on making bread led by Sister Elizabeth Ann.*
BOTTOM: *Class on art as prayer in the refectory.*

seventy-five. While a few women each year have an interest in exploring the religious life, and some in fact have entered the Sisterhood, others find ways to take the spiritual practices and monastic values they have learned into the context of their own lives as mothers, grandmothers, and career women. Many have become associates and oblates, some alongsiders; others have remained close friends of the sisters, and all in their own way have been ambassadors for the Sisterhood. The program continues to be a strong and popular one.

As part of the sisters' continuing desire to meet people's spiritual hunger, more training was offered to the sisters in spiritual direction. In 1996, a number of sisters began to do spiritual direction for theological students at Wycliffe College (part of the Toronto School of Theology) and out of that experience grew courses in contemplative prayer and monasticism taught by Sister Constance Joanna. The ministry of spiritual direction continued to grow both at the convent and in the branch houses in Montreal and Victoria, where sisters also received specialized training.

During Sister Constance Joanna's time in office, the sisters continued to enrich their worship as new music was introduced and an inclusive-language psalter was produced by a group of sisters including the poet-theologian Sister Rosemary Anne.

The tradition of teaching Sunday school, so long a part of the Sisterhood's ministry, was renewed as the community accepted an invitation in 2002 to teach at St. James Cathedral in Toronto. Sister Louise was the first, and remained in that role over the next six years as other sisters joined her for a year or two at a time: Sisters Dorothy, Anne, Jessica, Margaret, and Sarah Jean. They brought the same spirit of enthusiasm for helping children grow in their faith as sisters had throughout their long history of education.

The new millennium arrived and "Y2K" as it was known, came and went without so much as a peep. But the process of preparedness — the focus of every household and organization on Earth it seemed — helped the sisters upgrade their emergency plans; and as a bonus, new duvets were

Sister Constance Joanna teaching a class on prayer at the Toronto School of Theology.

purchased for sisters' and guest bedrooms, generators were installed, and practice drills were held to deal with potential power failure. The sisters held a vigil of prayer for peace at midnight on December 31, 1999, as the new millennium stretched before the world with seemingly irrepressible opportunities. Some things did come to an end, however. Shortly after Cana Place closed, in November 2001, St. John's Priory in Edmonton closed — not for lack of work but because the Diocese of Edmonton could no longer support the sisters' ministry of hospitality, and the sisters did not have the financial resources or appropriately trained personnel for the ministries that would have fulfilled the priorities of the diocese at that time.

Wonderfully, the sisters received an invitation shortly after that to begin a new ministry in the Diocese of British Columbia, where (as with the house in Montreal) Bishop Barry Jenks wanted the sisters to be a "praying presence." In the fall of 2002, Sisters Doreen and Valerie moved to Victoria, B.C., to begin this new ministry. They lived for a short time at Queenswood, a retreat centre in Victoria run by the Roman Catholic Sisters of St. Anne, and the following year moved into a house that the diocese found for them and which is supported by many parishes as well as the diocese. With the help of a number of sisters and an oblate, Doreen Davidson, the sisters developed a strong ministry on Vancouver Island and also on the mainland of B.C. in the Diocese of New Westminster. The ministry there continues to thrive.

But the biggest change was yet to come.

The decision to move from Botham Road had been weighing on the community's collective mind for a number of years. Three major issues contributed: the increasing noise and air pollution from eighteen lanes of traffic on the 401; the increased numbers of

TOP: *St. John's House in Victoria, BC.* BOTTOM: *Doreen Davidson, an Oblate, with Sisters Louise, Jocelyn, Jessica, and Doreen.*

guests and the consequent need for more meeting and bedroom space; and the need for more accessible facilities for the sisters (the fondness in the 1950s for split-level architecture made it impossible to install an elevator that would serve all parts of the building). The community debated its options: was it better to stay and renovate, or to sell the Botham Road property and construct a purpose-built convent? If so, where?

At chapter in 2001, the sisters began serious discussions. They revisited their vision and mission statement in order to determine what kind of building would give shape to the work God called them to perform. Dr. Peta Dunstan, of the Faculty of Divinity at Cambridge University and an expert on Anglican religious orders, spent ten days with the sisters and associates in 2002, helping them with the visioning process. The sisters brought in volunteer experts in finance, fundraising, real estate, and building construction in order to assess their options. They studied how to avoid future civic development that would impinge on the land around a new convent. They prayed and talked and consulted. Sister Constance Joanna put on soirées and the sisters organized other events purely for fun, which reduced stress and helped to keep the community grounded during a time of upheaval.

In the end, practicalities and common sense swayed the decision: it was cheaper to build than to renovate; the land on which they were currently sitting was prime real estate; and the Sisterhood owned another prime piece of property next to St. John's Rehab.

Birchall-Bainbridge Hall had been built in the 1950s as a residence for hospital staff and sisters. The residence and the eight acres of land on which it stood had already been transferred to the Sisterhood's ownership. The site met the goals of the sisters: it was urban, convenient to public transportation, in a quiet residential neighbourhood, and had sufficient space to build a new convent attached to the old residence, which would be renovated to become the new guest house. Architects Montgomery Sisam and construction managers Dalton Engineering were soon on board, and suddenly the sisters became adept at reading architectural drawings and understanding the tender process. They broke ground on September 18, 2003.

The decision to move necessarily meant a decision to do some serious fundraising. One of the major changes in Sister Constance Joanna's tenure was in the Sisterhood's attitude to fundraising. Mother Hannah had stipulated from the start that sisters were not to do fundraising themselves; that job would be left to the community's associates. However, throughout the history of the Sisterhood, the sisters themselves had had many appeals for funds, especially for the Botham Road convent and its extensions and also for various missions along the way.

The sisters engaged Dan and Janice King as their consultants, and put together a stellar "Campaign Cabinet," headed up by long-time friend and associate the Reverend Canon Tim Elliott. The sisters had to raise $2.5-million — the amount remaining after they had sold the Botham Road property and received a major grant.

While funds were being raised and building plans progressed, organizing the big move was also taking shape. As with any transition, it was chaotic and at times disorienting. Botham Road, after all, had been the sisters' home for fifty years. But move they did. A process of decluttering began, and a decision was made corporately to allow each sister to move a maximum of forty-five cubic feet of belongings (this was visualized in terms of forty-five bankers' boxes per sister!). Closets were emptied, belongings donated, books culled. Boxes were collected, lists made, and stickers and labels purchased. Committees (how the sisters love committees!) were formed to take care of every detail: a Simplicity and Moving Committee; a Furnishing and Decorating Committee; a Celebrations Committee; a Chapel Committee, a Landscape Committee, and so forth.

While this sounds daunting, in fact the sisters who headed up each of the committees enabled a huge move to take place with a minimum of stress and strain. In particular, Sister Margaret Mary (who oversaw the actual move) freed up Sister Constance Joanna to attend to the planning and pastoral needs of the community, and to oversee the builders.

On September 8, 2004 — almost exactly a year from the day ground was broken — the sisters moved into the new guest house (following the renovation of Birchall-Bainbridge Hall) and in January, 2005, into the new convent.

When her second term as Reverend Mother ended, Sister Constance Joanna wondered if her old hopes of ordination would be merely a dream, that she might be too old to begin the process. However, her vocation, like Sister Rosemary Anne's before her, was deemed genuine, and after study and preparation she was ordained to the priesthood in 2008.

Competent and organized, imaginative and passionate about the Sisterhood's mission, Sister Constance Joanna infused the community with a revitalized purpose. When she left office in 2005, the community was poised to make the new building a real home while the sisters continued their mission to reach out beyond the convent walls.

6 *A Stabilizing Step Forward, 2005–2015*
Sister Elizabeth Ann

To observe Sister Elizabeth Ann buzzing around the new convent in her Birkenstocks, a pager clipped to the waistband of her skirt, you would be tempted to marvel at how far the Sisterhood has evolved since the days of Mother Hannah. And you would be correct, to a point. The atmosphere is more casual and collegial, and the convent itself, with its great expanse of windows and its light-filled corridors, registers a brightness and cheerfulness that contrasts significantly with the more austere times of decades past. In an era where transparency is a political buzzword, the Sisterhood lives it literally and philosophically. But the essence remains the same: it is a contemporary community grounded in the monastic traditions and values developed by St. Benedict almost 1,500 years ago. After a decade of change and the upheaval of a major move, Sister Elizabeth Ann's term of office has helped to stabilize the community and re-root it in the Benedictine tradition.

Elizabeth Ann Eckert was born to Grant, a family doctor, and Theda, a registered nurse, on April 7, 1957. The family worshipped at the Church of the Resurrection in Sudbury, Ontario, and Elizabeth Ann eagerly took part in many church activities. After being confirmed as a young teen, she began attending the mid-week Eucharist in addition to the Sunday services. It was clear that faith was being nurtured deeply within her. When Dr. Eckert took a position at the newly opened North York General Hospital, the family moved to Toronto and joined the local parish church, St. John's York Mills. Its youth group turned out to be a formative experience for Elizabeth Ann: at one event she heard the Reverend Margery Pezzack, the first woman to be ordained in the Diocese of Toronto, talk about a recent retreat she had taken at a convent. It was, she told the assembled group of teens, like emptying the pockets of her life, setting them aside while she was held in God's love throughout the weekend, then taking up the pocket contents at the end of the retreat to find them more orderly than when she had left them. Inspired by this, sixteen-year-old Elizabeth Ann made her first retreat at the same convent Pezzack had visited — the Sisterhood of St. John the Divine.

The call to monastic life did not come immediately. Sister Elizabeth Ann attended Lakehead University to study forestry and worked summers for the Ministry of Natural Resources.

Her immersion in the beauty and mystery of nature only deepened her longing to know more of the mystery of its Creator. She continued to make occasional retreats at St. John's Convent, and spent a month there during the summer of 1981. She fell in love with the silence, the music, and the dedicated life of prayer and service.

In the fall of 1987, she was admitted to the community. Along with her smiling freckled face, wavy ginger hair, and quick gait, she brought along her six-foot cross-cut saw and her photographic and dark room equipment.

There was no shortage of work for a young and eager novice. She used her creative energy in the garden, the kitchen, as a pastoral visitor at St. John's Rehab Hospital, and at the sisters' branch house in Edmonton. In 1998, Sister Elizabeth Ann was chosen along with three other sisters to set up the sisters' new branch house in Montreal. That experience, along with five years as Assistant to Sister Constance Joanna in her second term as Reverend Mother, helped develop her own leadership skills. Just as construction on the new convent neared completion, Sister Elizabeth Ann was elected the sixth Reverend Mother in January 2005.

Sister Elizabeth Ann.

Photo by Michael Hudson.

Like any family who moves house, the sisters found their transition to the new convent an uprooting challenge. Sister Elizabeth Ann used her calm voice, her can-do spirit, her humour and warmth, and her intuitive clarity to help stabilize the community. She understood that this was the first priority of her new role.

The support of friends outside the community also assisted the sisters in appropriating their new space and finding ways to live out their ministry in a new context. One of the most supportive events at the beginning of Sister Elizabeth Ann's term was the open house and ribbon cutting in October 2005, attended by hundreds of people who came to see the new convent and offer their enthusiastic support.

Outside the convent the world looked as if it had undergone a massive move, too, one that had left it wondering what box to unpack first. The first full year of Sister Elizabeth Ann's time in office was the year

Photo by Michael Hudson.

TOP: *The Reverend Margaret and Jim Fleck speaking at the opening of the new convent before the cutting of the ribbon.*
BOTTOM: *Archbishop Colin Johnson and Sister Elizabeth Ann cutting the ribbon.*

YouTube was launched, and the word "viral" took on an entirely new meaning as videos posted by private citizens suddenly captivated audiences around the world. It drove the phenomenon of celebrity worship to ever greater heights in the Western world, but it also allowed monastic communities to share the beauty of Gregorian chant and made celebrities of peace out of religious leaders such as the Dalai Lama, who visited Toronto in 2005.

The decade following has been a time of unprecedented technological advances, and the challenge to religious communities and the Church in general is to use the technologies and the social media they support in a way that reinforces the value of human relationships.

As previous Reverend Mothers had deduced, change was inevitable and even necessary, and there was no way to avoid it but to steer into it. And so did Sister Elizabeth Ann. During her time in office, the sisters have broadened their "household of God" to include an online community which is far-reaching. Through the community's website, Facebook, and monthly e-newsletters the sisters reach thousands of people with spiritual resources, reflection on contemporary issues, and prayer support.

Many other changes have been ushered in during Sister Elizabeth Ann's time in office.

Bishop Hill died in 2006 after a long period of declining health, during which he lived with the Basilian Fathers at their residence at St. Michael's College, but remained closely connected to the sisters. It was the end of an era for the Sisterhood because he had been such a strong influence in the sisters' ecumenical ministry.

Sister Constance Joanna was ordained to the diaconate in May 2007, and to the priesthood in February 2008 — the first ordained member of the community since Sister Rosemary Anne, who had been ordained in 1977 and died in 2001.

The ordination of Sister Constance Joanna.

Photo by Michael Hudson.

Sister Elizabeth Ann guided the community through a discernment process that led the sisters to close the branch house in Montreal, a ministry they loved. But neither the Diocese of Montreal nor the Sisterhood had the resources to continue beyond 2008.

An even bigger challenge confronted the sisters in the spring of 2010 when the CEO of St. John's Rehab, Malcolm Moffat, brought forward the possibility of a merger between the hospital and Sunnybrook Health Sciences Centre. Over the next year and a half, a committee of sisters and members of St. John's Hospital board worked hard to arrive at an amalgamation agreement that enshrined some of the most

TOP: The last Annual General Meeting before the merger of St. John's Rehab Hospital and Sunnybrook Health Sciences Centre: MPP David Zimmer, with Barry McLellan (CEO of SHSC), Sister Elizabeth Ann, and Malcolm Moffat (former CEO of St. John's Rehab). BOTTOM: Sisters Elizabeth Ann and Constance Joanna with Hilary Short and Joyce Bailey, members of the board of Saint John's Rehab Hospital.

important values of the Sisterhood: preservation of the parkland around the hospital for its ongoing therapeutic properties; requirements for consultation around any building that might happen on the hospital property that could have a negative impact on the convent next door; agreement that the sisters would continue to form the heart of the spiritual care team at St. John's Rehab (one of the most important contributions they had made over the seventy-five years of the hospital's history); and other agreements that would ensure the hospital remained a strong presence in Ontario health care. At the last Annual General Meeting of St. John's Rehabilitation Hospital, immediately preceding the amalgamation, Sr. Elizabeth Ann was honoured, on behalf of the Sisterhood, with the Queen's Diamond Jubilee Medal — the fourth such medal received by the Sisterhood across its 130 years and a recognition of the esteem in which the sisters' work in health care has been held.

St. John's Rehab had always had a significant ecumenical and multi-faith ministry and the amalgamation agreements ensured that would continue. Since the founding of the hospital, the sisters have visited every patient, regardless of their faith, and they arrange for representatives of other faiths to visit as well. Patients who profess no faith or say they don't believe in God nevertheless have spiritual needs: they may need to grieve the loss of a limb, adjust to limitations in mobility, or find the courage to face life positively. Meeting those needs is an important part of helping patients on the "road to recovery," as the main hospital drive is called.

Through discussions with her sisters, Sister Elizabeth Ann has shepherded new initiatives.

When the community first moved into the new convent in 2005, neither of the courtyards had been landscaped. Finding the resources and making plans to do this had been one of the sisters' priorities. They planted flowers in the summer, and the grass was kept mowed, but the expanse of lawn in both the sisters and the guest courtyards were not developed except for a pond dug by the sisters in 2009. Sister Elizabeth Ann headed up a committee to make initial plans for landscaping not only the courtyards but the grounds around the convent. In 2010 a generous anonymous donation made it possible to develop the guest courtyard, and the "outdoor rooms" that the architects had envisioned began to take shape.

They have since become places where sisters and guests gather, where barbeques are held in the summer; they are also oases of contemplative peace where one can sit and read a book, pray, or simply enjoy the beauty of the gardens.

Under Sister Elizabeth Ann's leadership, the sisters decided to have a weekly period of corporate Contemplative Prayer. Held each Thursday in place of Morning Prayer, it is a way of finding space in the sisters' lives for them to pray silently as a group. "We take very seriously our life of prayer," says Sister Elizabeth Ann. "While the sisters have always been faithful to their private daily prayer and to our corporate worship, we needed to renew the opportunity for communal silent meditation. Praying together in silence is extremely powerful."

Following the successful capital campaign for the new convent, the sisters' campaign advisors had encouraged them to build on that momentum and take on a longer-term approach to fundraising, to take ownership and responsibility for the survival and sustainability of the community. It was an enormous culture shift for the sisters, and their staunch sense of self-reliance melted into humility as they mustered the confidence to ask people for help in fulfilling their mission work.

At the suggestion of the Reverend Canon Tim Elliott, the sisters' capital campaign chair, a group of women was brought together to offer continuing support to the sisters, to be ambassadors for their work, and to be a support to each other in their faith journeys. This Women's Roundtable meets once or twice a year to worship together, enjoy a special meal, and hear a speaker who inspires the faith journey of the sisters and the "women of the roundtable."

The women and other advisors have encouraged an annual fundraising campaign, and in addition, Sister Elizabeth Ann has continued the new direction set by her predecessor to seek help and funds when needed. Sister Doreen was placed in charge of fundraising, and under her leadership, with the assistance of Sister Wilma and Lynne Samways-Hiltz (the Sisterhood's fundraising assistant), the community's financial outlook has stabilized. A new dishwasher was required for the kitchen, and barely had the need been expressed when the necessary funds came in from a number of donors.

A larger and riskier project involved the installation of solar panels. It was as much a decision to save energy and money at the convent as it was a desire for the Sisterhood to demonstrate its environmental responsibility and stewardship. In fact, so passionate were the sisters about this project that they were prepared to take a financial loss until the savings kicked in. What happened instead was quite remarkable: after careful deliberation, the sisters decided to put a notice in *The Eagle* about their plans to install the panels. *The Eagle* was barely in the mail when people came forward to offer help. What looked to be a fundraising drive lasting many years was completed in a matter of weeks. It was nothing short of astonishing — perhaps even miraculous. Then again, people who know the sisters know the great love and willingness to help that comes from beyond their immediate community.

The sisters had moved past Mother Foundress' reserve about "begging" for money and embraced a spirituality of fundraising that has been influenced by the words of Henri Nouwen:

> Fundraising is precisely the opposite of begging ... we are declaring "We have a vision that is amazing and exciting. We are inviting you to invest yourself through the resources that God has given you — your energy, your prayers, and your money — in this work to which God has called us."[1]

A happy group of women attend the Women's Roundtable.

Sister Elizabeth Ann has also brought a genuine enthusiasm to her role as an ambassador to the wider church. Whether as a delegate to General Synod or sitting on various diocesan and national committees, she has cultivated a reputation as a conciliator, an intent listener, and a woman of deep spiritual understanding. Other sisters have also served on diocesan and national groups. Sister Elizabeth serves as chaplain to the Council of General Synod. Sister Constance Joanna

serves on the Postulancy Committee for the Diocese of Toronto, helping to discern and support the vocations of those who are selected as candidates for ordination. A number of sisters have worked with Momentum, the program for ongoing formation of new clergy in the Toronto Diocese, as well as being assessors for the Advisory Committee on Postulants for Ordination. Sisters Brenda, Louise, and Dorothy in Victoria, B.C., have participated in the Truth and Reconciliation Commission and other programs to promote listening and understanding among First Nations Canadians and others. The monastic values of listening and prayerful discernment are offered as a gift to the church.

But let's go back to Sister Elizabeth Ann and that quick gait, smiling freckled face, and wavy ginger hair for a moment, because they hint at her playful, mischievous side,

TOP: *Sisters and associates are seen worshipping in the chapel during the Gathering.*
BOTTOM: *Bishop Gordon Light presided at one of the Eucharists and accompanied us on the guitar for one of the hymns.*

which endears her to those with whom she lives and those she meets day to day. She most definitely does not have the intimidating and imperious presence one expects from the superior of a religious order, and this has served her and her community immensely well. Her ready smile and easy-going approach, with a song at the tip of her tongue for every occasion, lightens the mood and gives joy to the community. And it helps expand the Sisterhood's sphere of influence by building bridges between the religious and secular worlds. Indeed, this fresh approach has contributed to committed women, strong in their faith, arriving at the door of the Sisterhood of St. John the Divine to test their vocation.

Much as the Associate Assembly had done in 1995, the Gathering of associates and (now) oblates in 2009 brought fresh energy and new ideas to the Sisterhood. Eighty-four associates, oblates, and sisters gathered to listen to author Margaret Silf talk about "Something More" — the desperate need of people in the twenty-first century to find a connection with the Divine even when they don't realize it is God whom they are seeking. The Gathering gave fresh impetus to developing an alongsider program and strong support to continuing the oblate program that had started about ten years earlier. And it reinforced the importance of places like the convent where quiet, peace, stability and space offer an opportunity to explore the meaning that people are seeking in their lives.

In 2010, the sisters agreed in chapter (after a number of years of discernment) to launch an alongsiders' program, an opportunity for women to live, pray, and work with the sisters for a fixed period (usually a year). The purpose of the alongsider program is two-fold. First, it provides an opportunity for the alongsider to seek a deeper relationship with God within the context of a Christian community, to learn about the monastic life, to explore and better understand the importance of a balanced life of prayer, work, study, and community, and to take some of the core values of monastic life back out "into the world." And second, it enriches the sisters' extended-family unit, and enhances the way the community is modelled for the church and contemporary culture by including women who can act as ambassadors for monastic values and the simplicity of life in Christ.

During Sister Elizabeth Ann's time as community leader, the sisters formed a relationship with the Reverend Claudine Carlson, a pastor of the Evangelical

Lutheran Church in Canada, which is in full communion with the Anglican Church of Canada. Through Claudine's monthly presiding at the Eucharist for the sisters, other friendships with Lutherans both at the convent and in the branch houses, and the community's use of the new *Evangelical Lutheran Worship* book, the Sisterhood has become increasingly familiar with the Lutheran church and intentionally contributed to the building of relationships as encouraged by the Waterloo Accord of Full Communion which had been approved by both church bodies in 2001.

A historic moment occurred in 2010 when Debra Johnston, an experienced Lutheran pastor, was admitted to the Sisterhood. Sister Debra has been an ambassador for the monastic life among her Lutheran colleagues and has helped the Sisterhood understand the subtle differences and similarities between Lutherans and Anglicans. She presides once a month at the sisters' daily Eucharist as well as assisting in a local Lutheran parish and a local Anglican parish. She has served as a pastoral visitor at St. John's Rehab and is currently part of the sisters' household in Victoria, where she and the sisters there will have an opportunity for mutual learning among Anglicans and Lutherans in the Diocese of British Columbia.

Sister Elizabeth Ann receives Sister Debra, a Lutheran pastor, as a novice of our community.

Relationships with other communities have also thrived during this period. In 2009 several sisters from a French Roman Catholic order, the Xavières, Missionaries of Christ Jesus (they have a house in Toronto), came to St. John's Convent for their annual retreat. That visit resulted in a friendship that has involved shared visits to each other's homes, meals and barbeques, and the sharing of music and liturgical traditions.

The sisters have also shared ministry with two male Anglican communities, the Order of the Holy Cross and the Society of St. Francis. As a member of the Executive of the Conference of Anglican Religious Communities in the Americas (CAROA), Sister Elizabeth Ann has helped forge relationships of mutual learning and support among the communities. CAROA has also reached out to another organization, the National Association of Episcopal Christian Communities (NAECC), to see what these dispersed and non-traditional communities share in common with the more traditional monastic communities.

Reaching even farther, in 2014 the House of Bishops Standing Committee on the Religious Life, headed by Bishop Linda Nicholls of Toronto, convened a consultation between the traditional communities in Canada and the "new monastic" communities. In some ways these new monastic communities are visibly different from the traditional communities; they include married couples and families as well as single individuals and many live at a distance from one another — although others may live communally. But the similarities are more striking than the differences. In many ways their sense of mission is nearly identical to that of the communities formed in the time of the Oxford Movement, when the church rediscovered the call of the poor and established parish communities in the poorest urban districts of the big cities of England (and later in the U.S. and Canada).

Some of the francophone Xavière sisters join us for choir practice as we seek to learn one another's music.

As the sisters offer support and mentoring to some of the new monastic communities, especially in Toronto and Victoria, they also have much to learn from them, to see how the Spirit may be calling Christian communities to live out their values and mission in a highly secularized and quickly changing world.

"I hope to live long enough to see how this community fares in the next fifty years, and to see how the Sisterhood continues to respond to the needs of the wider church and community," Sister Elizabeth Ann says. "I expect that there always will be a core group of sisters who

are a praying presence surrounded by a growing company of people responding to that life of prayer and service as associates, oblates, alongsiders, as I did almost thirty years ago."

As the Sisterhood goes forward into the future, the circle of sisters and their friends and their extended family carries forward the monastic values of prayer, community, simple living, communal decision-making, and service to the poor and to all who are seeking God in our increasingly secular society. The early days of the Sisterhood of St. John the Divine were not unlike some of the new monastic communities today — opening clinics and hospitals, providing food and clothing for the poor, attending to the physical and social needs of those in the poorest parts of our cities, and offering hospitality to all who were seeking spiritual nourishment. The future for the Sisterhood will lie in an adaptation of those very same values, as these words from the Sisterhood's mission statement express: "Our community is called to be a stable and radiating centre of the presence and power of Christ, within the church and society. We are called to be a sign of Christ, and by our lives of prayer and service to witness to the power of God's reconciling and forgiving love."

Members of CAROA and NAECC who attended a joint meeting at the convent in 2014.

Sisterhood of St. John the Divine - *Houses and Works 1884–2014, Part 1*

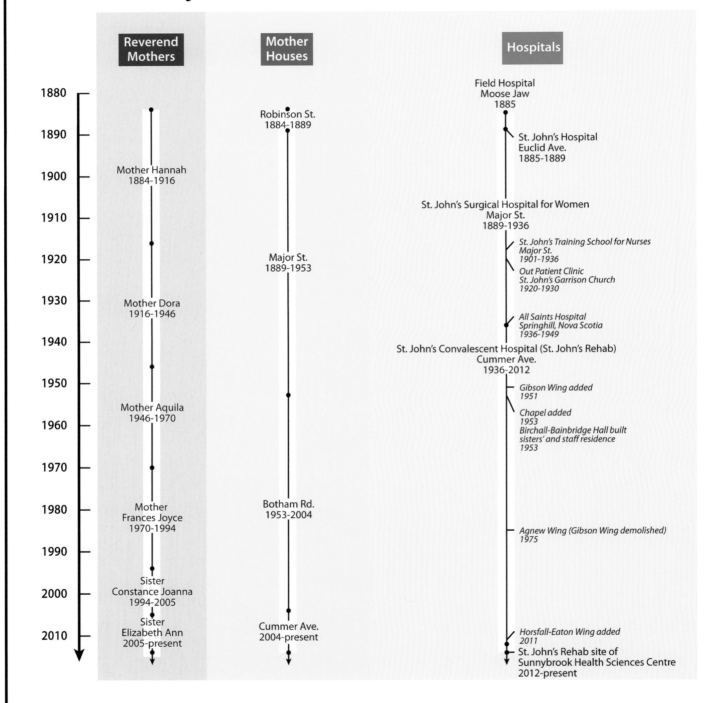

Reverend Mothers

Mother Houses

Hospitals

1880

1890

1900

1910

1920

1930

1940

1950

1960

1970

1980

1990

2000

2010

Mother Hannah
1884-1916

Mother Dora
1916-1946

Mother Aquila
1946-1970

Mother
Frances Joyce
1970-1994

Sister
Constance Joanna
1994-2005

Sister
Elizabeth Ann
2005-present

Robinson St.
1884-1889

Major St.
1889-1953

Botham Rd.
1953-2004

Cummer Ave.
2004-present

Field Hospital
Moose Jaw
1885

St. John's Hospital
Euclid Ave.
1885-1889

St. John's Surgical Hospital for Women
Major St.
1889-1936

St. John's Training School for Nurses
Major St.
1901-1936

Out Patient Clinic
St. John's Garrison Church
1920-1930

All Saints Hospital
Springhill, Nova Scotia
1936-1949

St. John's Convalescent Hospital (St. John's Rehab)
Cummer Ave.
1936-2012

Gibson Wing added
1951

Chapel added
1953
Birchall-Bainbridge Hall built
sisters' and staff residence
1953

Agnew Wing (Gibson Wing demolished)
1975

Horsfall-Eaton Wing added
2011

St. John's Rehab site of
Sunnybrook Health Sciences Centre
2012-present

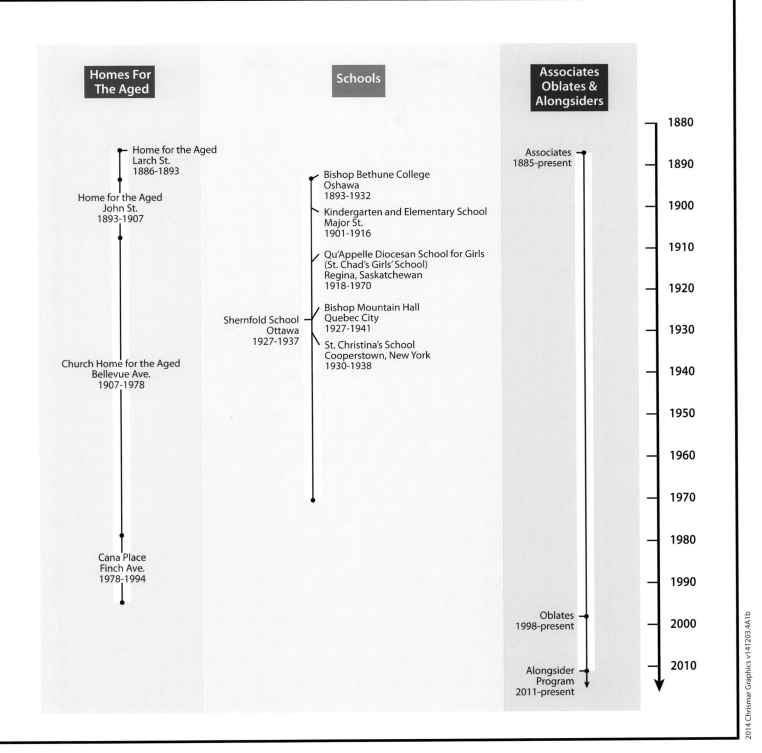

Homes For The Aged

Home for the Aged
Larch St.
1886-1893

Home for the Aged
John St.
1893-1907

Church Home for the Aged
Bellevue Ave.
1907-1978

Cana Place
Finch Ave.
1978-1994

Schools

Bishop Bethune College
Oshawa
1893-1932

Kindergarten and Elementary School
Major St.
1901-1916

Qu'Appelle Diocesan School for Girls
(St. Chad's Girls' School)
Regina, Saskatchewan
1918-1970

Bishop Mountain Hall
Quebec City
1927-1941

St. Christina's School
Cooperstown, New York
1930-1938

Shernfold School
Ottawa
1927-1937

Associates Oblates & Alongsiders

Associates
1885-present

Oblates
1998-present

Alongsider
Program
2011-present

1880
1890
1900
1910
1920
1930
1940
1950
1960
1970
1980
1990
2000
2010

Sisterhood of St. John the Divine - *Houses and Works 1884-2014, Part 2*

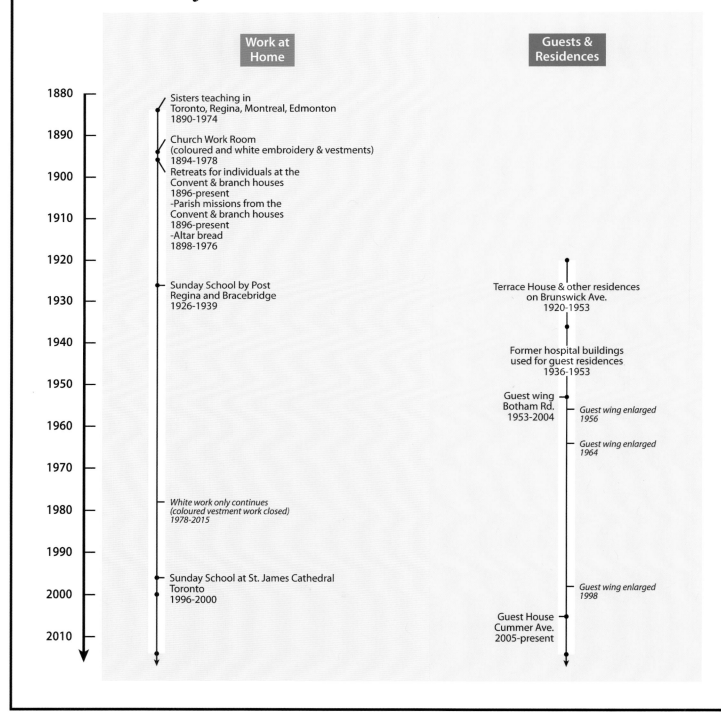

Work at Home

Guests & Residences

1880 — Sisters teaching in
Toronto, Regina, Montreal, Edmonton
1890-1974

1890 — Church Work Room
(coloured and white embroidery & vestments)
1894-1978
Retreats for individuals at the
1900 — Convent & branch houses
1896-present
-Parish missions from the
Convent & branch houses
1910 — 1896-present
-Altar bread
1898-1976

1920 — Terrace House & other residences
on Brunswick Ave.
Sunday School by Post
1930 — Regina and Bracebridge
1926-1939
1920-1953

1940 — Former hospital buildings
used for guest residences
1936-1953

1950 — Guest wing
Botham Rd.
Guest wing enlarged
1960 — 1953-2004
1956

Guest wing enlarged
1964

1970 —

White work only continues
1980 — (coloured vestment work closed)
1978-2015

1990 —

Sunday School at St. James Cathedral
2000 — Toronto
1996-2000
Guest wing enlarged
1998

Guest House
Cummer Ave.
2010 — 2005-present

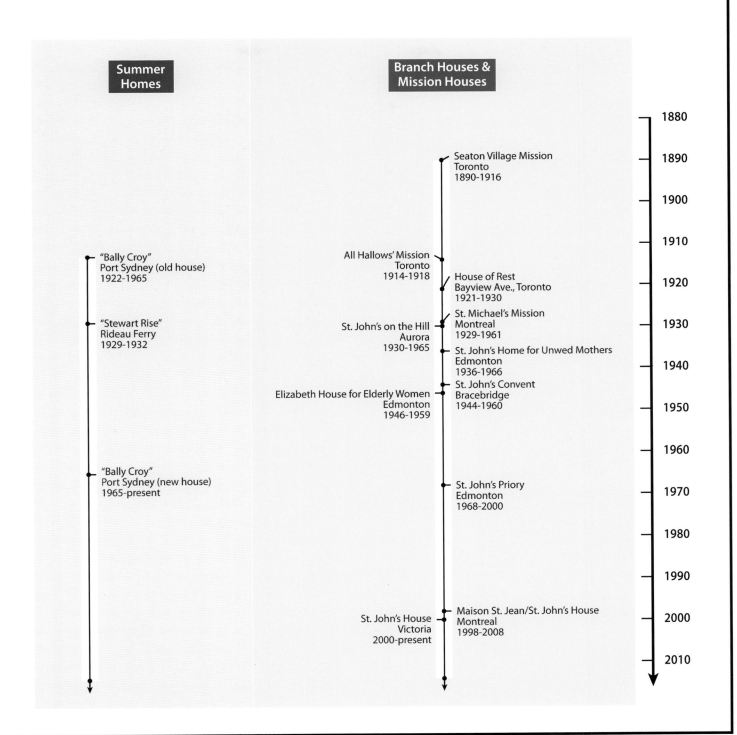

Summer Homes

Branch Houses & Mission Houses

"Bally Croy"
Port Sydney (old house)
1922-1965

"Stewart Rise"
Rideau Ferry
1929-1932

"Bally Croy"
Port Sydney (new house)
1965-present

Seaton Village Mission
Toronto
1890-1916

All Hallows' Mission
Toronto
1914-1918

House of Rest
Bayview Ave., Toronto
1921-1930

St. Michael's Mission
Montreal
1929-1961

St. John's on the Hill
Aurora
1930-1965

St. John's Home for Unwed Mothers
Edmonton
1936-1966

St. John's Convent
Bracebridge
1944-1960

Elizabeth House for Elderly Women
Edmonton
1946-1959

St. John's Priory
Edmonton
1968-2000

St. John's House
Victoria
2000-present

Maison St. Jean/St. John's House
Montreal
1998-2008

1880
1890
1900
1910
1920
1930
1940
1950
1960
1970
1980
1990
2000
2010

2014 Chrismar Graphics v141203.4B1b

Part II
Sacred Space

INTRODUCTION

A new and creative opportunity opened for the Sisters of St. John the Divine when, in 2002, they started talking seriously about moving to a new location and building a new convent and guest house. Taking a large step of faith in God's plan for the future, they considered the mission they felt called to and dreamt of how that might shape a new building. They drew on the accumulated wisdom of sisters who had lived at the Botham Road convent since 1953, who had witnessed first-hand a number of additions and renovations to the building, and who knew what its benefits and challenges were.

The sisters chose Terry Montgomery and his colleagues at Montgomery Sisam Architects, because of their understanding of the importance of sacred space as well as the practical experience the firm had in designing buildings that were both functional and beautiful. When they first started working with Montgomery Sisam, they had already chosen the Cummer Avenue site, which met their needs: a quiet, developed neighbourhood where there would be no surprises affiliated with the construction of large condo towers in the coming decades, accessibility to public transportation, and a large enough space (eight acres) to provide a buffer between them and the hospital next door.

The next step was to consider the building plan itself. They were well aware of the traditional architectural dictum that "form follows function." They had already tried on Botham Road to fit the growing guest and retreat ministry into a building that didn't quite fit the current needs. The guest and meeting areas were spread around the sisters' areas, and there simply wasn't enough space.

While it was important for the sisters to balance Benedictine values of simplicity, privacy, and hospitality when they envisioned a convent, St. Benedict hadn't had to contend with Wi-Fi, elevators, and closets for modern secular clothing. The new building had to be functional and accessible for all.

Other needs had changed since the move to Botham Road in 1953. There were more sisters with mobility issues who couldn't access the library on the ground floor. The convent offices didn't have the necessary space for computers, which had become a necessity in virtually all the work of the community. As with any family that lives in the same house for fifty years, the needs had changed and the physical space was no longer entirely adequate or appropriate. The functions of the monastic life were having to adapt to the building, rather than the other way around.

Knowing what they needed for living simply in the new century, the sisters in 2003 had the opportunity to design a purpose-built home. Together with the architects, they read about traditional monastic architecture and looked for new ways of realizing their goals: to provide appropriate and adequate space for groups and guests; to provide privacy for the sisters' community life while sharing common space like the chapel, refectory, and library; to provide lots of light and space, bringing the outdoors in; and to incorporate treasured items from the previous convents (especially stained glass and other works of art).

On the floor plan that follows, you will see highlighted all the traditional spaces and functions of a monastery. From the sixth century to the twenty-first, certain elements are always present — a church or chapel, which is the central focus of the building; a chapter house or room for the community to gather; a private enclosure with individual cells (bedrooms) for the sisters; a novitiate space for new members; an infirmary for those who are ill or need assistance; a gate house or foyer where guests are welcomed and from which the monastic community comes and goes; a guest house; a refectory and kitchen; a library; a scriptorium for writers; arts and crafts rooms; and gardens.

And now, let's take a tour of the convent to get a sense of how these various spaces define the life and work of the sisters past, present and most importantly, future.

FLOOR PLAN OF THE CUMMER AVENUE
CONVENT AND GUEST HOUSE

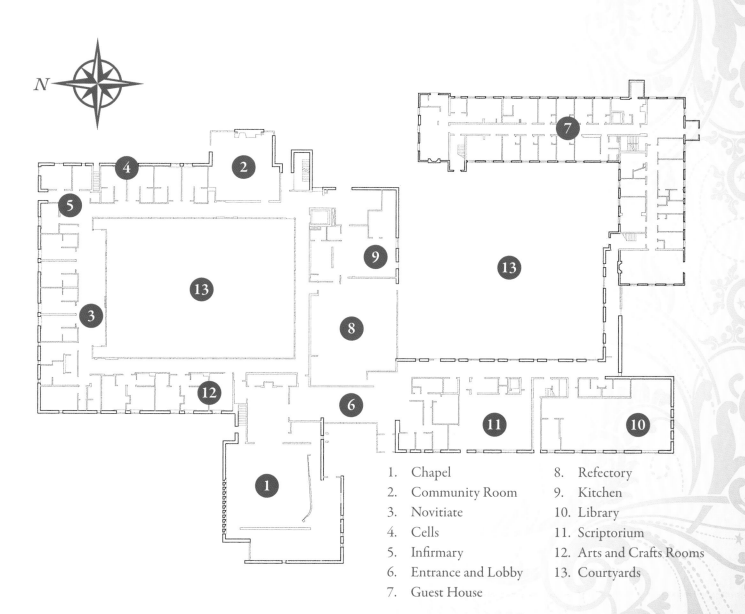

1. Chapel
2. Community Room
3. Novitiate
4. Cells
5. Infirmary
6. Entrance and Lobby
7. Guest House
8. Refectory
9. Kitchen
10. Library
11. Scriptorium
12. Arts and Crafts Rooms
13. Courtyards

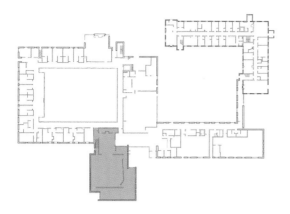

CHAPEL 7

Like living stones, let yourselves be built into a spiritual house, to be a holy priesthood, to offer spiritual sacrifices acceptable to God through Jesus Christ. (1 Peter 2:5)

In the lobby of St. John's Convent, just outside the chapel, hangs a large and colourful icon of St. John the Divine. It was painted for the sisters by Archimandrate Felix Dubneac, a Romanian Orthodox priest, to honour his friendship with Bishop Henry Hill, who lived with the sisters on Botham Road. Like all icons, it is highly symbolic, and it especially resonates with the Sisterhood. On the right side of the icon is a representation of the convent on Botham Road, and on the left are depictions of various buildings on Patmos, the island where, according to legend, St. John was exiled.

In the centre of the icon, St. John is receiving from God the vision of heaven and of the church described in the Book of Revelation, while a scribe, surrounded by baskets of scrolls, writes down the words. In this icon is represented the whole Johannine tradition — from the Revelation, the gospel, and the letters. It is an icon of

Outdoor photo of chapel.

Photo by Tom Arban.

the Sisterhood's spirituality, based on St. John's inspiration to pursue the "vision of heaven and the life of love," as one of the Sisterhood's prayers expresses it.

The Sisterhood of St. John the Divine holds in a creative tension these two phrases: the "vision of heaven" is a reminder of the importance of prayer as the foundation of our relationship with God; and "the life of love" is a reminder that out of our prayer comes our inspiration to share God's love with others.

The same balance is seen in the convent narthex and chapel. As you enter the narthex (the entry room of the chapel), to your right is a handsome limestone fireplace. It is a cosy place to sit and read or pray on a cold winter day, but more than that it is a symbolic reminder that our Christian journey begins at the hearth — in the homes where we were born and nurtured from infancy, and where we return for comfort and friendship. The hearth also symbolizes vividly the communion of saints — the sisters who have gone before and been part of this family of God for 130 years.

As you turn toward the chapel you see a limestone baptismal font. It stands on the axis between the hearth and the altar and symbolizes the link between the secular and sacred, the transformation of our lives in Jesus Christ, and our call as

Christians to embrace and protect all of God's creation.

The font is filled with colourful stones that shimmer under the water. They remind all who enter that the monastic community is made up of "living stones," that is, the people who come together to worship God in the sacred space of the chapel — the sisters, all of the monastic "household of God" (associates, oblates, alongsiders), and the guests who come for a shorter or longer period of time.

Opposite the font, at the west end of the chapel, is the limestone altar designed by Toronto-based sculptor Jacobine Jones. The three carved panels of the altar depict three feminine images of God. The phoenix is a symbol of the Resurrection, as this mythical bird sacrifices herself and is reborn out of the ashes. The pelican is a symbol of the Atonement, as a mother pelican is said to feed her babies from the blood of her own breast when food is scarce. And the eagle is both a symbol of the Ascension and of St. John. According to tradition, the eagle is the only creature that can look directly at the sun and not be blinded; here you see a mother eagle teaching her babies to fly toward the sun.

TOP: *The narthex.*

BOTTOM: *The Chapel of St. John the Divine.*

The altar is the culmination of our journey from the hearth, through the waters of baptism, to the altar, which represents both sacrifice (as we are called to take up our cross and follow Christ) and the nourishment that Christ gives in the bread and wine of the Eucharist. As we gather together around the altar at the time of Communion, we understand the meaning of "living stones, being built into a spiritual house."

> The Spirit and the bride say, "Come." And let everyone who hears say, "Come." And let everyone who is thirsty come. Let anyone who wishes take the water of life as a gift... Amen. Come, Lord Jesus! (Rev 22:17, 20)

Details of the altar panels: the phoenix, the pelican, and the eagle.

In the Book of Revelation, John the Divine presents a picture of the newly born Christian church that both challenges Christians to live the values of the

Gospel, and draws us deeply into the mystery of union with God. The book ends with the invitation of Jesus to us, "Come!" and is answered by that most primitive cry of the human heart to Jesus — "Amen. Come, Lord Jesus!" Come into our lives, our hearts, our communities; and bring us into your presence.

The sisters' dedication to contemplative prayer as well as to public worship is reflected in this chapel full of the light of God.

Every home of the Sisterhood has contained a chapel as the central focus of its building, whether a tiny room fitted out with altar and chairs as in the sisters' first convent on Robinson Street, or an imposing gothic space as in the chapel in the Major Street convent, or a modest but beautiful chapel as in the sisters' home in Victoria, B.C. The chapel is always at the heart of the community's buildings, just as the sisters' commitment to prayer is at the heart of their lives.

Corporate and Personal Prayer

At the beginning of the Sisterhood in 1884 a daily rhythm of prayer set the schedule for the day, which began at 5:45 a.m. and ended at 10:00 p.m. Between these times, the sisters came together in chapel seven times for the "Divine Office" — the round of prayer marking the hours of the day — and once a day for a celebration of the Holy Eucharist. They listened to scripture, sang hymns, and prayed for the needs of the world. When it was time for chapel, everything else had to be dropped. Novices in the community were warned of "the lust to finish" their work: a sign of detachment from worldly concerns was the ability to lay down your work and pick it up again after the chapel service.

Everything else — meals, work, recreation, study of scripture and other topics, personal prayer, spiritual reading, and

Easter Vigil, 2014.

sleep — revolved around these times of communal prayer. And all this happened in the midst of a full work schedule, with sisters working in the hospital, the Church Home, the school, and the missions.

Today, 130 years later, the sisters still rise early and continue to gather for corporate worship, though only four times a day, including the Eucharist, with two hours allotted each day for private prayer and spiritual reading. Centering prayer, Christian meditation, Ignatian prayer with scripture, *lectio divina*, walking the labyrinth, and praying with the rosary are all prayer forms that sisters find helpful. Spiritual reading is also an important part of the two hours of daily prayer.

The sisters' current *Rule of Life* states that "prayer is God's gift, enabling growth in our relationship with Christ in every aspect of life, and releasing creative power into the world for the glory of God."[1] The challenge remains the same as it was for Mother Hannah — not to let the sisters' work co-opt their prayer, but to be sure that prayer is the grounding for all of the community's active work.

CORPORATE PRAYER AND MUSIC

Mother Hannah had written in the Sisterhood's first *Rule of Life* that "the Life of Prayer and Devotion must come first."[2]

The Reverend J.D. Cayley, rector of St. George's Church in Toronto, concurred with this statement at the April 15, 1882, meeting of the Sisterhood's founding committee at which Mother Hannah was present: "I believe the chief work [of the Sisterhood] to be the life of prayer, whereby such a society becomes a centre of blessing to all around it."[3]

Such was the vision and the foundation of the Sisterhood, to be a centre of prayer from which sprang the ministries or works the sisters would take up.

From the beginning until the early 1960s, the community relied for its corporate prayer on the *Monastic Diurnal, The Hours of Prayer,* and *The Day Hours* at different times interchangeably. These books contained all the readings, psalms, hymn texts, and prayers necessary to pray the traditional Benedictine seven-fold office. Lauds (morning) and Vespers (evening) were the major offices of the day. The minor offices of Prime, Terce, Sext, None, and Compline were short, lasting from ten to fifteen minutes each.

Early service books show that the community was concerned with the beauty and dignity of the music and used predominantly chants when singing the Divine Office.[4] Miss Rose Grier, elder sister of Mother Hannah and retired headmistress of Bishop Strachan School, helped to form the musical tradition of the community in the early years. She had been an organist and choir-mistress as a young woman, and during her retirement she collected and copied hymns and other music for the sisters to sing.

Sister Eva was in charge of music during the 1920s and wrote some music for the community. In 1929, she was succeeded by the Reverend Alfred L. Rose of the Society of St. John the Evangelist's Canadian congregation in Bracebridge, Ontario. An expert musician and composer, Father Rose held a quarterly choir school for the sisters. He also composed a number of masses, motets, *faux bourdons* and hymn tunes for the community. He has had a lasting influence on the Sisterhood; two of his compositions, "The Dedication Motet" and "The Life Profession Motet," are regular parts of the sisters' repertoire to this day.

Sister Agnes served as the community's organist and choir mistress for the next thirty years. She was active in the newly formed Canadian Gregorian Association and pursued her study of plainsong at the Choir School of St. Michael's Cathedral in Toronto. Sister Agnes died in 1964, just as the sisters were entering an era of liturgical renewal.

Sister Thelma-Anne succeeded Sister Agnes as the sisters' music director and was well suited to carry the community through a period of significant change. When Vatican II was ushered in (in the early 1960s), the sisters began to talk about changing from the seven-fold office to a four-fold office, consisting of Morning Prayer (8:30 a.m.), Noon Office (12:00 p.m.), Evening Prayer (5:00 p.m.), and Compline (8:30 p.m.). Part of the motivation for this change came from a desire for the Sisterhood's prayer to reflect more closely the prayer of the Church as a whole. With the revision of the Canadian *Book of Common Prayer* in 1962 and the inclusion of a noon office and night office (Compline) as well as Morning Prayer and Evening Prayer, it was possible to use the common prayer of the Church as the office book for the Sisterhood. One of the results of this shift was a new emphasis on private prayer for the sisters: reducing the number of chapel offices meant there was more time for the sisters' contemplative prayer and reading.

After using the new *Book of Common Prayer* for a while, the sisters found it did not have enough variety for daily use, and so they drew on resources from other communities, from the American *Book of Common Prayer* (1976), from a series of experimental liturgies published in Canada (especially the Qu'Appelle liturgy), and from texts and music written by Sister Rosemary Anne and Sister Thelma-Anne.

A gifted organist and composer, Sister Thelma-Anne began to compile modified psalm tones for use in Evening Prayer and to introduce the community to the Gelineau psalter for Compline. She also composed, modified, and rearranged tones that the community still uses for the Introductory Responses, Venite, Jubilate, Song of Zechariah, Song of Mary, and Song of Simeon. She introduced the sisters to resources from Taizé and the Orthodox tradition for the litanies and responsories that are in current use in the daily offices. She found and composed new settings for the Eucharist on Sundays and major feast days. The community used several hymn books during this period: *The English Hymnal* (1933), *The Book of Common Praise* (1938) published for the Anglican Church of Canada, and *The Hymn Book* (1971) published jointly by the Anglican and United churches. In 1984, the Sisterhood's centennial year, a collection of hymns was published called *Songs for Celebration*, featuring texts by Sister Rosemary Anne and music by Sister Thelma-Anne.

When the Canadian *Book of Alternative Services* (BAS) was published in 1985, the Sisterhood was among the first communities and churches in Canada to order copies and to adopt the book for its regular worship. It contained generous options for canticles, responsories, litanies, and other music for the Divine Office and the Eucharist. Musicians active in the church at the time, like George Black, William Buchner, and the community's own Sister Thelma-Anne began writing musical settings for the texts in the BAS, and the sisters suddenly found themselves with a wealth of new music for the Divine Office and the Eucharist. Because the BAS did not include an order for Compline, the sisters supplemented it with forms of Compline from the American *Book of Common Prayer* (1976) and *A New Zealand Prayer Book* (1988) until the Anglican Church of Canada published an order for Compline, *Night Prayer* (2001).

Sister Thelma-Anne continued to be a leader in music and liturgy into the 1980s and 1990s, both for the Sisterhood and for the Anglican Church of

Canada. She became a member of the Hymn Book Task Force, which developed a new hymnal to complement *The Book of Alternative Services* and *The Revised Common Lectionary* — the three-year cycle of scripture readings used by Anglicans as well as Roman Catholics, Lutherans, and the United Church. When *Common Praise* (1998) was published, the community adopted its use entirely for both the daily offices and Eucharist. Two of the hymns from *Songs for Celebration,* "Sing Hallelujah," (words by Sister Rosemary Anne and music by Sister Thelma-Anne) and "Apostle of the Word" (words by Sister Rosemary Anne set to a traditional tune) were included in *Common Praise.*

Hal Gober with the new Gober organ.

In 2000, Sister Thelma-Anne was assigned to St. John's House in Montreal where she continued her musical activities and retreat leadership in that diocese. Her departure from the convent left a void that needed to be filled, specifically an organist to play at the convent's Sunday Eucharist. The Sisterhood was fortunate to find some gifted musicians to fill the vacancy: Julie Deck (2000–02); Don Willis (2002–03); and beginning in 2003, Stephanie Martin. Stephanie was with the community during the move from Botham Road to Cummer Avenue.

During Stephanie's time the sisters explored music from many other sources, including new hymn books from other denominations. In 2001, the Waterloo Declaration brought the Anglican Church of Canada and the Evangelical Lutheran Church in Canada into full communion, and in 2006 the sisters began to use worship resources and hymns from the newly published *Evangelical Lutheran Worship.*

During construction of the new chapel, the sisters received an unexpected and generous gift from an anonymous donor to build a new organ, as the organ in the Botham Road chapel was not able to be salvaged and moved. Working with the Sisterhood's organ committee, Stephanie assisted in choosing Hal Gober Organs, based then in Elora, Ontario, to build a tracker-action organ. (A tracker-action organ is fully mechanical; the only electricity used is to run the wind motor.)

The glorious new organ was dedicated in 2006. Shortly afterward, Stephanie, who was also a professor of music at York University, was offered the position of music director at the Church of St. Mary Magdalene, Toronto, and so reluctantly had to end her time with the sisters. She left a beautiful legacy in the form of an "Alleluia" written and dedicated to the sisters — one of the favourite pieces sung in the Easter season.

In 2007, Daniel Norman was hired as convent organist and choir director. A talented musician who also works at Church of the Redeemer in Toronto, Dan has enhanced the sisters' repertoire by composing inspiring music for the Divine Office and the Eucharist. The choir practices, which he leads every Friday morning, are full of energy and inspire the sisters' best singing.

Many of the sisters are musical and enjoy playing recreationally, and a few also take leadership in the community's worship. Sister Anne, a talented violinist, has played in community orchestras and often teams up with Dan Norman for special services. A number of sisters have beautiful voices and serve as cantors. Sister Constance Joanna serves as pianist at many of the services when Dan is not scheduled. Sister Sue is a talented poet who, like Sister Rosemary Anne, has set many of her poems to music — some composed by Sister Thelma-Anne, some by Dan Norman and others, and some of her own composing.

Dan Norman playing the organ with Sister Anne on the violin.

In 2011, the sisters looked for a supplementary hymnal that would allow them to incorporate more contemporary music into their worship. After trying out music from various hymnals in several choral workshops, they chose the third edition of the popular Roman Catholic *Gather* (GIA Publications, 2011) and have integrated it into their worship. Since 2012, the words and music of *Gather* have given the Sisterhood fresh expression to the Divine Office and Eucharist.

At the beginning of Lent in 2013, the community revised the Divine Office binder containing the music and texts for Morning Prayer and Evening Prayer, together with canticles and the inclusive-language psalter produced by the Sisterhood back in 1995. The sisters have a strong commitment to using gender-inclusive language in public worship and often use the *Inclusive Bible* (2007) for public reading of scripture. They also have a commitment to sing the Divine Office whenever possible, following the old proverb that "whoever sings prays twice." While this is not always possible in smaller branch houses, where the number of singers is smaller, even then the sisters sing when they can. At St. John's Convent, virtually all the offices are sung. The gift of music and prayer is offered to all who come.

With such a rich, dynamic, and eclectic musical tradition the sisters can't help but feel a natural and easy resonance with the words of Psalm 149:

> Hallelujah! Sing to God a new song;
> sing praise in the congregation of the faithful.
> Let Israel rejoice in the Creator;
> let the children of Zion be joyful in their Sovereign.
> Let them praise God's name in the dance;
> let them sing praise with timbrel and harp.
> For God takes pleasure in all people
> and adorns the poor with victory. (Psalm 149:1–4)

Hymns

"Anniversary Hymn"[5]
By Sisters Rosemary Anne and Thelma-Anne

ANNIVERSARY HYMN

1 Lord Almighty, King eternal,
   Help your servants and defend.
   By your Holy Spirit lead us,
   Be our dear and constant friend;
   Keep aflame one living passion,
   Love for you and all mankind.
   Grant our needs of soul and body
   And bestow the Christ-like mind.

2 Bless us in our life and labours,
   Strength for every task renew;
   Kept in patience, faith, obedience,
   May we render service true.
   While our eyes in faith behold you,
   Draw us closer to your side,
   That at last our hearts may know you,
   And your love be satisfied.

RA, SSJD

158

"O God, Who Moves the Stars Across the Heavens"[6]
By Sisters Sue and Thelma-Anne

1. O God, who moves the stars across the heavens, _____ you set us on the earth to do your will, _____ through countless ages, e-ons, e-vo-lu-tions, cre-a-ted, birthed, e-volved for good or ill.

2. We know our on-ly re-course is your mer-cy, _____ O Mother, our sal-va-tion's by your grace; _____ so act with-in us, through us and be-yond us, that in your love we may find each our place.

3. Not like the stars that etch the night's clear dark-ness, _____ o-bey-ing laws they do not un-der-stand, _____ we live in free-dom, free to work a-gainst you, or free to nest-le close with-in your hand.

4. You sent your Law and prophets to defend us,
Uplift us from our willful, selfish goals;
You sent your Son, your very Self, among us,
O Father of our Saviour and our souls.

5. He lived with us that we may live in freedom;
He taught us, healed us, loved us, without cease.
He led us to the Cross that's heavenly wisdom;
He moves us, like your stars, into your peace.

6. Grant us the will to use our freedom wisely;
Grant us the power to turn from power's allures;
Grant us the peace of stars, the strength of eagles;
Grant us the grace to find our will in yours.

Text : Sr. Sue Elwyn, SSJD
Tune: Sr. Sue Elwyn, SSJD & Sr. Thelma-Anne McLeod, SSJD
Harm: Sr. Thelma-Anne McLeod, SSJD

CASCADE 11 10 11 10

"DAUGHTER OF GOD"[7]
By Sisters Rosemary Anne and Thelma-Anne

1 O God, whose all-redeeming love
  Crowns every saint in light,
  On this your servant's festal day,
  We sing with heart's delight.

2 In joyful praise our songs ascend,
  For this most loving grace:
  Your daughter stands among the blest
  Within the heavenly place.

3 Among the blest, in radiant peace,
  Yet still a servant true,
  Her strength and beauty perfected,
  Her vision ever new.

4 Once, she had known temptation sharp,
  The doubts that shake the mind,
  Yet laboured still in love and prayer
  Eternal life to find.

5 **(This verse for a martyr:)**
  She gave her life in steadfast love
  And knew that death was gain,
  That in the purposes of God,
  No sacrifice is vain.

6 Assist us in our stumbling walk
  And aid each humble vow,
  For you are speaking through your saints
  In ages past, and now.

"CREATOR, GOD"
By Sisters Sue and Thelma-Anne

1. Cre - a - tor, God, my gov - er - nor, my guide, you
2. I've been your ser - vant; still I serve and will, from
3. You send me forth, each vow and pro - mise kept, ac -
4. You've brought sal - va - tion clear, de - li - ve - rance sure, to

give me leave at last to go to that great space where
birth un - til all a - ges end, and then, in peace and
cor - ding to the pro - phets' word. My eyes, which searched so
eve - ry na - tion, set - tled, wild, for Is - rael's glo - ry -

e - ven stars do hide, their fire in your more bril - liant glow.
love, will I serve still, nor cease when time it - self you rend.
long, so oft - en wept, are o - pened now in joy as - sured.
hope of rich and poor - is God, em - bo - died in a child.

Text: Sr. Sue Elwyn, N/SSJD
Music: adapted from DRESDEN, J.S. Bach, (*E.H.* 515)
    by Sr. Thelma-Anne McLeod, SSJD

SEBASTIAN
84 84
© SSJD, 2002

"A Hymn for the Holy Women of the Old Testament"
By Sisters Sue and Thelma-Anne

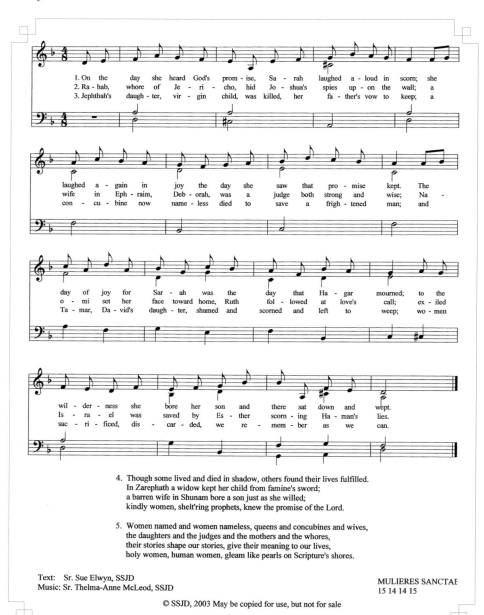

1. On the day she heard God's prom - ise, Sa - rah laughed a - loud in scorn; she
2. Ra - hab, whore of Je - ri - cho, hid Jo - shua's spies up - on the wall; a
3. Jephthah's daugh - ter, vir - gin child, was killed, her fa - ther's vow to keep; a

laughed a - gain in joy the day she saw that pro - mise kept. The
wife in Eph - raim, Deb - orah, was a judge both strong and wise; Na -
con - cu - bine now name - less died to save a frigh - tened man; and

day of joy for Sar - ah was the day that Ha - gar mourned; to the
o - mi set her face toward home, Ruth fol - lowed at love's call; ex - iled
Ta - mar, Da - vid's daugh - ter, shamed and scorned and left to weep; wo - men

wil - der - ness she bore her son and there sat down and wept.
Is - ra - el was saved by Es - ther scorn - ing Ha - man's lies.
sac - ri - ficed, dis - car - ded, we re - mem - ber as we can.

4. Though some lived and died in shadow, others found their lives fulfilled.
   In Zarephath a widow kept her child from famine's sword;
   a barren wife in Shunam bore a son just as she willed;
   kindly women, shelt'ring prophets, knew the promise of the Lord.

5. Women named and women nameless, queens and concubines and wives,
   the daughters and the judges and the mothers and the whores,
   their stories shape our stories, give their meaning to our lives,
   holy women, human women, gleam like pearls on Scripture's shores.

Text: Sr. Sue Elwyn, SSJD
Music: Sr. Thelma-Anne McLeod, SSJD

MULIERES SANCTAE
15 14 14 15

"My God Made a World That Changes"
By Sisters Sue and Thelma-Anne

Text: Sr. Sue Elwyn, SSJD
Music: Sr. Sue Elwyn, SSJD and Sr. Thelma-Anne McLeod, SSJD

MUNDUS MUTANS
PM

8 COMMUNITY ROOM

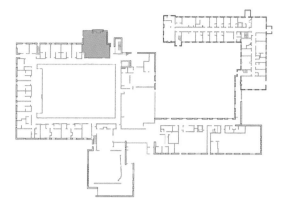

Oh how good and pleasant it is,
when families live together in unity!
It is like the dew of Hermon
that falls upon the hills of Zion.
For there God has ordained the blessing:
life for evermore. (Psalm 133:1, 4–5)

LIVING INTENTIONAL COMMUNITY

The community room (called the chapter room in some communities) is the place in a monastic building where the members most directly confront the reality of relationships. In St. John's Convent, it is where the sisters gather informally for coffee, to read the newspaper or to chat, for a Saturday night movie, or for evening recreation; and more formally for the daily conference, house meetings, and chapter meetings. It is a place to sit in front of the fire in winter, or to gaze out at the beautiful grounds through vistas of windows in the summer. The newest books in the sisters' library are kept in this room, along with newspapers and snacks.

But the room itself is also a place of work, because building community requires an intentional commitment to deepening relationships, learning to love people who are very different from you, listening to each other's stories, asking forgiveness, and seeking reconciliation.

Intentional community understands the values of love, commitment, and interdependence as normative and not optional. It is a model of relationship that expresses itself in surprise, wonder, and gratitude for the gift of God's love. This kind of community is not about being a club or interest group, but a loving, extended family where alienation and differences are met with friendship and acceptance. Members of monastic communities are not forced to live together; they choose to do so in response to God's call.

So how do the sisters manage it? What does it take to live like this?

They spend time together, listen to one another, and care about each other's growth and well-being. Like marriage, community living is not easy. In fact, living with twenty-five or more women can be rather more complex than living in a small family unit. It requires a balance of privacy and togetherness. Just as the Sisterhood's ministry will not flourish without the commitment to prayer, so community life will not flourish unless there is also a commitment and space for privacy. Finding the balance is crucial. Each person participates in three sets of relationships that intersect: a relationship with oneself, a relationship with others, and a relationship with God. If one is neglected, the whole will fall apart.

We live in a world that hungers to belong and to be accepted and yet demands independence and values the individual. It is also a broken world, and sisters can and do unintentionally bring some of that brokenness into

Sister Constance reading the newspaper.

community, which is why forgiveness and reconciliation are crucial to a healthy community life. They learn to live fearlessly, not by walking away from differences of opinion and misunderstandings but by working through them. The reward is deeper understanding and acceptance. Being actively open to the needs of others while also being honest about one's own needs and failings may seem like a paradox, but it is the warp and woof of community living.

A Day in the Life of a Sister

The rhythm of the day makes this paradoxical balance not only possible but creative, as sisters find new ways to integrate their prayer and work. The Sisterhood of St. John the Divine lives the "mixed" life, as do most of the religious communities in the Anglican Communion (whether they are called Episcopalian in the U.S.A. and Scotland, or Anglican in most other places). The term "mixed" is intentional, signalling a creative tension between contemplation and action, between work and prayer — a balance that has been part of the Benedictine tradition since its inception in the sixth century.

Most sisters begin their day before 6:00 a.m., with some rising much earlier. This ensures that the sisters begin the day by attending to God's "still small voice" with at least two hours for prayer and meditation, spiritual reading, prayer with scripture (*lectio divina*), and other forms of contemplative prayer as the sisters find most helpful. Night owls may choose to have part of their prayer time in the evening after Compline. The sisters keep the Great Silence from 9:00 p.m. to 9:00 a.m. (a tradition that has not changed since the founding of the Sisterhood) so that everyone is able to read, pray, and sleep in a spirit of quiet. However, the silence may be broken to speak to staff or to meet the needs of a guest or another sister.

A Bible study in the community room.

All three meals are eaten in silence, except for Sunday supper, holidays, community celebrations, and special occasions when family and friends join the sisters for conversation. The midday and evening meals follow worship in the chapel, and the silence is a reminder that just as God feeds our spirits through our prayer and worship, so God provides physical nourishment for our bodies.

Three times a day — morning, noon, and evening — the chapel bell rings to signal the praying of the Angelus[1] at the beginning of the sisters' worship together. At night prayer (Compline), a tune is played on the chimes instead of ringing the chapel bell — a quiet and peaceful beginning to the last corporate worship of the day.

Morning Prayer begins with the words, "Open our lips, O God." And all respond: "And our mouth shall proclaim your praise." These are often the first words spoken in the morning following the Great Silence. It is the first corporate check-in with God, and a commitment to truly lift hearts and voices in worship.

Following Morning Prayer, the sisters go to the community room for the morning conference. They begin with one of several prayers for the community's "Household of God" (which includes the sisters, associates, oblates, and along-siders), and a short reading from the *Rule of Life*. They acknowledge special anniversaries of sisters living and departed and share necessary information with one another about the day's doings. A scribe keeps notes from these meetings so that sisters who are unable to attend because of their work or for other reasons may keep up with what is happening.

It is also at this conference that apologies may be made for not observing some part of the *Rule of Life* or for sharp words spoken. These moments of apology are vital to ensuring a healthy community where problems and hurts are not allowed to fester, where issues are sorted out, and where peace with one another may prevail.

After conference the sisters go to their assigned areas of work. All the sis-

A party at recreation.

ters have responsibilities according to their gifts and abilities: it could be in the chapel or refectory, the infirmary or guest house, at St. John's Rehab or out in a community mission, in the library or administration offices or reception desk. It takes a village to run a convent, and in many ways the convent is both the sisters' village and their home.

The sisters stop work at noon and go to chapel for the Eucharist, followed by dinner (the main meal of the day). Following dinner, they may have a time of rest, go for a walk, or do something else that refreshes them, and then return to their assigned work until Evening Prayer at 5:00 p.m., followed by supper. Some sisters may be out for the day or part of the day. One sister works as a parish priest, several sisters work at St. John's Rehab, and still others go out to lead workshops and preach at local parishes. It is sometimes necessary for a sister to miss a meal or a chapel service, but in general the sisters are committed to participating in chapel and communal meals.

After supper, some sisters clean up in the refectory and kitchen while others complete the various duties of the day before gathering in the community room at 7:00 p.m. for recreation. This often involves lively conversation or reports from sisters about their activities during the past week, while many enjoy handcrafts like knitting, crocheting, or making rosaries. One evening a week, sisters meet in smaller groups to play board games, go for a walk, listen to music, watch a DVD, or exercise in the therapeutic pool at St. John's Rehab next door.

At 8:10 p.m., everyone returns to the chapel for Compline, the final office of the day. In contrast to the relative liveliness of Morning Prayer, Compline is a gentle, more subdued service in which to thank God for the day, to ask for the blessing of peace and a quiet night, and to pray for others — especially those who work while others sleep. Compline ends, the Greater Silence begins, and the sisters return to their individual rooms for well-deserved sleep.

COMMUNITY DECISION-MAKING

The community room is often called the chapter room in monastic houses because the chapter (the official decision-making body) of the community meets there. The chapter of SSJD is made up of the professed sisters, but members of the novitiate attend chapter meetings with an invitation to speak but not to vote on constitutional matters. In less formal gatherings, everyone, even the newest postulant, has a voice and a vote in community meetings — although the sisters try to minimize formal voting and work toward consensus.

Meetings of the sisters, both formal and informal, take place frequently. The daily conference described above is one of those. Once or twice a month the sisters hold house meetings to discuss current topics or issues that concern their life together. A house meeting might include a discussion of the menu in the kitchen and whether (and which) changes need to be made; plans for an upcoming event or special liturgy, with an opportunity for everyone to share in the plans and set task groups and timelines; a report from a sister who has been to an interesting conference on a topic of relevance to the sisters' life and worship. These are just a few examples of the many and varied topics that may be brought to a house meeting. Decisions are made by consensus and include all the sisters present from the newest to the most senior.

The annual general chapter takes place over a week or ten days, usually in August, and is the time in the year when the sisters hear reports of the various ministries of the Sisterhood, evaluate the progress of the sisters in formation (postulants, novices and first-professed), discuss issues of strategic and current significance to the Sisterhood, and consider future directions and possible changes in ways of doing things or in the ministries of the Sisterhood. The Sisterhood also gathers annually as the legally constituted corporation of the Sisterhood. Like the annual general meeting of any corporation, members receive the annual reports of the president (the Reverend Mother), the treasurer (an elected member), the auditor, and the director of fundraising (a sister). The

Sisters meeting in chapter.

sisters discuss the community's financial situation, and make plans as necessary for the future. Everyone attends this meeting, but only the life-professed sisters are voting members according to the corporate by-laws of the Sisterhood.

The sisters have profited greatly from some of the newer forms of communal decision-making that have come from the world of business as well as the church. The ORID process was introduced by Sisters Thelma-Anne and Constance Joanna after they learned about it at a workshop at the Canadian Institute of Cultural Affairs.[2] ORID is an acronym for Objective, Reflective, Interpretive, Decisional. It is a process of strategic questioning in which a group first asks what the relevant objective facts are, then asks reflective or feelings-based questions, then interpretive or value-based questions, and finally asks questions that lead to a decision. It has been a major help to the Sisterhood as it has dealt with all kinds of change — small ones such as changes in the daily timetable, and big ones such as moving to a new location and building a new convent, opening new ministries, or bringing a gracious end to a previous ministry.

More recently, the Sisterhood has had training from Rob Voyle in the process of Appreciative Inquiry. Like the ORID method, Appreciative Inquiry is based on asking creative questions and helping a group appreciate its strengths in order to know how to move into the future.

Whether the decisions the sisters make are small or big, strategic or practical, all members of the community are involved. The community room becomes symbolic of this commitment.

ADMINISTRATION AND FUNDRAISING

Many aspects of community life do not physically take place in the community room itself, but in offices in the administrative wing of the convent, which are spiritually a part of the commitment to communal life that the community room represents. Bills have to be paid, budgets made up, investments monitored, insurance provided, computers maintained, staff payroll and benefits looked after, and building maintenance attended to. All these nitty-gritty aspects of community life may not seem exciting, but they are what enable the communal life, prayer, and ministry of the sisters to continue.

An important and often overlooked aspect of the monastic life is the need to steward resources responsibly, and to invite others to join in the Sisterhood's mission by helping to make that financially possible. When the Sisterhood was founded, Mother Hannah insisted that those who were part of the organizing committee and had the original vision for a women's religious community in Canada, must themselves take on the responsibility for establishing an endowment fund and undertake ongoing fundraising to allow the sisters to do the ministry to which they were called.

For many years the sisters who worked in the hospital, the Church Home, the schools, and the missions received no salaries and were entirely dependent on the maintenance allotted in the budgets of these facilities and on fundraising done by others on behalf of their work. Today, the sisters who work at the hospital or outside the community do receive honoraria or salaries. But this constitutes a fraction of the cost of running and maintaining a modern convent, and the sisters subsidize the guest house, where expenses always exceed revenue from the modest accommodation fees. Thus, the Sisterhood continues to rely on the generosity of associates, oblates, and friends who believe that communities of compassion and hospitality are needed in the world today. The sisters' ministries of hospitality, pastoral care, teaching, and caring for those God puts in their path make a difference in the lives of many women and men seeking "something more" in a world hungry for meaning, acceptance, love, peace, and justice.

The sisters live and work, trusting in the gospel value that if they openly give and share what they have they will receive enough and more than enough: "Give and it will be given to you. A good measure, pressed down, shaken together, running over, will be put into your lap; for the measure you give will be the measure you get back." (Luke 6:38)

These principles underpin the Sisterhood's approach to fundraising. They have had the help of fundraising experts, but in the end it is the sisters themselves who know their donors and who can best witness that fundraising is an important ministry in its own right. It is a way of sharing the vision and inviting other people into the mission. As Henri Nouwen has said, "fundraising is proclaiming what we believe in such a way that we offer other people an opportunity to participate with us in our vision and mission."[3]

9 NOVITIATE

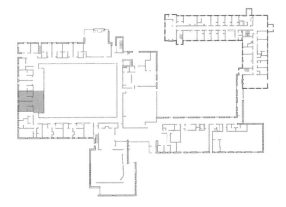

How dear to me is your dwelling, O God of hosts!
my soul has a desire and longing for your courts.
Happy are they who dwell in your house;
they will always be praising you.
Happy are the people whose strength is in you,
whose hearts are set on the pilgrims' way. (Psalm 84:1, 3–4)

The word *novitiate* traditionally refers to the place where new members of a monastic community live and study. It also refers to the group of new members (postulants and novices). But its more important meaning is the period of formation and training of new members. No monastic community can survive without a constant flow of new members, and without a focused time of spiritual formation, study, and reflection on important issues of our time through the lens of the monastic life.

At one time, novices and postulants were segregated from the professed members of a monastic community. This is no longer the case. In St. John's Convent there is a room where new members gather for classes and discussion, but the important focus is the process of formation rather than the place where it happens.

FORMATION IN THE RELIGIOUS LIFE

Whatever we decide to do in life, there is almost always a period of training. We may need to study for several years at a technical training school or college or university after completing high school or we may be apprenticed to someone or simply learn from one who is more experienced. Some skills may be learned from a book but personal contact or mentoring is almost always necessary. When Mother Hannah was asked to found the Sisterhood of St. John the Divine, she went to the Community of St. Mary in Peekskill, New York, to be formed in the religious life. Her training there as a novice was just over two years and was more extensive than for an average novice as she was also being prepared to found a new community. The first women who joined Mother Hannah as postulants and novices would have learned directly from her and from the work they were given to do. Initially, Mother Hannah was also the Novice Mistress (in the terminology of the time), until she asked another life-professed sister to take on the care of the postulants and novices. As the number of new members grew, they were housed in a separate part of the convent with their own common room for conference, recreation, and classes, although they prayed and worked with the professed sisters.

There would have been benefits to this partial separation: the new members were able to bond; they were not troubled by the concerns of the professed sisters (for example, whether to start or close a ministry); and they could have some fun times together such as a picnic, a walk in a park, or an excursion somewhere. However, by the 1990s, when there were fewer novices, it became impractical to have the members of the novitiate living separately and so they became fully integrated into the community, attending conference, recreation, and chapter meetings with the professed sisters. There are benefits to this arrangement too, especially as women entering the community these days are older on average than many of the novices in Mother Hannah's day, and have the wisdom of life experience to bring to community decision-making.

So what kind of formation is needed today to prepare women to live in intentional community under the vows of poverty, chastity, and obedience? Initial formation begins with postulancy, a period of approximately six months when the

Early novices having recreation with Sister Margaret Ann.

new member experiences the joys and challenges of living in community. It is a time of learning and discernment, often an eye-opening experience of discovering that the reality of the religious life is not the same as the ideal one may have formed before entering the community.

At the end of approximately six months, the postulant may ask to become a novice. If the Reverend Mother and Novitiate Director agree, she will be formally received as a novice and given the community habit as a sign of her promise to live by the Sisterhood's *Rule of Life*. This is followed by an ongoing time of formation and discernment, approximately three years, as the novice seeks to understand the responsibilities and privileges of a monastic vocation. She accepts all the challenges of living in community and seeks to balance the common life with personal development, spiritual growth, study, ministry, and recreation. This calling requires ongoing inner change and conversion of life, as St. Benedict referred to the process of spiritual growth. The hope is that the novice will discover inner freedom within the framework of community life which will enable her to choose first profession (often referred to as first vows).

The Sisterhood's *Rule of Life* begins with the following intention:

> The Sisters of Saint John the Divine, in the spirit of their patron, are called to live to the glory of God in fulfillment of the two-fold law of love. Each sister will seek to do everything as one who has been baptized into Christ's death, and has entered into the new life of his resurrection, by the power of the Holy Spirit. We are committed to lifelong conversion and to growth in union with God through the life of prayer and the undivided service of Jesus Christ. In Christ we are both called and sent to be open and responsive to the needs of the church and of the world, and to pray and work for peace, justice, unity and the integrity of creation.[1]

This intention describes the purpose of the Sisterhood and therefore also the goal of the novitiate period. The formation program provides opportunities, challenges, and directions for growing into a deeper relationship with

TOP: *A current novitiate class with Sister Elizabeth.*
MIDDLE: *The novices on an outing in 2012.*
BOTTOM: *Sister Susanne helping our associate Anne Day in the kitchen.*

God and with the community through personal and communal prayer, following the community's daily rhythm, joining in the work of the community, enjoying times of recreation together, having regular novitiate classes, weekly guidance from the Novitiate Director, spiritual direction, and learning about the religious life from more senior sisters. Most of the women who enter will also take the four-year Education for Ministry program, which is a college-level course of religious education and teaches the basics of biblical scholarship through a study of scripture, church history, theology and ethics. New members learn and practise different forms of prayer and meditation and gradually take on various roles in chapel as they feel comfortable and have the ability — reading, cantoring, serving at the altar, leading the intercessions at the Eucharist, and others.

All the women in the novitiate meet regularly to study and discuss the Sisterhood's *Rule of Life*, to learn the ways of prayer, and to study books that help in living the monastic life in the contemporary world.[2] There may also be classes on the Enneagram or the Myers-Briggs psychological types to help the sisters understand themselves and others better, and to give them insights into how they relate to other people.[3]

Every few years there are opportunities to attend a workshop sponsored by the Conference of Anglican Religious Orders in the Americas (CAROA). For example, in October 2013 the members of the novitiate attended a workshop entitled: "Becoming Fire: Discovering Intimacy with God, with Others and with Ourselves." The women in the novitiate also participate in the Inter-Novitiate program with novices of other Anglican and Roman Catholic communities in the Toronto area for worship, discussion, and fellowship. It helps to know that others are sharing the same challenges, difficulties, and joys, and there is a great deal to be learned from each other's traditions.

At the end of three years, a novice needs to decide whether she is ready for her first profession of vows. If she requests it, the Reverend Mother will ask for input from the whole community. At the service of first profession, the novice promises to live according to the three vows of poverty, chastity, and obedience for the following three years.

> The vow of poverty is grounded in the simplicity of life which
> Jesus lived and taught.... In poverty we bear witness that God
> is our whole support.[4]

The vow traditionally called "poverty" might well be expressed as the vow of generosity. Conscious of the great division in the world between rich and poor, the sisters hold all their possessions in common and try to live a simple and ordered life, freeing them to give generously of their time and resources. Financial decisions are made as a community. The sisters participate in an annual budget process, estimating their personal needs and the resources required for their areas of responsibility (for instance, infirmary, guest house, financial administration). The community's understanding of poverty also means being ecologically aware, aware of the limitation of the earth's resources, and doing what they can to reduce their call upon those resources. (Among other things, the sisters have installed solar panels that not only reduce their hydro-electric bill but also put power back into the grid.)

> The vow of chastity is grounded in the wholeness of life with
> which Jesus embraced humanity and all creation.... In chastity
> we bear witness that God is our whole love."[5]

The vow of chastity for the Sisterhood and all traditional monastic communities is expressed in the celibate life. The sisters live by the gospel imperative implicit in the baptismal promise to love God above all else and to love others as one loves oneself, leaving them free to serve others while also maintaining relationships with their family and friends (including the children of sisters who may have been married before they joined the community). They work hard at relationships within the community, and as their *Rule of Life* expresses it, "Friendship is a gift of God, to be developed responsibly and thankfully, for the enrichment of the whole community."[6]

> The vow of obedience is grounded in the singleness of purpose
> with which Jesus lived in order to accomplish the will of the

One who sent him.... By our obedience we bear witness that God is our whole life."[7]

Obedience is an expression of the baptismal promise to seek and follow God's will. The word "obedience" comes from a Latin word, *obaudire*, which means "to listen and respond." Obedience means to listen and then respond to the leading of God. The will of God is discerned in the context of the community constitution, including the *Rule of Life*, in the direction and counsel of the elected leadership of the community, through the chapter (the decision-making body of the Sisterhood); and through ongoing discernment in the sisters' common life. Learning to respond to the voice of God in the heart as well as in the circumstances of daily life requires faithfulness and courage — a lifelong challenge to love.

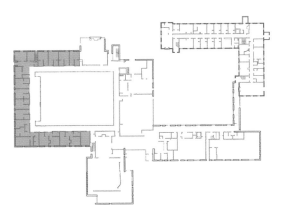

When you pray, go into your room, close the door, and pray to your Father who is unseen. (Matthew 6:6)

At the north end of the convent is the sisters' quadrangle, with bedrooms facing out to the gardens. As you walk through the corridors, light streams in from open doors and large windows. The floor is carpeted. There is quiet and peace. It is what is called in monastic jargon the sisters' "enclosure" — that part of the convent which, according to the Sisterhood's *Rule of Life*, "provides a place apart for the sisters for silence, prayer, and the privacy and quiet necessary for the stability and development of our common life in Christ."[1] When the sisters leave this part of the convent, or return to it, there is a very clear sense of leaving home or coming home.

Within the enclosure, each sister "has a separate room where she may have privacy and silence for rest, prayer and study." (*Rule of Life*, 9). Traditionally, these rooms have been called "cells" as they are so much more than merely bedrooms.

Each door has a name — a saint's name or the name of a virtue (St. John, St. Mary, Patience, Joy, Love, etc.). The furnishings of each room are comfortable and homey, but simple. Useful extras are present, but they are useful only as they help the cell-dweller to meet with the Spirit of God. Aside from a radio or CD player (used with earphones so as not to disturb others), electronic devices are reserved for offices where the sisters work.

At night, the sisters finish the prayers of the community in chapel, and then it is time for the cell and for personal prayer. The sisters follow the example of Jesus, who prayed on his own in quiet places as well as with others in the synagogue.

How does one learn to pray? How can one become a man or woman of prayer? How does one overcome attacks from inside the heart that are reminders of the failures of that day, doubts about vocation, the monotony of obedience, and other such temptations? The answer that faith gives is the reminder that God is truly present in the monastic cell. Thomas à Kempis said, "Shut yourself in, and call the well-loved presence of Jesus to your side; let him share your cell with you; nowhere else will you find such peace."[2]

Probably there is confidence and determination at the time of closing the door, and even more in calling for Jesus to come and share the prayer. After a time, the familiar struggle begins, and confidence is replaced by doubts and dislike. It is painful to acknowledge one's failures but it is the road to forgiveness and reconciliation. It is easy to forget the strength that comes from expressions of gratitude. Spiritual restlessness urges one to leave the cell, and do something important. But the cell is the very place where interior work can be done. To remain in place, while offering a listening ear to truth at a more costly level, is going to be rewarded.

The former Archbishop of Canterbury Rowan Williams wrote that "truthfulness given to human beings and sustained in them, as a constant, self-critical, alert, prayerful and receptive turning-back to Jesus is the gift of the indwelling Spirit."[3]

The monastic cell is a place that may be small and simple, and yet it contains the mysterious presence of God. Any room that is used as a dwelling-place or a meeting place with God will become home. Anyone who spends time there faithfully will find healing for life's hurts and, even more, discover her true self.

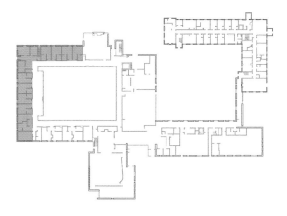

INFIRMARY

11

Your loving-kindness is better than life itself;
my lips shall give you praise.
So will I bless you as long as I live
and lift up my hands in your name.
My soul is content, as with marrow and fatness,
and my mouth praises you with joyful lips,
When I remember you upon my bed,
and meditate on you in the night watches. (Psalm 63:3–6)

Infirmaries have been an integral part of the monastic tradition since the early monasteries of the fifth and sixth centuries. The late Ellis Peters, in her historical medieval mystery novels, introduced readers to the delightful Brother Cadfael, an herbalist and infirmarian at a large Benedictine monastery. While it is a rather romantic portrayal, it gives insight into a vital aspect of monastic life. The infirmary allows members of the community to be cared for at home and to remain at home until their death.

When Hannah Grier Coome entered the novitiate at St. Mary's Convent in Peekskill, she received excellent training in a variety of medical, surgical, and other nursing skills. No doubt her own earlier experience of being hospitalized for a miscarriage and later caring for her beloved cancer-stricken husband reinforced her dedication to health care. It certainly had an impact on the Sisterhood's earliest ministries. At the same time, she would have been equally dedicated to ensuring the highest quality care for her own sisters as they became ill or frail.

In the early days of the Sisterhood, the infirmary would have been only a room or two in the convent for someone who was ill, and since St. John's Hospital was right next door, sisters who needed more intense care would have been cared for in the hospital. While it is not clear exactly when an infirmary was first organized in the convent, it most likely grew as the need arose. It wasn't until the early twentieth century that there was a need to care for elderly sisters.

The religious life has always been about intergenerational "family" living where sisters care for each other. It is a gift but it does not come easily: the sisters have to work at it through their life of prayer. The infirmary in a monastic community illustrates this well, as Sister Jessica notes:

Sister Jessica and Florencia Delgado.

It is one of the many things that endeared this life to me. When I was sixteen, I helped care for my dear granny in Scotland when she was dying at home. I wasn't a trained nurse then but I seemed to have natural nursing skills, and a year later I formally began my vocation in nursing. I had seven years of training in many different areas of nursing, from infectious diseases to midwifery. I loved it. When I was admitted as a postulant in 1983, my first job was in the infirmary at Botham Road. I will always be grateful to our former Sister Janis Mary, who was then the Infirmarian (sister in charge of the infirmary). She was an excellent nurse who taught me a lot about running the infirmary and the care of the elderly sisters. More importantly she helped me understand how a balanced life of prayer and work is the kernel of ideal monastic living.

Sister Jessica discovered that both the caregiver and the sister living in the infirmary had to keep this balance of life.

At the time she arrived in the community in 1983, the infirmary at the Botham Road convent accommodated nine sisters, but without private washrooms, and the working area for the nursing staff was very small. A planning committee was set up in 1990 to renovate the infirmary and the renovations were completed in 1991. The sisters were thrilled. The working space was much better for all of the staff, and there was more private space for the nurse-infirmarian to conduct confidential visits. A beautiful sunroom facing the ravine allowed invalid and elderly sisters to spend time enjoying the birds, flowers, and visits with friends.

When the new convent was built in 2004, there was an opportunity to make it even more serviceable and up-to-date for nursing care, and at the same time incorporate the sisters' values of hominess, comfort, and beauty. The infirmary in the new convent has eight homey, single rooms with space to accommodate wheelchairs and walkers, ensuite washrooms, floor-to-ceiling windows that look out on to the grounds, and flower boxes outside the windows. There are also four "flex" rooms that can be used as overflow for sisters or physically challenged guests or associates. The rooms are arranged around a beautiful courtyard garden for strolling, exercising, bird watching, or meditating. The sisters have delightful memories of Sister Helena, who was legally blind, using her white cane to guide her daily walk around the courtyard regardless of rain or shine, and her twice-daily sessions of outdoor Tai Chi.

Some of our caring infirmary staff.

The infirmary allows sisters to stay at home when it is time to die. As Sister Jessica has said, "one becomes fond of those we care for when they are most vulnerable, and I experienced much sadness and grief at so many losses. I was deeply moved then and I still am today by the way the sisters are upheld in prayer as the community gathers around them as a family to pray with them and support them when they are near death."

For the past twenty years, the sister assigned to be Infirmarian has worked alongside a professional nurse manager, together with a team of personal support workers. They arrange medical appointments, visit with the sisters, ensure their physical needs as well as spiritual needs are met, and coordinate transportation and accompanying arrangements for the sisters.

While there are fewer nursing sisters and more staff than twenty years ago, the staff too have come to be part of the family and care deeply about the sisters they nurse. Younger sisters participate in supportive ways in the infirmary, taking their sisters to appointments, helping with heavy lifting, giving haircuts, social visiting, reading to sisters with impaired vision, taking sisters around the grounds in their wheelchairs, or taking them on drives — these are things that generally enrich the sisters' lives. Most important, the sisters who are cared for in the infirmary may either attend chapel services or listen over the PA system in their rooms, and attend functions as they are able with the sisters.

Our oblate, Chris Hooker, chatting with Sister Merle over a glass of sherry.

The health field has changed greatly today so hospital stays are much shorter and patients return home in need of a continuum of care. The sisters' infirmary, because it is considered part of a private home and not an institution, is eligible for community support. In addition, a doctor visits the sisters monthly and is on call for emergencies.

Intentional visiting in the infirmary is an important value for the sisters, to ensure that sisters who are elderly or infirm do not feel isolated from the community as a whole. In addition to ensuring the sisters are able to attend events with the whole community, sherry and tea parties in the sunroom and other gatherings are very popular with everyone.

We live in a time where countless elderly men and women spend the end of their lives in nursing homes, often not of their own choosing. More often than not, their children and other family members and friends are scattered across Canada and even further afield, or have pre-deceased them. The health system in Canada does its best to provide good care for the elderly, but the need is enormous.

Monastic infirmaries like the Sisterhood's are in the minority today. The sisters are indeed blessed to have such a wonderful facility where they "stay home" and are given excellent, loving care until they die. Sisters who have worked as Infirmarians have expressed their gratitude to God and to the community for the privilege and blessings they receive in that role, and the many sisters whom they look after are similarly grateful to have a monastic infirmary where they can remain an integral part of the community even when ill or coming to the end of their days.

Sister Margaret Mary enjoying a cup of tea in the infirmary sunroom.

12 ENTRANCE AND LOBBY

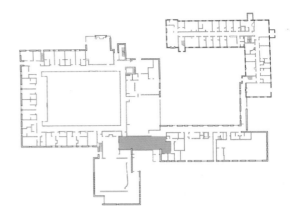

"Everyone who calls on the name of the Lord shall be saved." But how are they to call on one in whom they have not believed? And how are they to believe in one of whom they have never heard? And how are they to hear without someone to proclaim him? And how are they to proclaim him unless they are sent? As it is written, "How beautiful are the feet of those who bring good news!" (Romans 10:13–15)

The entrance and lobby of a monastic house functions as a threshold — a place where people come and go bringing the good news of God's love, peace, forgiveness, and reconciliation. The sisters go out "on mission" to parish churches and other groups, preaching on Sundays, leading retreats and workshops, perhaps teaching Sunday school or speaking at a diocesan synod.

As the sisters go out, others come in to the convent — alone, seeking personal renewal, or as part of a group. All kinds of people enter to worship with the sisters, attend retreats or workshops, join in the life of the monastic community, and then go out to share the good news of what they have found.

Several categories of people are affiliated with the Sisterhood: associates, oblates, and alongsiders. They are "liminal" people, threshold people, sharing the life of the sisters for an hour, a day, a week, or a year. They bring gifts from outside the convent — creative gifts, gifts of knowledge and wisdom, gifts of love and prayer. And they take gifts out into the world when they return — gifts of acceptance, discernment, guidance, and prayer.

ASSOCIATES

First there were associates — the men and women behind the founding of the Sisterhood. Then there were sisters, supported by the associates in a myriad of ways. Today, the associates continue to promote and assist the community. While the earliest associates were Anglican women, associates today include women and men, lay and ordained, of all Christian denominations, who seek to enrich their spiritual lives through having a close connection with the Sisterhood. Prayer is the chief bond that binds the sisters and associates together.

Associates follow the associate *Rule of Life*, which provides guidelines for living an intentional Christian life in the midst of the secular world. The *Rule* encourages associates to speak with others about the monastic life, to share their experience of community with others, to meditate and pray, to read and study scripture, to participate actively in their local church, to make an annual retreat, to support the sisters with their resources of time, talent, and treasure, and to reflect on their lives as associates in an annual letter or conversation with the Associate Director. The *Rule* recognizes that each associate's circumstances are unique and that, as one's life situation changes, it may be necessary to adjust the practice of the *Rule*.

The first formal admission of associates occurred in 1885, shortly after the Sisterhood began. These were women who were part of the group who were instrumental in praying and fundraising for the founding of the Sisterhood. The most notable was Georgina Broughall, who worked tirelessly on the founding committee of the Sisterhood, and who became the first Convenor of associates in 1893. Over time, priest-associates were introduced and later, lay men became associates. From a start of five, the associate numbers grew to seventy-five in 1891, to 250 in 1923, and peaked in the late 1970s at nine hundred. In January 2014 there were 840 associates.

Sister Christabel with some associates at the convent on Major Street in the 1930s.

In the beginning, the Mother Foundress took responsibility for all associates. Later, sisters were appointed as Wardens (later called Associate Directors); these sisters were able to devote more time to nurturing those under their care. At various times there have been regional Associate Directors in places where the sisters have had branch houses. The directors maintain contact with associates in their areas, arrange for quiet days and retreats, and communicate with associates by phone, email or regular mail, and personal visits.

As the Sisterhood established institutions and missions across the country, associate vocations grew as more people came to know about the order. One associate remarked, "I remember admiring the calm and spiritual bearing of a woman in my church. When I commented on it, she explained that she was an associate of the Sisterhood. I decided then I would become one." Associates helped the sisters in whatever way they could — by working in missions, procuring furniture and supplies, donating money, fundraising, etc. Nowadays, the Sisterhood is engaged in different work than in the past, yet still needs the practical assistance of associates as well as their prayer. Most of the volunteers at the convent are associates. They act as receptionists, help with registration of retreatants, lead quiet days, assist at the hospital chapel services, provide spiritual direction, and do many of the jobs that would otherwise suffer because of lack of sister power.

Associates have been equally important in the branch houses — cooking, looking after the house when the sisters are away, allowing sisters some time off, looking after the library, writing letters, and many other daily tasks.

But it is even more important that associates, like sisters, have time just to be – to pray, rest, and be spiritually refreshed. For some associates, especially those living near Toronto, the convent is a spiritual home. However, physical proximity is not essential to maintain a close connection, particularly in these days of email. In times of trouble or distress, sudden illness, death of a loved one,

Sister Brenda, Sarah Clarke, an associate, Sister Dorothy, and Sister Louise.

TOP: *Associates Rachael Boles and
Anne Day greeting associate Kay Jolly
arriving for a special event.*
MIDDLE: *Sister Margaret Mary chatting
with associate Ruth Corstan.*
BOTTOM: *Sister Elizabeth Ann
admitting Andrew Mugford and
Louise Simos as associates.*

189

associates know they can turn to the convent or branch house for prayer and strength.

Before anyone becomes an associate, he or she undergoes a period of discernment. This usually lasts a year and is the opportunity for individuals to try out living by the associates' *Rule of Life*. During this period they communicate with the Associate Director either in person or by letter to share their experience and how the *Rule of Life* may be a support not only to their spiritual life and Christian commitment, but to all the areas of their lives. At the end of the discernment time, the person may be admitted as an associate at a service in chapel. The new associate receives the silver associate cross, and is encouraged to wear it as a witness to his or her commitment. The simple cross, engraved with the initials SSJD, identifies the wearer and has often sparked conversation or recognition of affiliation with the Sisterhood.

As the Sisterhood's ministries evolve, the community hopes that associates will continue to give their time, talents, and most importantly, their prayers, to support the sisters. The one constant, prayer, remains at the heart of the relationship.

Oblates

Oblates with Sister Constance Joanna at the Trienniel in 2010.

An oblate of the Sisterhood is a woman who feels called to a life of contemplative prayer and active service and who is closely affiliated with the Sisterhood's monastic life while living outside the community.

What's the difference between an oblate and an associate, you may ask? The short answer is that the oblate is a woman called to live the monastic life in the world and who might have become a sister had her personal circumstances been different (age, family commitments such as dependents, husband, young children, etc.).

Both oblates and associates are bound to the Sisterhood by prayer, but the oblate's self-offering (the word *oblate* means "offering") to God is alongside and in partnership with the Sisterhood.

Among other things, the oblate commits to residing with the sisters for two weeks annually, entering their rhythm of prayer and work, and has the opportunity to make a long retreat with the sisters at the convent. In consultation with the Oblate Director she writes a personal *Rule of Life* that outlines her practice of prayer, as well as other aspects of her life. She gives service to the Sisterhood and her local community as she is able.

The impetus for having oblates grew out of the 1995 Associate Assembly. A pilot program was started in 1999, which included two women who had specifically asked to be oblates and had already formulated their tentative Rules of Life, and five others whom the sisters invited to consider an oblate vocation. The first oblate, Caroline Hamilton, was received on May 1, 2000, at Saltspring Island, B.C. Three others were admitted that year, and three more the year after.

Top: *Oblates Chris Hooker and Lynne Van der Hiel gardening while at the trienniel in 2013.*
Bottom: *Oblate Lynne Samways-Hiltz working in the fundraising office.*

After the pilot program was evaluated in 2002, it was agreed to continue it and to invite applications from other women who were drawn to it. The number of oblates increased gradually as the program became known, but the sisters limit the numbers. As of 2014, twenty-two oblates from Nova Scotia to British Columbia live an intentional monastic life in their own context and spend committed time each year living, working, and praying among the sisters at the convent or in a branch house.

The oblate discernment period lasts between one and two years, after which she may be formally admitted as an oblate and receive the oblate cross. The oblate promises are signed at the altar, signifying the depth of commitment. As a general rule, oblates make annual promises for three years, and then have the option, in discussion with the Oblate Director and the Reverend Mother, to proceed to life promises.

As time passes, and with the advantage of electronic communication, the oblates are forming their own close-knit community. They are in touch with and support each other in their chosen lifestyle. Every three years there is an oblate gathering at the convent, which fosters the development of close relationships among them as well as with the sisters. Facebook, email, and Skype help keep oblates connected who are scattered from the West Coast to the East Coast and offer some creative ways of sharing the oblate journey — for instance a weekly time to pray Compline together via Skype.

In a homily at the reception of an oblate, the Reverend Susan House described the oblate vocation as "a new venture in faith and a new commitment..... Becoming an oblate of SSJD is not so much a question of undertaking new tasks as of being in new relationship."

The Reverend Frances Drolet-Smith says, "As oblates we are engaged in a covenant relationship with the sisters with some mutually beneficial expectations, such as accountability and commitment."

Sister Constance Joanna has noted:

Mary L. Stewart and Sandi Austin cutting the cake after making their Life Promises.

Oblates expand the circle of the monastic life. Throughout history, monastic life has always been "for the other." Those of us called to the professed life in community are given a precious gift that is meant to be shared with others. In sharing our prayer, our community life, and our work and leisure with oblates, we enable them, in turn, to share those things with others.

During the past twelve years, the sisters have been immeasurably enriched by the presence of oblates, and the oblates have found their offering of themselves to God in this partnership with SSJD to be a fulfilling way of living out their baptismal covenant.

Alongsiders

During the past seventy years or so, the Sisterhood has been blessed with alongsiders — women who lived and worked and prayed with the sisters. They did not have the official title of alongsider until 2011, but these women resided at the convent for differing periods of time and for differing reasons. They contributed to the sisters' life and helped out in various areas as they were able, thereby freeing up sisters to be more directly involved in missions, hospitality, or other work. In August, 2005, one of the sisters presented at chapter a proposal for intentional alongsiders. The inspiration came from the U.K., where religious orders were being greatly helped by the presence of alongsiders. They provided extra hands and minds and voices and in return they benefitted by learning about prayer and community living.

After a time of discernment, the official SSJD alongsider program began in September 2011, with Susan Murphy, a woman who had lived in the guest house

Oblates Nancy Scott and Lynne Van der Hiel enjoying a meal with Sister Louise in the refectory.

while pursuing theological studies. Susan was a part-time alongsider. She continued to attend university, had obligations at her church on Sundays, resided in the guest house and was not able to participate in community life as much as alongsiders do now. However, during that year, Susan served as volunteer coordinator, set up and produced an electronic newsletter, "Home for the Heart," for the guest house (which she continues to maintain), and did some beautiful photography.

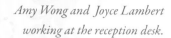

Amy Wong and Joyce Lambert working at the reception desk.

As the first alongsider, Susan made some very valuable suggestions on ways to improve the program. It is still in the early stages and the sisters anticipate its continuing evolution as they make changes to enhance the program from both the sisters' and the alongsiders' points of view.

Susan described her experience as an alongsider: "It's a very interesting psychological and spiritual study: identifying the ingredients I can take into the secular world; how priorities compete in my head; recognizing my absolute need for God.... This place has a huge potential for changing lives. The sisters are role-modelling a lot of stuff for me. They are just so real, and it's OK to be real!"

Since 2012, the alongsiders have resided in the enclosure with the sisters, after having spent a month in the guest house to give them and the sisters a time of adjustment. They define their personal and spiritual goals for their time with the Sisterhood, and are assigned a mentor to accompany them on their community journey. They attend the sisters' daily conference, participate in most of the chapel and community activities and share in household tasks. Alongsiders are committed to a daily practice of personal prayer, spiritual reading, and reflection on sacred scripture. They have study and work periods like postulants and novices, but have more spare time. Individual financial arrangements are made with each woman depending on her personal situation.

From September 2012 through August 2013, Joyce Lambert and Amy Joy Wong were alongsiders. Joyce served as volunteer coordinator for the year, took sisters who couldn't drive to medical appointments, and helped in many other ways. Amy Joy served as an assistant in the guest house and as a spiritual director (she has an M.Div. with a speciality in spiritual direction from Tyndale University). Amy Joy served a second year as an alongsider and her main assignment was pastoral visiting at St. John's Rehab.

Although an alongsider may decide to apply to enter the community, the program is not an internship for prospective sisters. It is a temporary interlude in the life of a woman seeking to deepen her Christian life, an opportunity to live and learn in community. There is no alumni association yet but both Susan and Joyce continue to volunteer in creative ways. As for Amy Joy, she joined the Sisterhood in September 2014.

13 GUEST HOUSE

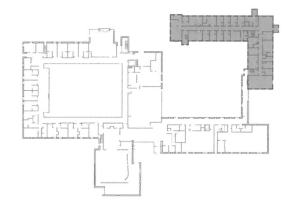

All guests who present themselves are to be welcomed as Christ, who said, "I was a stranger and you welcomed me" (Matthew 25: 35). Once guests arrive they are to be met and treated with all the courtesy of love.[1]

A HOME FOR THE HEART

From the earliest monasteries in the fifth and sixth centuries, space for guests, pilgrims, and spiritual seekers has always been a priority. The Sisterhood's intention as described in their Constitution is to live by the two-fold law of love as Jesus taught it:

> Hear, O Israel, the Lord your God, the Lord is one. Love the Lord your God with all your soul, with all your mind, and with all your strength. The second is this, Love your neighbor as yourself. There is no commandment greater than these. (Mark 12:29–31)

This intention is lived out in many ways, including the community's ministry to guests, who have always been welcomed to the sisters' homes in Christ's name. For many years before the convent moved to Botham Road, houses on Brunswick Avenue that had previously been used as nurses' residences provided accommodation and welcome for women who desired a quieter and more home-like life than what was offered in the typical boarding house.

The calm and peaceful atmosphere of these guest houses attracted and was appreciated by the guests, both transient and permanent; by associates and friends, university students and business and professional women who found a true home there.

In 1912, the houses were combined into one and became 49 Brunswick Avenue. When Saint John's Hospital on Major Street was closed and Saint John's Convalescent Hospital opened in 1937, the former wards were transformed into comfortable guest rooms. During the Second World War, the sisters welcomed English refugee children and the Korean sisters of the Community of St. Peter, Woking, U.K. The Sisterhood also assisted the Order of the Holy Paraclete, an Anglican sisterhood in England. Its boarding school in Whitby, England, was evacuated during the war and temporarily relocated to the University of Toronto's St. Hilda's College. The Sisters of St. John the Divine provided a home away from home for the Whitby sisters who came for time away from the children and the school.

AN EXPANDED GUEST WING

Although beautifully appointed, the number of guest rooms was limited when the sisters moved to Botham Road. As generous donations allowed the sisters to add an extension to the convent in 1956, the number of guest rooms grew, and in 1964 an unusually large legacy from the Larkin estate was used for a new wing, including a guest wing, the Chapel of the Holy Spirit (used by guests for meditation), and a new kitchen and refectory, as well as an addition to the infirmary. This last extension was dedicated on May 19, 1964. It included twenty single rooms and two double rooms, and over time it accommodated an average of five hundred guests annually, who came for retreats both individually and as part of a group. The sisters were glad to find that the guest wing was used by women and men, young and old, rich and poor, students, mothers, and others in need of rest and quiet, as well as by associates and retreatants. A special joy was the use of the guest wing by people of other denominations and faiths, witnessing to the community's growing ecumenical interests.

A New Guest House

In 2005, when the sisters moved to Cummer Avenue, one of the key reasons for the new building was to provide more space for guests to meet the growing demand. The sisters designed the building not only with more space for guests but also to allow privacy for both sisters and guests. Shared facilities (chapel, refectory, kitchen, conference room, and library) connect the public and private parts of the building. The guest house, as it is now called, has thirty-one single rooms, five double rooms, and a few "flex" rooms available to sisters or guests as needed. The convent and guest house offer ample and well-planned facilities, including large and small meeting rooms. The ministry of the guest house has flourished and grown more than four-fold since the move from Botham Road. Today, the Sisterhood welcomes about 2,500 guests annually, either individually or in groups, and serves up to fourteen thousand meals for them.

The guest house ministry is powerful in its very simplicity. In the Sisterhood's communications (such as brochures, website, Facebook, and e-newsletters), the words "recharge," "refresh," "reflect," "reconnect," and "redirect" are used, and those are precisely the gifts that the sisters offer their guests, It perhaps also helps guests understand the reason for their attraction to the convent and to

St. Philip, one of the sitting rooms in the guest house.

its Food for the Soul program, which includes weekend retreats, Quiet Saturdays, Quiet Garden Days, and workshops. Guests come from across Canada, the United States, and around the world, and there are many reasons that they come. Some may be at a crossroads and need a "time out" to discern or come to terms with changes or transformation that may be happening to them on their life journey. Some come for spiritual direction, or to seek insight and guidance when they feel disconnected from God. Some are grieving the loss of a loved one or the loss of health or a job or even loss of their sense of who they are, where they are going, and how they can transform their lives. Some may feel disconnected from God and/or family and are experiencing an ineffable sense of aloneness.

Sometimes family members of patients at St. John's Rehab next door stay while their parent, spouse, child is in the hospital, and find it not only a convenience to be close by, but also discover a source of strength and peace during a difficult time for the family.

And then there are those who value the peace and quiet of the guest house, and so they come to work on their thesis, dissertation, or manuscript, or they are caregivers who come for a few days of respite, or they come as part of a sabbatical. One person comes at the same time every year just to do his Christmas cards! Many make silence and solitude part of their monthly or annual spiritual practice.

Not all who come are Christian. Jewish and Buddhist friends regularly have times of quiet reflection at the convent, and some join the sisters for holiday meals. People who have no faith, or have lost theirs, come seeking for meaning in their lives. The search for truth and wholeness is universal.

One of the bedrooms in the guest house.

Many people come with a group, sometimes for their own programs and sometimes for Food for the Soul retreats and workshops offered by the sisters: lay people, clergy and religious individuals from many dioceses, guests from multi-faith or non-faith backgrounds, those on discernment retreats and pre-ordination retreats, youth groups, interfaith church communities and their ministry teams, as well as Buddhist and other meditation groups. There is a constant coming-and-going of people attending workshops, planning sessions, and education meetings. Food for the Soul events include dynamic speakers, authors and artists, and are often sold out. One of the most popular annual events is a retreat that coincides with New Year's Eve for those seeking a more spiritually focused ushering in of the New Year than the usual Times Square countdown.

Whatever their reasons for coming, guests are invited to take time out from the world of "muchness" to empty themselves into the quiet and the silence, and to be open and responsive to what comes out of the depths of that stillness. The gentle rhythm of daily life at the convent often draws people to pray and worship with the sisters in chapel and to experience the rhythm of the common life as the power of the Holy Spirit works within and around us.

The guest house has come to be known as the "Home for the Heart," and could well be called the "Home of the Many Hands." Sisters, alongsiders, oblates, associates, friends, staff, volunteers, in-house guests, and day visitors contribute to the holiness and spirit of this place. The thirty-nine-room, wireless-enabled guest house is part of the very large "whole" of the sisters' home. Whether they come for few hours, a day, several days, or longer, guests enjoy simple but comfortable rooms, beautiful grounds, an ample library, and the opportunity to worship with the sisters when they desire, allowing the daily rhythm of the sung offices to nourish their spirits.

Letters, emails, and notes arriving regularly from guests testify that they have reconnected with God and with their spiritual life in new ways. Some have been able to clarify the changes they needed to make in their lives. Others discovered a book in one of our two libraries that resonated with them and unblocked their thinking. Still others are simply grateful for a place where they can simply "be."

To be an ear to listen, a hand to help or hold, a heart and mind to be open to one another. This is what we are all invited to do if we are to evolve into that world of unity and peace that we all pray for so fervently.

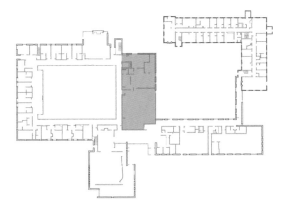

REFECTORY AND KITCHEN 14

I saw a stranger yestreen,
I put food in the eating place
drink in the drinking place
music in the listening place
and in the sacred name
of the Holy Trinity
He blessed my house,
my cattle and my dear ones,
and the lark sang her song:
Often, often, often
goes the Christ in a stranger's guise.
(A Celtic Rune of Hospitality, traditional)

The sisters process in silence from chapel to the refectory, the large communal dining room, mindful that they move from one sacred table (the altar) to another. The refectory is an important place of intersection for sisters and guests, where the body is nourished and fed to strengthen it for the work of prayer and the work of service to others. Bright, open, and simply furnished, its wall of windows looking out onto the guest courtyard dramatically brings the outside in.

In most monastic houses meals are eaten in silence and one person reads aloud from a book while the others eat, so that both mind and body are nourished. Reading aloud however is not the custom at St. John's Convent. Instead, the tables in the refectory are furnished with a shelf below the tabletop where reading material is stored for reading after a person has finished eating and before the formal thanksgiving prayer at the end of the meal.

The way sisters eat together has changed over the years. At one time the sisters sat in strict seniority order with a head table for the leaders of the community. When all were assembled, the Reverend Mother said grace and all would sit, waiting for the meal. Plates were filled in the kitchen and taken to guests and sisters by the servers of the week. Toward the end of the meal, the Reverend Mother rang a bell and the sisters appointed removed the plates, brought in dessert (when it was provided on a Sunday or feast day), and served tea and coffee. At the end of the meal a final bell was rung for all to rise for a thanksgiving prayer.

Guests sat separately from the sisters. A sister sat with the guests to attend to their needs. At one time men were served apart from the sisters and other guests. Priests and the servers and acolytes (all male in those days), following an early morning Eucharist, would be taken to a private dining room and served a full breakfast — hot oatmeal, eggs, bacon, toast with marmalade, and hot coffee with cream — while the sisters and other guests ate oatmeal and toast with tea in the refectory. The heartier breakfast for the priests was not offered out of deference but as thanks: priests who came early in the morning to preside at the Eucharist never received any compensation but the sisters provided a special breakfast (along with the morning newspaper) as an expression of gratitude.

In the 1970s, men were integrated into the refectory with the other guests. Guests still sat apart from the sisters in the refectory, and on those days when the sisters were in retreat a folding divider-wall could be pulled across.

There is less division in the refectory now, although the sisters are seated at their own tables. Today, all meals are served buffet style. There is always a vegetarian option, lots of fresh fruits and vegetables, more options than in days when everyone was expected to eat what was put before them, and generous accommodation for special diets.

Silence throughout the meal gives one time to slow down and enjoy what is being eaten, rather than rushing on to the next thing to do. On Sunday evenings, holidays, and special occasions, sisters and guests enjoy meals with conversation. Sometimes in the summer, barbeques provide even more informal occasions to relax and talk with each other. Other special days, such as the annual picnic for associates and families, mean that sisters can invite their families and friends. Really special dinners — for the Women's Roundtable, for volunteer recognition evenings, or for celebrating a sister's profession of vows — merit a call out for the white linen tablecloths and table napkins.

Sister Elizabeth Ann carving a turkey at Thanksgiving.

Many years ago, paper table napkins were changed to cloth napkins in response to environmental fragility. The sisters have also declared the convent and guest house to be a water-bottle-free zone, and groups and guests are asked to drink the tap water. In small ways like these the sisters support social justice issues such as safe drinking water for all.

Breakfast begins the day with a choice of hot cereal, and a variety of cold cereals, yogurt, fresh fruit, bread for toasting, peanut butter and jams, and juices. Always available is fresh hot coffee and tea, with a choice of several herbal teas. Hot breakfasts with free-range eggs, bacon, sausages, or waffles and syrup, and other items are available on weekends and special feast days.

The main meal for the sisters is at noon, a hot dinner that includes fresh fruit, canned fruit, and often a dessert for a special occasion. In the evening after Evening Prayer, the meal is a lighter supper, usually consisting of a homemade soup, sometimes a casserole or other hot dish, and lots of salads, cheese, vegetables, a variety of breads, and fruit for dessert.

The sisters once did most of the cooking, washed the dishes, pots and pans, and kept the kitchen and refectory in order. Eventually a cook and assistant were hired to help, in order to free up sisters for outside ministries. Since the guest house ministry has expanded, employees now do most of the cooking. Sisters clear up after the evening meal when the staff has gone home for the day, and they prepare food for parties and special occasions. Many of the sisters are great cooks and bakers and share their talent when time permits, to the delight of sisters and guests. The bread-makers among the sisters are especially appreciated.

So are those who harvest vegetables and fruits from the sisters' gardens — among them fresh rhubarb, blackberries, cherries, tomatoes, lettuce, potatoes, onions, Swiss chard, bush and pole beans, asparagus, and squash.

In branch houses, sisters cook in a smaller quantity and food is served family style. In these circumstances,

TOP: *Sister Jean preparing the broccoli for Christmas dinner.*
BOTTOM: *Sisters Beryl and Doreen making rolls for a special event.*

sisters sometimes take it in turn to cook, or sometimes one sister is assigned as the main cook for the household. But in all the houses of the Sisterhood, eating together has been a strong value and remains so in a society which values slow eating and family time less and less. Having meals together and inviting others to join in corporate silent meals is a witness to this value of taking time to slow down, and be really present to the moment. It is also scientifically proven to be better for one's overall digestion and health!

Gone are the days when food was merely a necessity for the body to keep it strong for work. Now the refectory, full of light, reflects a new understanding of Christ calling people to live life abundantly. The sisters and their guests gratefully enjoy the variety of healthy food choices and give thanks to God for this place and space.

Sister Brenda preparing a meal at St. John's House.

Recipes

WHITE BREAD OR CRACKED WHEAT BREAD

Sister Elizabeth Ann

3 cups white flour
2 ¼ cups warm water
2 tsp salt
⅓ cup oil
1 tbsp instant yeast
2 eggs, slightly beaten
⅓ cup honey
1 tsp cider vinegar

Mix flour, salt, and yeast together. Mix all liquid ingredients together, and add to flour to form sponge.

Let sit for 15 minutes, then add an additional 2–3 cups flour. Knead 15 minutes. Let rise, punch down, and form into two loaves. Bake at 350°F for 45 minutes or more.

To make cracked wheat bread, replace 1 cup white flour with 1 cup cracked wheat. Soak the cracked wheat in 1¾ cups boiling water for 5 minutes, then add the rest of the ingredients to form the sponge. Continue as for white bread.

CELERY SEED SALAD DRESSING

Sister Rosemary Anne

1 cup sugar
2 tsp dry mustard
2 tsp salt
2 tsp paprika
½ cup vinegar
2 cups salad oil
2 tsp celery seed
1 tbsp grated onion

Combine sugar, mustard, salt, paprika, and vinegar and stir well. Add the oil very slowly and beat well. Stir in the onion and celery seed. Let the dressing stand 24 hours before using. This recipe works well using a food processor and pouring the oil down the spout while mixing. Makes about 3 cups.

SONG OF INDIA RICE

Traditional convent favourite

Cook together:

1¼ cups brown rice

2 tbsp soy grits

Sauté:

1 tbsp butter

1 tbsp curry

½ cup nuts

½ cup raisins or currants

1 apple, sliced

1 onion, sliced

Add and mix with rice. Add salt and pepper to taste. Serve with yogurt.

TRI-GINGER COOKIES

Sister Elizabeth

¾ cup butter, room temp

1 cup packed brown sugar

¼ cup molasses

1 large egg

2¼ cups flour

2 tsp ground ginger

2 tsp baking soda

1 ½ tbsp finely chopped fresh ginger root (peeled)

½ tsp salt

½ cup finely chopped crystallized ginger

Cream butter and sugar. Beat in molasses and then the egg. Sift flour, ground ginger, baking soda, and salt together. Beat into butter mixture only until blended. Add the fresh and crystalized ginger and stir until well mixed. Cover dough and refrigerate at least 2 hours or overnight. Shape the dough into 1 inch balls and place about 2 inches apart on a lightly greased baking sheet. Bake at 350°F for about 10 minutes until browned. Remove to a wire rack for cooling. Yields 3 ½ to 4 dozen cookies.

WINDBLOWN CAKE

Sister Doreen

1½ cups white sugar
1 tsp baking powder
3 or 4 eggs, divided
pinch of salt
⅔ cup water
1 tsp vanilla
1½ cup flour

Beat egg whites stiff (not dry). In another bowl beat egg yolks with cold water to 5 times their bulk. Add sugar. Beat. Add flour, baking powder, and salt. Beat. Fold in egg whites and vanilla. Place in an ungreased tube pan. Bake at 350°F oven for 50 minutes. Take out of the oven and invert on table for 1 hour to cool. Remove from pan and frost. This cake is sometimes called a Depression cake as it is like an Angel Food cake but does not use as many egg whites.

HILDEGARD'S SPICE COOKIES

Hildegard of Bingen

In her 1157 treatise Physica: Liber Simplicis Medicinae, *Hildegard provides a recipe for spice cookies: "Eat them often," she says, "and they will calm every bitterness of heart and mind — and your hearing and senses will open. Your mind will be joyous, and your senses purified, and harmful humours will diminish." The following recipe is adapted from Hildegard's.*

¾ cup butter or margarine
1 cup brown sugar
1 egg
1 tsp baking powder
¼ tsp salt
1 ½ cups flour
1 tsp ground cinnamon
1 tsp ground nutmeg
½ tsp ground cloves

Let butter soften and then cream it with the brown sugar. Beat in the egg. Sift the dry ingredients. Add half the dry ingredients and mix. Add the other half and mix thoroughly. Dough may be chilled to make it workable. Heat oven to 350°F. Form walnut sized balls of dough, place on greased and floured cookie sheet, and press flat. Bake 12–15 minutes (till edges are golden brown). Cool for 5 minutes, remove from cookie sheet, and finish cooling on racks.

15 LIBRARY

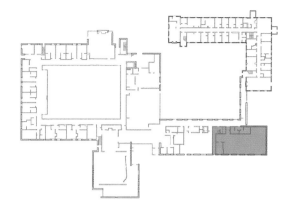

For some of us, books are as important as almost anything else on earth. What a miracle it is that out of these small, flat, rigid squares of paper unfolds world after world after world, worlds that sing to you, comfort and quiet or excite you. Books help us understand who we are and how we are to behave. They show us what community and friendship mean; they show us how to live and die. (Anne Lamott)[1]

You will find bibles in a convent library, even books to help you to understand the Bible, but they are only a small part of the great range of books that provide learning, friendship, consolation, challenge, and enjoyment to the mind and heart.

The library is an important centre in all monastic houses and has been so at least since the time of St. Benedict. Before the great universities of Europe were established in the thirteenth century, monastic libraries were centres of learning. It was there that the clever people went to study and to augment their education. It was where books were kept, because there were no other places for books, and most of the population was illiterate. Today, there are public libraries and university libraries everywhere, but the libraries of religious communities remain crucial to the ongoing education and wisdom-gathering of its members, as well as to its members' leisure and entertainment.

The Sisterhood's *Rule of Life* highlights the community's commitment to reading and learning:

> A strong community life, hospitality and lifelong learning are
> the principles that undergird our call.... Effective action must

be informed by awareness of the world's need. Opportunities for ongoing education, study, and training are provided for the adequate fulfillment of the community's ministry, and the creative enrichment of each sister's life.[2]

Daily reading, personal time for study and reflection, concern for world and local news that informs and makes real our prayer — all are part of our life.

Reading is an important measure of the community's spiritual discipline, a focus for ongoing education, and a source of entertainment as well. Even in the sisters' branch houses there have always been libraries, with books on spirituality, prayer, the Bible, theology and literature, but also excellent collections of non-fiction as well as fiction. The convent library offers a good reference section, study tables, comfortable reading chairs, wireless internet connection for laptops, and two desktop computers for the use of guests.

The main convent library houses about sixteen thousand volumes. Some of the newest books are kept in the sisters' community room and may not be available in the library until the sisters have had a chance to read them.

There is also a library in the guest house, with another two thousand volumes, specifically for associates and oblates, because their rules of life emphasize the importance of spiritual reading. They may take books home; other guests

TOP: *The sisters' library.*
BOTTOM: *The associate library in the guest wing.*

are welcome to use both the sisters' library and the associate/oblate library while they are at the convent.

While lifelong education is both a personal and communal foundation of the sisters' lives, it is this same passion for learning that has enabled them to develop spiritual, educational, and vocational discernment programs. In addition to sisters who teach and lead retreats inside and outside the community, the Sisterhood offers some special programs, including Education for Ministry, the Alongsiders, and Women at a Crossroads. All of these benefit from a good library.

The Women at a Crossroads program is held during the month of July each summer for women who are at a crossroads in their life, and want to discern where God may be calling them. The response to each of these different programs indicates that there is a great hunger and search for a deeper spiritual life and a desire to commit to "something more" in the lives of many people. The sisters' libraries make an important contribution to helping people find this.

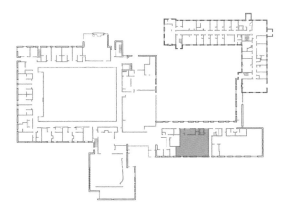

SCRIPTORIUM 16

In the beginning was the Word, and the Word was with God and the Word was God.... And the Word became flesh and dwelt among us. (John 1.1, 14)

If you are a fan of medieval mysteries or old *New Yorker* cartoons, you may already know what a scriptorium is. It's the room set aside for the copying of manuscripts. Monks or nuns would put in their several hours of manual labour, not in the fields or the laundry, but in the scriptorium, copying the Bible or the Rule of Benedict or even the works of pagan philosophers or poets. The most famous of these manuscripts is the *Book of Kells*, a beautifully copied and illustrated version of the four Gospels created sometime around 800 CE in Ireland. Most people think of the scriptoria (the works produced in the scriptorium) as copies; in fact, there were original documents written by the members of those old communities: commentaries, poetry, hymns, essays, and accounts of dreams and spiritual experiences. One of the most prolific of these writers was a woman, Hildegard of Bingen, an abbess who lived in Germany in the twelfth century (and whose recipe you read in a previous chapter).

While we tend to think that every medieval monastery and convent had a room set apart as a scriptorium, it seems that was the exception rather than the rule, in the Middle Ages at least. According to Dom David Knowles, in the twelfth century monks copied and illuminated manuscripts in the cloister – a garden of sorts with a walk around all four sides, one of which ran along the length of the monastery church. Desks would have been set up there in all but the coldest weather, when the monks either had to abandon the work until the days became warmer; or if the monastery was well-provided, they would have worked in the single room which had a fireplace (shared with other functions of the monastery). It wasn't until the thirteenth century that cloister walks were enclosed and wooden carrels were provided for the monks and later still that most monasteries had rooms dedicated to the work of writing.[1]

A similar situation exists for the Sisterhood today, where the sisters use multi-function spaces. The sisters write in their cells (bedrooms), in their private offices, or in shared office space; they write in the library, in the community room, sometimes in the gardens or the meeting rooms. But they do write.

The earliest writings of the Sisterhood are found in the first *Rule of Life*, adapted by Mother Hannah from the Rule of the Life of the Community of St. Mary in Peekskill, New York, where she did her novitiate; in the surviving letters of Mother Hannah and other sisters; in the Sisterhood's early newsletter, *St. John's Messenger*; and in the minutes of early annual chapter meetings. Except for letters, which were addressed and signed, it is not always easy to identify the author of a given piece of work. If you look through the copies of the *Messenger*, published from 1891 until 1961, you will see that associates, priests, bishops, and friends of the community are named as author of this article, that letter, or that piece of poetry, but if a sister was the author, as often as not the attribution reads "SSJD" or is lacking altogether. It was an intentional anonymity, a custom of the time, because sisters did not draw attention to themselves. It was not until 1971, under the leadership of Sister Frances Joyce, that *The Eagle* (which replaced the *Messenger* in 1961) consistently notes the names of the sisters responsible for the articles and the poetry.

Until 1918, the reports presented by sisters at chapter were read aloud; notes were taken by the chapter secretary as to the content of the reports but the reports themselves were not preserved. From the first chapter in 1889 until 1918, all the chapter minutes were handwritten (in beautiful and legible copper-plate handwriting) by the chapter secretaries (Sister Gertrude, Sister Fanny, and Sister Eva). From 1918, the chapter minutes are typed and the names of the sisters who wrote the reports are recorded in the minutes.

Until the common use (and affordability) of the telephone in recent years, and now of email and social media, the sisters were encouraged to keep in touch with their families and friends by letter. Unfortunately, most of those letters have perished; judging by what writing has survived, however, the letters, like the chapter minutes, would have been written in careful copper-plate writing, setting out the daily activities — work, prayer, community life — thoughts and feelings of the individual sister sending the letter.

Just as the medieval scriptorium was often a place for copying manuscripts, in the history of the Sisterhood a good deal of the calligraphic writing done by the sisters has consisted of copies of works they have admired or found inspirational. One such work has an interesting history. In 1891, to celebrate the first reception of a novice to take place in the newly consecrated chapel at the Major Street convent, a

Sister Miriam's calligraphy: St. John the Apostle of Love.

poem was written by the first warden of the community, the Reverend Ogden P. Ford. The poem was printed in the *Messenger* (Epiphany 1892). Over 120 years later, you can find, on the wall of the chapel narthex, a copy of that poem in delicate calligraphy with illustrations in gold and red and blue and yellow. On the back of the frame are found the words "To Sister Beatrice: on her Golden Jubilee, July 17th, 1949, with loving greetings from Dorothy, SSJD."

The archives of the Sisterhood hold a wealth of fascinating writings of the sisters over the years. Issues of the *Messenger* from the 1930s contain reports on the founding of St. John's Convalescent Hospital that make you feel as if you were there. Sister Beatrice (who was the first sister in charge) wrote of planting a vegetable garden to provide food for the patients, the staff, and the sisters. There are descriptions of cooking and planting, of raising the money to furnish the hospital, of the daily lives of the sisters assigned there — how they worshipped, how they prayed, how they worked together, and how they met for meals and recreation.

In the same pages, over the years, you can read essays and poetry and reports of the other ministries of the Sisterhood

— schools in Oshawa and Regina and Ottawa, the Church Home, Seaton Village Mission, Sunday School by Post, and many more. It's a way of living into the past, or of bringing that past into the present. As time progresses, *St. John's Messenger* becomes *The Eagle* and eventually the names of the sisters who wrote the report or the homily or the poem can be seen at the end of the piece.

In addition to short pieces found in their newsletters, various sisters have written historical books: *Memoir of Mother Hannah*, written in the 1930s by Sister Eleanora, who had been a novice in the first years of the community (although in keeping with the practice of the time her name does not appear on the title page); the *Brief History*, first published in 1931, revised several times, and updated in 1984 for the Sisterhood's Centennial; and *Story of a School* by Sister Lydia and others, a history of the Qu'Appelle Diocesan School. They have written autobiographies and autobiographical accounts: *Other Little Ships* by Sister Constance in 1997 and *In Age Reborn, By Faith Sustained* by Sister Thelma-Anne in 2007. The Sisterhood published two other books in the centennial year: *Wings* (a collection of poetry written by sisters) and *Songs for Celebration*. Sister Constance Joanna published *From Creation to Resurrection* in 1989, a study of the scripture readings from the Great Vigil of Easter. Many sisters have written articles and reflections for *The Anglican Journal* and diocesan newspapers. They have kept diaries, given homilies, delivered retreat addresses, and recorded talks for the national church website Lenten series — all of which are expressions of the gift of writing. And the writing of poetry, articles, lectures, and addresses continues as the sisters carry their scriptorium with them wherever they go.

In the 1970s, the writing of journals (an ancient form of reflective writing) emerged as a widespread practice in the Sisterhood. There were workshops on journalling, and retreats on journalling. Sisters went on retreat and were encouraged to journal. Many of the sisters find writing down their thoughts, their feelings, their prayers in journals is of great benefit in discerning God's will for them, maintaining a disciplined life of contemplation, and (for some) staying cool in the hot-house atmosphere of the religious life.

On special occasions (sisters' birthdays or anniversaries, Christmas, Easter, leaving for a branch house or going on long retreat), it is a custom for sisters to give cards to one another. Sometimes these express simple sentiments — "May God be with you as you travel," "Happy Birthday," "Welcome Home." At other times the sisters use this occasion to write heartfelt messages to their "Sister in Christ" or write a poem to celebrate the Life Profession of a sister. The lives of the sisters are filled with words and with writing.

You may be wondering why the sisters put so much emphasis on the written word, whether it be community records, copies of great (or not so great) authors, or creative works by the sisters. At the beginning of this essay you saw the quote from the Gospel according to St. John: "In the beginning was the Word, and the Word was with God and the Word was God ... and the Word became flesh and dwelt among us." (John 1.1, 14) For all Christians, the Word of God, Jesus the Christ, Brother and Friend, Saviour and Redeemer, is central to their faith. For modern members of monastic orders as it was for the earliest nuns and monks, Christ the Word is to be found (among

Sister Thelma-Anne signing a copy of her book, In Age Reborn, By Faith Sustained.

other places) in words — spoken words, sung words, and written words. To copy the words of scripture is, in some sense, to copy the Word of God. To write a poem inspired by prayer is, in some sense, to put the Word of God onto the paper in black and white, to make those words and that Word available to others. To write a report on a ministry is to remember how the Word of God was present in that ministry over the previous year.

The Scriptorium may be more a place of the heart than a specific area of the convent, but for the Sisters of St. John the Divine, as for countless other monastics through the centuries, the Scriptorium is one of the places where God is found, worshipped, expressed, and cherished.

Poetry

THE JOYFUL MYSTERIES: FIVE SONNETS[2]
By Sister Rosemary Anne

THE ANNUNCIATION

The angel Gabriel was sent from God...
And Mary suddenly became aware
of his unearthly presence. Shining, fair,
divinely beautiful, his swift feet shod
with flame, his countenance as morning light,
he knelt before her motionless. His eyes,
calm as the quietness of summer skies,
glowed with immortal radiance, clear and bright.
He stayed a moment silent at her feet,
and Mary looked on him and made no stir.
Then, as she wondered at the cadence sweet
of his "all hail," she gave with demur
her free submission, humbly as was meet,
because she knew the Lord had need of her.

THE VISITATION

And Mary in those days arose with speed,
turning, as one who steadfastly fulfills
a destiny, toward Judean hills.
There dwelt Elizabeth, and Mary's need
was ardent longing in herself to pour
her heart out on her gentle cousin's breast;

to find there sympathy and love and rest,
to share the wondrous tidings that she bore.
Swift were her eager feet upon the road,
swifter her heart that hurried on apace;
yet One before her found the blest abode
and filled it with his presence and his grace –
and he it was, when Mary came, who showed
the meaning of the light upon her face.

The Nativity

Mary was tired, being very young,
Now that the anguish of her travailling
had come at last, she heard no angel sing;
she did not see the shining glory flung
across the sky, within the stable room
she was alone with pain. The whole vast earth
held only the tense agony of birth,
and Joseph, standing silent in the gloom.
Until at length the shadows drew apart,
the early banners of the dawn unfurled,
and Mary worshipped Jesus in her heart,
holding him close to kiss the small hands curled
against her breast, she sang with untaught art
for joy a Man was born into the world.

The Presentation

Old Simeon was one who waited long
the advent of Messiah, and his prayer
ascended daily in the Temple, where
his lifted heart made supplication strong.
To him the Holy Spirit had revealed
the breaking of shadows, and the morn
of brighter hope for ages yet unborn –
the secret of the love of God unsealed.
Thus, Simeon it was, when Mary came,
who marked her purity and how she trod
with reverence, and softly spoke the name
of Jesus. Then he knew that Jesse's rod
had blossomed, and with joy like mounting flame,
stretched out his arms and took the Son of God.

The Purification

Then were accomplished the appointed days
for purifying, as the Law commands.
And Mary, with the white doves in her hands
for sacrifice, trod the accustomed ways
of Israel. As Joseph held the child
asleep against his breast, she slowly turned
toward the bright, undying fires, that burned
in ritual pleading for a race defiled.
Now, as prophetic utterance had shown
so long aforetime in the written word,
came suddenly and softly to his own,
and all unheralded, the mighty Lord;
entered his Temple, and to man unknown,
was yet by angels worshipped and adored.

GOD'S CALL[3]
By Sister Lydia

I stood upon the threshold of the years,
My hand in Thine.

The call of Love was sounding in mine ears,
The Call divine.

Fearless, I entered on the glorious Quest,
At Thy behest.

In lightsome places with Thy face ashine,
Thou wast with me.

In darksome places still Thy hand held mine,
I could not see.

But feeling for the print of pierced feet,
Found Love most sweet.

Ah! Lovely are the years I spend with Thee
Who bidst me "Go!"

For Thou dost travel all the way with me,
And this I know,

That when at last I hear Thy voice say "Come!"
Thou wilt be Home.

NOT I — BUT CHRIST[4]
By Sister Nora

I am blind, and yet I see,
Deaf, and yet I hear.
My tongue is silent, yet I speak.
I doubt, I question, yet I know,
Fearful am I, yet unafraid.
I am alone, I am with friends,
Weary, yet filled with strength.
I am to creatures tied and to the world,
Yet I am free.
Lost, yet I surely know the way,
Confused, and yet all things are clear.
Poor, yet I have all things.
Unclean, unworthy — chaste and pure,
I live — not I, but Christ!

Autumn in Muskoka[5]
By Sister Rosemary

There's a beauty in the northland that sets all my blood afire,
for the lift of it and swing of it like music from a lyre,
set all my pulses leaping to a gypsy sort of beat,
a tune that's irresistible and ravishingly sweet.

For autumn brings a loveliness, a magic all her own,
a lavishness of colour, an extravagance of tone
and hills are wearing drapery in every faery hue,
lifting flushed and happy faces to a sky of azure blue.

Now the evergreens stand straight and tall in sombre overcoats,
while maples flaunt their scarlet gowns and golden petticoats,
and along each winding pathway, crowds of black-eyes Susan's nod
and try their naughty best to flirt with stately goldenrod.

There's a faint and subtle perfume from the balsam and the pine,
a wistful haunting fragrance that intoxicates like wine;
for September weaves enchantment that I cannot but confess
as she holds me in the mystic spell of her own loveliness.

CONTEMPLATION[6]
By Sister Rosemary Anne

God's presence is a quietness,
a still desire
that holds the heart in silence.
It is fire
of love so tender, so intensely
true, that all
the holiness of common things
and small
deliciousness of human loving
have their place
within the spacious kindliness
of his embrace.

THE NEOPHYTE[7]
By Sister Rosemary Anne

Upon election to Profession — April 12th, 1951

Here is finality: I hold my life
With all that has been there of storm and strife,
With all of joy and all of painfulness,
The upward struggle and the inward stress,
All peace and passion, tenderness and tears,
The bitter-sweetness of the ended years —
Years now remote, yet still a part of me
With all they had of living destiny —
I hold as full-mixed wine within a cup
And humbly, with my heart, I offer up.

Yet not alone the past, today I give
Whatever now remains of life to live.
I turn my steps one way, my will I bend
To hold the course unswerving to the end.
The future lies mysterious between
This moment and my death and all unseen.
Shall I grow old? Today I yield old age
and its infirmities. The unwritten page
I yield to hands that mightier are than mine,
The Author's, to inscribe his own design.

THE GARDENER[8]
By Sister Anitra

Rich, ripe fruit glowing
red-gold in the sunlight.
Deep purple shadows
velvet soft and silken.
Fresh crisp leaves
dancing green in the wind.
Strong gnarled trunk
scarred and vibrant with life.

Tenderly His hand
caresses the vine
expertly examining
each branch and twig.
Frowning, he pauses
then
with love afire He
slashes
the withered twig
close to the branch.
Shuddering the branch sways
for a moment,
then peacefully surrenders
to the healing touch
closing the wound.

A flash of steel —
blackened diseased
leaves, misshapen
shriveled fruit
another branch
falls to the fire.

The whole vine murmurs
shakes with the blow.
Again the Hands strong and
sure seal with love
the surgeon's mark.

He pauses, smiles,
dazzling light
dances on His hands
and vine as uncurling slowly
pale and fragile
soft spring-green
tiny leaves
reach to the Light
energy surging forth
in waves of joy and love.

He touches
lovingly
once more
each scar
ancient and new.
A long last
gentle caress
of each new leaf
and silently
He moves on.

The vine
glowing more richly
from within
tranquilly patiently
awaits His return.

17   ARTS AND CRAFTS ROOMS

Art is a collaboration between God and the artist, and the less the artist does the better.

— *André Gide*

An ancient Christian motto, *Ad Majorem Dei Gloriam* — "To the Greater Glory of God" — holds a special meaning for religious communities; for each one has had not only a history of service in the name of God, but also a desire to give expression to the beauty of God's creation through the many forms of creativity with which God has endowed human beings. Just as music is a creative expression at the heart of the chapel, and words provide the expression at the heart of the scriptorium, so the visual arts give expression to the joys and sorrows, the longings and fulfillment of the human heart.

At St. John's Convent special rooms are dedicated to the creation of visual arts, but throughout the houses of the Sisterhood, you can see the works of others hanging on the walls or visible around the building — paintings, mosaics, icons, sculpture, and fabric art. Both the works done by others and those created by the sisters illuminate the way in which God has designed human beings to be co-creators of a world of beauty, and nourishes the sense of wonder and gratitude that this inspires.

WORKS OF ART CREATED BY OTHERS

In the 1950s Canadian sculptor Jacobine Jones created the magnificent bas-relief sculpture of St. John the Divine that graces the exterior wall of the chapel, watching and welcoming all who approach the sacred space of St. John's Convent. As a sentinel denotes watchfulness and vigilance, this stone carving reminds all who look upon it to watch for those in need and to offer their service to one another with humility and grace.

Jones also sculpted the three panels that grace the front of the altar, depicting feminine images of God as a phoenix, a pelican, and an eagle (see image on page 150). Both the statue and the altar panels were created for the convent on Botham Road and have travelled with the community to their new home on Cummer Avenue.

Above the altar is a large wooden crucifix flanked by figures of Mary and John — the two whom scripture records stayed at the foot of the cross with Jesus. These pieces date from around 1889, and were carved in Oberammergau, Germany. Later, two kneeling wooden angels from Exeter, England, were added to the group. At one time they topped the chancel screen that divided the sisters' choir from the congregation. These pieces have been with the community since the early twentieth century when they were first installed in the convent chapel on Major Street.

Another focus for beauty and reflection in the chapel is a mosaic triptych of the Mother and Child surrounded by various Christian symbols. It was made in 1979 by much-loved Canadian artist Doris McCarthy, who gave it to the sisters for Cana Place, the seniors' residence in Scarborough that the sisters administered until 1994. McCarthy also designed a large wall hanging with pieces which were sewn by the residents of Cana Place, along with staff, friends, volunteers, and visitors. With gentle humour, the hanging depicts The Wedding at Cana, complete with a blushing bride with downcast eyes.

A mosaic triptych created by Doris McCarthy.

On the wall near the fireplace in the narthex is a large, framed, crocheted hanging of The Lord's Prayer. This impressive piece, made by one of the Sisterhood's Newfoundland associates, Mary Pike, was donated following her death in 2009.

A convent without stained glass just wouldn't be a convent, would it? The sisters have some extraordinary pieces dating back to the Major Street convent. Visitors are

first greeted in the convent lobby by five panels, each portraying an angel with a musical instrument — cymbals, portable organ, lute, trumpet, and harp — which honours the music that figures so prominently in the sisters' prayer. These panels were originally installed in the narthex of the chapel on Botham Road.

Somewhat hidden from public view — but not intentionally! — is the extraordinary Mary Window that has been with the community since 1889. It first had pride of place above the altar of the chapel on Major Street before being moved to the west wall of the Botham Road chapel. It now resides in the Lady Chapel of the new convent and has been installed at eye level. It is an exquisite piece with rich, jewel-like colours, created for the community in memory of the Reverend Ogden P. Ford, the first warden.

The main portion of the glass, with its rounded top, depicts John guiding Mary to his home following the crucifixion, in response to one of Jesus' last words from the

IN PIAM MEMORIAM SACERDOTIS O P FORD HUIUS SOCIETATIS AUCTORIS DILECTI DIE VIII MENS SEPTR AD 188

TOP: *The angel windows in the foyer.*
BOTTOM: *The Mary window in the Lady Chapel.*

232

cross: "Mother, here is your son" and "Here is your mother" (John 19:26). To the sisters, the window has become a symbol of their ministry of hospitality.

The five panels below chronicle the "joyful mysteries" — major events in Mary's life: the Annunciation (the angel announcing to Mary that the Holy Spirit would come over her and she would become pregnant), the Visitation (Mary's visit to her cousin Elizabeth who was pregnant with John the Baptist), the Nativity (Mary with her newborn baby), the Presentation (the infant Jesus being blessed by Simeon in the temple), and the Purification (Mary carrying a pair of turtle doves, the sacrifice required of poor women after childbirth according to the ancient law of Israel).

In St. Margaret's Chapel (the retreat chapel of the guest house), there is a large and striking panel designed by Ellen Simon and created in stained glass by Yvonne Williams, both Toronto artists. It shows the risen Christ with St. John the Divine on the left and St. Margaret of Scotland on the right. It was a gift to the Sisterhood by St. John's Anglican Church in Carrying Place (near Belleville, Ontario) when that church closed in 2004. The panel has special significance because it was dedicated to the memory of the Reverend John Grier (who was the first rector of the parish) and Rose Margaret Grier, father and niece respectively, of Mother Hannah.

Two other beautiful stained glass windows crafted by Yvonne Williams are on either side of the sanctuary in the chapel of St. John's Rehab hospital just opposite the guest house — one depicts the nativity, with a sister in the black habit of earlier days (most likely intended to be Mother Hannah) watching from a slight distance; the other depicts St. John receiving the Revelation, a more mysterious window, splendid in hues of blue, purple, and red.

In the 1970s and 1980s, making banners was a popular creative activity. Many were beautifully executed and they enlivened the refectory and other locations in the convent. The former Sister Mary Katherine (now Katherine McDonald), a calligrapher and artist, created a number of

The Risen Christ window in St. Margaret's Chapel by Yvonne Williams, originally located in St. John's Anglican Church, The Carrying Place, Ontario.

beautiful banners; by far the most striking are four large hangings depicting the traditional canticle from "Song of the Three" in the Apocrypha: "Glorify the Lord, every shower of rain and fall of dew, all winds and fire and heat; winter and summer, glorify the Lord, praise and exalt God forever."

A large and striking banner that now hangs in the chapel narthex was originally designed for the chapel of St. John's Priory in Edmonton by an SSJD associate in the 1970s (see image on page 95) It symbolically depicts seven "Amens" from the book of Revelation, replete with magnificent blue-and-purple satin streaks of

Two windows designed by Yvonne Williams in the chapel at St. John's Rehab:
LEFT: *St. John writing the book of the Revelation to John.*
RIGHT: *The birth of Jesus.*

234

lightning on a silvery-grey background, and containing in the centre a free-hanging roundel surrounding a majestic Lamb clothed in a fleece of French knots:

> Worthy is the Lamb that was slaughtered
> to receive power and wealth and wisdom and might
> and honour and glory and blessing!
> (Revelation 5:12)

Another example of fabric art is a gift of four tapestries on permanent loan from the Cariboo Stitchers of Grace Church-on-the-Hill in Toronto that depict The Four Seasons, based on designs by textile artist Elizabeth Taylor[1] in 1988 for an altar hanging at St. Paul's Cathedral, London, Ontario. This piece was supported by a grant from The Anglican Foundation's Sacred Arts Trust.

In 2005, a beautiful oil painting, *From the East,* was given to the sisters by Janet Read of Markham, Ontario, for the new chapel. The beauty of the light penetrating a dark blue and cloudy sky is both restful and energizing, and a fitting symbol of the light of God that penetrates the chapel itself.

Janet Read's painting, From the East.

The Sisters as Artists

Sister Miriam's statuette of the Madonna and Child.

Many sisters over the years of the community's life have been skilled and talented artists who left an important legacy to the Sisterhood. In the 1930s, Sister Miriam sculpted a foot-tall statuette of Madonna and Child. Its simple lines and Mary's interesting pale-green cloak have never ceased to attract the attention of those who view it. More recently, Sister Rosemary Anne sculpted small figurines, some of which are displayed in the cases in the front lobby of the convent. If you look closely you'll also spot the figurine of a sister in a traditional habit, made by Sister Anitra as a teenager in the 1950s in her art class at Toronto's Central Technical Collegiate — evidence that thoughts about the religious life were on her mind long before she entered a convent.

One oversized painting which strikes you as you walk down the corridor from the refectory to the guest house is by Sister Nonah. She has bequeathed to the community many beautiful watercolours done in the 1980s, and this was her first attempt at a large oil painting, though sadly she never did another one. It is a powerful yet subtle piece showing a carpet of brown, desiccated leaves after a harsh winter, and signs of new growth — you have to look long and hard at this painting to spot them — of greening moss on a log and tender shoots peeking between the dead leaves, heralding the start of spring. Sister Nonah's peaceful watercolour of an old metal garden gate which hangs outside the entrance to the refectory was greatly influenced by her teacher Carl Schaeffer, another Ontario artist.

In some of the guest house rooms you will find charming watercolours of the Muskoka landscape painted by Sister Jean during her stays at Bally Croy, the sisters' cottage in Port Sydney, Ontario. Sister Anitra also loves working in watercolours, and her inspiration derives from Doris McCarthy, whom she was blessed to have as one of her art teachers.

Sister Margaret Ann had a gift for creating pencil sketches, most of them with a delightfully humorous tone depicting convent events, sisters, and visitors. Her work illustrates the sweetness of the mundane — garden baskets propped up against a wall, a rocking chair, a garden bench, as well as sketches of her sisters with garden hoses or engaged in washing dishes. She also sketched a whole series showing the building of the new convent as she watched the daily progress of backhoes and hammers, drywall and stucco, steel frames and insulation — even

TOP: *Sister Nonah's painting of a carpet of leaves.*
BOTTOM: *A watercolour of the Muskokas by Sister Jean.*

the construction workers have been immortalized in a personal and gentle way that a photograph could never have captured.

Other less obvious artworks are the personalized greeting cards created by a number of sisters: Sisters Jean and Madeleine Mary painted flowered cards; Sister Joyce and Sister Helen Claire's cards use recycled materials such as pressed flowers to illustrate their subjects; Sister Elizabeth Ann has printed many cards using her own stamps and other printing tools; Sister Elizabeth and Sister Doreen's photo cards have delighted hundreds; while the calligraphers within the community — Sisters Joyce, Sarah Jean, and the former Mary Katherine — crafted beautifully scripted cards with life-affirming quotations and prayerful meditations.

And then there is flower arrangement — an art form that rarely gets its due. Over the years the sisters have quietly adorned the chapel, refectory, and other rooms with breathtaking flower arrangements, stirring the senses and reminding both visitors and the community of the sheer range of plants and colours that God has given humans for their delight and joy.

Collage of sketches by Sr. Margaret Ann.

Sister Anitra sums up this creative work: "All of it points to the fact that the sisters, as a community, value art, and we regard it as an extension of our prayer life. We pray when we draw, paint, sculpt, knit, crochet, sew or dye. By using the skills God gave us we reflect back to the world the generosity of our Creator and the beauty of our planet."

CREATIVITY IN COMMUNITY

When a woman finds herself called to the religious life, she brings with her a wealth of experience and gifts. Among these gifts is creativity, which can be already developed or a surprising new talent. All are blessed with some form of creative talent and all are encouraged to use it. One of the benefits of living in community is that the sisters often discover new gifts as they are mentored and encouraged by other sisters.

In the early years, all cards for birthdays and anniversaries were made by hand, although few of these are to be found now. Sister Edna did two illuminated versions of the beginning of St. John's gospel (traditionally used by priests as a post-communion prayer) in her beautiful calligraphy — they hang in the vestries of both the convent and the hospital chapel. Sister Rosemary Anne, also a beautiful calligrapher, created and illuminated the Bede Roll of the deceased sisters, which can be found just outside the main Chapel. Sister Margaret Ann and Sister Wilma are known for their cartoons, displaying a wonderful sense of humour in the ordinary. As Novice Mistress, Sister Margaret Ann encouraged the development of the arts in her novices.

CRAFTS

There is an imagined fine distinction between art and crafts: we tend to think of crafts as something an amateur can do and art as something more professional. But crafts can be as professional as whatever we deem to be "art." From the sisters' point of view, crafts are simply the arts people practise, but on a smaller scale, or those that don't need large amounts of dedicated time and space. Knitting, crocheting, and embroidery are often done during the sisters' evening recreation hour as they gather in the community room to chat and catch up on the day's activities.

There are, however, two arts and crafts rooms where the Spirit of God and the creative heart of the individual sister can meet. Martin Luther said, "God writes the gospel not in the Bible alone, but on trees and flowers, and clouds, and stars." This visual gospel is expressed in the creative work of the sisters, a tangible gift to those around them. In the craft room, in workshops, and in the fabric arts room, a sister with some intentionality invites the Holy Spirit through silence and prayer to kindle within her a spirit of creativity. What unfolds becomes a visible result of her inspired partnership with God.

The arts and crafts rooms hold all manner of useful materials. Here a sister may go on her grace day, retreat day, or during her time of intentional prayer and find a variety of media to express herself. Here she may unleash her playful side.

This room is also a place of prayer-filled inspiration. In this context a sister may enter the craft room as she would the labyrinth, pausing at the door to offer a silent prayer and waiting for the Holy Spirit to direct her to a particular section where she might use materials for painting, sculpting, creating a finger labyrinth, a knotted or beaded rosary, or another form of abstract art. What she creates becomes a means through which God speaks to her, or He may communicate to another through her work. It is a place where the sister invites God to collaborate with her through the inspired direction of her hands by her heart.

ROSARIES

For the past ten years the sisters have been involved in making Anglican rosaries and giving workshops on the making and using of them. Sister Sarah Jean attended a workshop with the Community of St. John the Baptist in Mendham, New Jersey, where she learned how to make rosaries from semi-precious stones. On returning to Montreal, she began making these rosaries, and found much interest for them in Canada. A few years later, a sister from the Community of the Transfiguration showed several SSJD sisters how to make knotted Anglican rosaries from colourful fishing twine. Once they started making them, the enthusiastic response was unbounded. Years later it is still difficult to keep up with the demand. The sisters also make beaded rosaries using wooden beads and crosses. When giving a workshop about how to make a rosary, the beaded ones are easiest. Sister Sarah Jean finds that in her workshops, people really have a lovely time making their rosary, having it blessed, and then learning how to use it. Sister Louise has been giving workshops in Victoria, B.C., and even did one with a Sunday school class of kindergarten children.

SILK DYING AND OTHER COTTAGE INDUSTRIES

Sister Jessica's annual "Mosaic of Colours" retreats help people express prayer in the dying of silk scarves. The retreats always draw a crowd, and yield sometimes exuberant, sometimes delicate creations that participants wear proudly themselves or give away as gifts. Sister Jessica and community friend Ros D'Costa create many beautiful scarves throughout the year, which are offered for sale in the Convent book room. Other items for sale are hand-knit dishcloths and crocheted angels at Christmas. Hand-knit teddy bears for Amnesty International are enormously popular and the proceeds from the sale of the Teddies has raised thousands of dollars to support the advocacy work of Amnesty International. The making of the bears is a creative expression of the sisters, who also have friends (some from the Order of the Holy Paraclete in England) who knit "bear skins" and send them to the sisters to make up.

Fabric Arts

Fabric art is an age-old creative form that often utilizes recycled materials. Indeed, it is one of the arts that has been practised since the beginnings of the Sisterhood.

In the 1960s, when the sisters needed rugs for their cottage, they requested old nylon stockings from the nurses at the hospital. These were dyed with natural vegetable dyes and then braided and sewn into rugs, which have lasted for many years.

Sister Sarah Jean recently discovered the art of smocking, and makes exquisite baby and children's dresses.

The fabric arts room contains a sewing machine, lots of yarn donated by friends, many sets of knitting needles and crochet hooks, crochet cotton, tatting shuttles, embroidery silks and supplies, and more. Embroidery, as the next section will show, has been one of the longest and most influential of the arts in the Sisterhood's history.

Coloured Church Embroidery and Vestments

Needlework, especially embroidery, was one of the community's first artistic offerings to the Church. Mother Hannah was an expert needlewoman, and this gift was passed on to other sisters, who joined her in liturgical embroidery. Churches in Toronto and across Canada have vestments and altar frontals made by sisters, especially by Sister Joanna.

Sister Joanna was the last to do coloured embroidery, vestments, and altar frontals. She created a series of vestments in the six major liturgical colours

(green, red, white, yellow, purple, and blue) that have been used at the Convent for many years. All done on Tudor Rose fabric, they exemplify her delicate work with flowers, leaves, and animals. Her light touch brought a sense of harmony, light, and colour not unlike that of illuminated manuscripts of the Middle Ages; she painted with a needle and silk.

In 1976, the sisters closed the coloured work room when Sister Joanna was no longer able to see well enough to do the fine embroidery. Gradually, the vestments she and other sisters made (Sisters Lilias, Edna, and Mary Ruth) have come to need restoration. Sister Anne, who joined the Sisterhood in 1994, has discovered a gift for embroidery that started as a hobby but has developed into professional-quality work. At the encouragement of a number of people, Sister Anne joined the Ecclesiastical Needlework Guild of the Diocese of Toronto, and she has received training and mentoring from the skilled artists in this group. She also began working with an associate of the Sisterhood, Dee Ford, who once worked with Sister Joanna in her workroom at the Convent on Botham Road. Dee has been mentoring Sister Anne as she learns Sister Joanna's techniques.

In 2013, when Sister Anne assumed the role of Sacristan for the convent, she became aware of the need to preserve and restore the vestments that are part of the Sisterhood's heritage, and together with Sister Louise she has started to restore some of Sister Joanna's work. Together with other members of the Ecclesiastical Needlework Guild, the sisters have participated in ecclesiastical embroidery workshops at the Community of St. John the Baptist in Mendham, New Jersey, and have learned a great deal both

TOP: *Embroidery by the sisters: Saint John's orphry.*
BOTTOM: *Lenten Orphry.*

about embroidery and about restoring vestments. The stunning festal gold altar frontal that was designed and worked by Mother Hannah, with a roundel of the Mother and Child worked by an early associate, is in the process of being restored by an Ontario artist who specializes in this craft, Seanagh Murdoch. The Sisterhood's legacy of beautiful coloured embroidery may well be in for a resurrection.

White Church Embroidery

White embroidery was another skill practised by the early sisters, and in 1971 Sister Jocelyn started to learn some of the altar linen work. In 1978, when Sisters Maribel, Grace, and Rosemary found the work was getting too much for them, Sister Jocelyn took on the art of creating beautiful white work — fair linens, purificators, baptismal towels, and others. The white embroidery work travelled with Sister Jocelyn as she moved between the different houses of the Sisterhood — from the Botham Road convent to St. John's Priory in Edmonton, to Cana Place in Scarborough, Ontario, to Victoria, B.C., and finally to the present convent. Wherever Sister Jocelyn went she found associates and friends of the Sisterhood willing to help with hemming. In 2014, after more than 120 years, the white work department closed. It was the end of an era, but Sister Jocelyn's work, and the work of earlier sisters, can still be found in churches both across the country and overseas.

Art as Prayer

Any form of creativity can also be prayer. In *lectio divina* one prays with scripture or some other form of spiritual reading. In *visio divina* one prays with icons or paintings or movies. In the same way, you can pray with whatever it is that you are creating — using crayons, coloured pencils, water colours or oils, pottery or clay. Art is one of the many ways in which we can get in touch with the unconscious, with that part of ourselves which we usually ignore. Many faith traditions use mandalas as a way of deepening one's relationship with God and the depths of one's own being. A circle, which has no beginning and no end, is a symbol of wholeness, perfection, unity, and eternity, and is often seen in Christianity in the form of rose windows. It is where the invisible is made visible.

A number of sisters use art in their personal prayer time, on quiet days or retreats. Some of the sisters have learned a great deal from retreats made with Sister Virginia Varley and others in sacred art. And the sisters teach others to use this form of creative prayer as well, in the annual Women at a Crossroads program and in courses and retreats on prayer offered by the sisters. It is amazing how often something from the depths rises to the surface through this form of prayer, and how it can lead people into a deeper relationship with God.

In the end, all art is prayer, whether intentional or not, because every creative work develops from the image of God stamped on that individual:

> In the beginning God created the heavens and the earth …
> Then God said, "Let us make humankind in our image, according to our likeness…."
> So God created humankind in … the image of God. (Genesis 1)

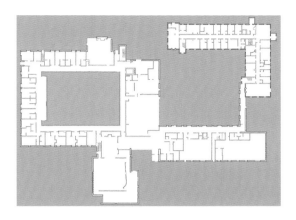

GARDENS AND GROUNDS 18

Awake, O north wind, and come, O south wind! Blow upon my garden that its fragrance may be wafted abroad. Let my people come to the garden, and eat its choicest fruits. (The Song of Songs, 4:16)

Gardens, courtyards and beautiful grounds have always played an important role for the Sisterhood, who regard nature as a source of spiritual and physical healing, a sign of hospitality, and a means of helping the human spirit transcend the confines of our technological and consumerist society. Gardening is also a form of art, and some sisters have a special gift in working with soil and seeds.

Since the first convent on Robinson Street and the first mission in Moose Jaw, the sisters have made a priority of creating and planting sacred space, places that are oases of calm in the midst of a noisy and destructive world. These are also healing spaces, where all the senses are stimulated by green vistas, by a profusion of colourful, cheerful flowers, by meandering paths, by space that is uncontaminated by distraction. Mother Hannah loved the outdoors and no doubt benefitted during her own early convalescence from walks through Kew Gardens and Hyde Park in London. In nature one not only sees the work of God but also feels God in the breeze, in the heat of the sun, in the chill of the air, and hears God in the whisper of the wind, in the crack of thunder, in the gentle rustle of the leaves.

The Sisterhood's earliest convent in Toronto had a kitchen garden, and during the 1930s at St. John's on the Hill some hardy sisters raised pigs and chickens, and grew crops to feed themselves and their patients.

Early pictures of St. John's Rehab show an almost denuded expanse of land, land that formerly housed a farm and then a golf course. That scene began to change in 1936 when Sisters Beatrice, Emily, Angela, and Vera started laying out the gardens and plantings, diligently following the plans of a landscape gardener who had cared for the former golf course.

Sister Emily had completed a course at the Guelph Agricultural College, obtained seedlings from the Ontario Department of Lands and Forests, and with the help of George Lockyer, the golf course gardener, she planted hundreds of Scotch pine, spruce, and eastern white cedar along both sides of the property. Flowering shrubs, a few apple trees, raspberry canes, and a vegetable garden were next. One of the sisters' friends, the Reverend Dr. Donald Anderson, recalls helping plant the trees.

For the next fifty years, the sisters continued to landscape the grounds. Norway and white spruce, Douglas fir, Carolina poplar, European larch, Siberian elm, and a native group of staghorn sumac have provided shelterbelts and windbreaks. Persian and black walnut, sugar maple, mulberry, mountain ash, black locust, weeping willow, birch, blue spruce, red oak, and white ash, along with herbaceous ornamentals, fruit trees, and shrubs have revitalized the landscape. Japanese crab apple, planted along the central driveway to the hospital in the 1940s, bloomed into a spectacular vision of pink and white and continues to make an impressive entrance to the hospital. The plants were all generously donated by the Hospital Auxiliary, the North York Horticultural Society, and by countless individuals in memory of loved ones.

Garden beside the entrance to the convent.

The result has been a remarkable transformation of both the land and the area. It has no doubt contributed to a transformation in the emotional and physical well-being of the patients at St. John's Rehab. To this day, the grounds provide a welcome refuge, not only to the patients and staff but to convent guests as well, who love to walk just next door to enjoy the beautiful grounds.

This mammoth undertaking could not have been easy. As any gardener can attest, you deal with what you have been given, do what you can, and then pray a lot. The sisters gamely wrestled with the heavy clay soil of north Toronto, and planted all the trees and shrubs, coaxing them along and gradually moulding the land into an urban Garden of Eden.

This commitment to natural beauty and to environmental stewardship was fundamental to the vision of the new St. John's Convent and Guest House, built in 2004. While there are many beautiful places of retreat in small towns and the country, St. John's Convent is the only "urban oasis" in Toronto where people can go for a day or an extended period and find the space and support to reconnect with the earth in the midst of the city. The sisters wanted to make it a place of beauty for all who come to join them for rest and retreat. They drew up a wish list that included a labyrinth, areas for quiet meditation, a water feature run on solar power, plants that would provide year-round interest and colour, and gardens that would be unfussy, easy to care for, and not overly cultivated. The challenge was working with the heavy clay soil of north Toronto.

The labyrinth was the first of the outdoor areas to be developed, in the fall of 2004. It is an eleven-circuit labyrinth, modelled after the one at Chartres Cathedral in France, and was designed by Heather Lindsay. The sisters chose to situate it outside the link (the glass-and-brick corridor that connects the convent to the guest house), so that it might be a focus of walking meditation for both sisters and guests. In medieval times, Christian labyrinths became an alternate way of pilgrimage for those who could not afford to journey to Jerusalem to follow the way of Christ. Today, the labyrinth is seen as a spiritual tool to connect people to the depths of our being, to the centre where Christ dwells. It can be walked alone, or in a group.

Heather had the assistance of the sisters and friends from her church. The area was first cleared and levelled, and an enormous piece of landscape cloth with the outline of the labyrinth was laid. Then came the task of using field stones of different sizes to outline the pathways. On a cold, damp, drizzly Saturday morning, some of the sisters, who were then living in Birchall-Bainbridge Hall, joined in the undertaking. At first, the task was prayerful and enjoyable: as each stone was selected for its shape and size a sense of ownership took hold as the labyrinth began to take shape. The task became less enjoyable after lunch when rain pelted down and the air became colder. Suddenly, the stones seemed heavier; several helpers drifted away. By nightfall, however, all the stones were in place, and everyone sighed with relief. The following week, wood chips were spread on the path inside the labyrinth. The labyrinth was complete, a sacred space ready

for guests and sisters alike. Because of good drainage it is usable most of the year (except when completely buried during some of Toronto's heavy snowstorms).

Many guests of the convent are drawn to the labyrinth. It is a pathway of contemplation, meditation and spiritual renewal, as well as one of mystery and power. Those who embark on a walk within the labyrinth are surprised and at times overcome at how deep, repressed feelings uncoil and complex problems untangle. Upon exiting the labyrinth, it is not uncommon to feel a sense of lightness and serenity.

The courtyards were designed later. Architects at Montgomery Sisam envisioned them as two outdoor rooms: the sisters' enclosed courtyard on the north side and the guest courtyard (shared by the sisters) on the south end of the building. But it took some years of hard, hands-on work as well as donations in order to bring these courtyards to life from the barren land. Sisters dug and planted. When Sister Brenda, with volunteers from Hands Across the Nation, dug a pond in 2009, the ground was so hard that they had to take turns breaking it up a little at a time using a pick.

In 2010, a generous donation allowed the sisters to bring in landscape designer Skai Leja. Through collaboration with the sisters she created a design plan and was contracted to landscape the guest courtyard. The plan succeeds in linking the indoor and outdoor spaces, and provides a sense of completion and integrity for the building.

Inside the guest courtyard is a patio (with a barbeque for picnic meals), a fish pond and waterfall, and beautiful perennial plantings that change colour with the seasons and and are as beautiful in the snow as during the lush periods of summer.

Part of the beauty of the gardens and grounds is the way they link the indoors with the outdoors. Approximately half of the guest rooms overlook the courtyard, as do some of the meeting rooms. All the corridors that link the guest house with the chapel, library, refectory, and reception area have large floor-to-ceiling windows that look out into the garden, as does the refectory itself. Thus, every guest who visits, by day or overnight, receives some benefit from the garden.

Over the years, the sisters have followed Leja's larger plan for the rest of the property, planting trees and bushes themselves in the chapel garden. Sister Sue in particular has shaped gardens in the sisters' courtyard. A recent donation of dogwoods has enabled the berm in the front of the convent to be planted. So the landscape progresses as time and generosity permit. Like all gardens, it is a work in progress.

There are also outdoor spaces beyond the convent's property that the sisters hold dear.

One is Bally Croy, the cottage in Port Sydney, Ontario, which the sisters have owned since the 1920s. This wooden, lakeside cottage is a true retreat, and each year the sisters choose their one- or two-week slot to visit it. Here they can unwind, read, flex their creative muscles, swim, or simply flop into a Muskoka chair and snooze. There is something about the scent of pine needles and the slap of a cottage's screen door that melts away tension and provides spiritual refreshment.

OPPOSITE TOP: *The central courtyard showing the circular pathway and patio outside the refectory.*

OPPOSITE MIDDLE: *The fishpond and bench.*

OPPOSITE BOTTOM: *A view of the courtyard after the ice-storm in 2013.*

ABOVE: *This shrine, shown here at the convent on Cummer Avenue, has had three incarnations in each of the three convents.*

The other outdoor space is actually two spaces, separated by many miles but consisting of a single entity nonetheless. It is the sisters' plots in two local cemeteries. Sisters do not retire; they are given gentler tasks as they age and their abilities decline. But eventually death comes to all of us. For those who commit themselves to monastic life, death is not marked as a loss but a transition to a fuller life and the hope of the resurrection. This does not mean that there is no grieving: sisters experience deep and profound sadness and loss when a sister dies, as one would expect from members in a close-knit community. But there is also a sense of victory: the deceased sister has persevered in her commitment to God and is released from any pain or distress that might have preceded her death. There is a sense of accomplishment and gratitude for a life lived deeply, honourably, and in the service of others.

The remarkable and accomplished sisters that have populated the Sisterhood's ranks are laid to rest in two cemeteries in Toronto: St. James Cemetery in downtown Toronto, where sisters were buried until the mid-1970s, and York Cemetery in north Toronto, near the sisters' current location, where more recent sisters are buried. Their graves are marked simply: no deeds are inscribed upon the markers, no accolades, only their names and dates of birth and death.

Funerals are usually held in the convent chapel, though there are exceptions: Mother Hannah's funeral was held at St. Thomas Church because there would not have been enough space in the convent chapel for all those who wanted to honour her. The funeral of Mother Frances Joyce, who fostered ecumenism, was held at St. John's Anglican Church York Mills, near the Botham Road convent. More recently, Sister Constance, who died in 2013 at the age of 109, had her funeral at St. James Cathedral due to the huge number of people from various walks of life who had been touched by her generosity and her work in the fields of education and gerontology.

Each month a special Eucharist is held in the convent chapel to remember sisters who have died in that month over the

St. James' Cemetery where many of our early sisters are buried, including Mother Hannah.

years. And each month the sisters gather as a family to celebrate anniversaries of those living and departed, and to remember those who have gone before them.

And from time to time, when sisters visit the cemeteries, they are reminded of the beauty of God's image, reflected in both in the natural beauty around them and in the lives of each of the sisters who have gone before.

GARDENING AS PRAYER

Whether working in the convent gardens, pulling weeds at Bally Croy, or planting flowers by the graves in the cemetery, gardening is a form of art, a way of co-creating with God, bringing forth beauty and joy in the sights and sounds, the textures and smells of the garden. And like the other arts, it can be an expression of prayer. Many sisters who love to garden feel closest to God in the outdoors. Sister Elizabeth, one of the community's most avid gardeners, says:

> As a child my favourite places were always outside rather than in the house. I particularly loved the chapels at Camp Artaban and at Guide Camp on the West Coast because they were hidden away and surrounded by tall cedars and fir trees, and all the furnishings were very simple and rustic. Just to be there was to be close to God. In *The Practice of the Presence of God*, Brother Lawrence of the Resurrection writes, "The most holy, the most general, and the most necessary practice in the spiritual life is the practice of the presence of God, whereby the soul finds her joy and contentment in His companionship, talking humbly and lovingly to Him always and at all times...."[1] The garden is where I feel closest to God and to work in the garden is to create something beautiful for God. Sometimes as I'm pulling weeds I ask God to pull the weeds out of my soul; as I prune shrubs I pray that I may be open to God's pruning of my wayward ways. But always the beauty of God's creation lifts my heart to God.

19 Branch Houses

Where you go, I will go;
where you lodge, I will lodge;
your people shall be my people,
and your God my God (Ruth 4:16)

Over the years, as ministries have developed outside the convent (the "mother house" of the community), the sisters have had branch houses. Sometimes they have been attached to an institution, as for example when sisters have lived with the people they served in their hospitals, schools, and homes for the aged. Other branch houses have been mission houses or houses of prayer, where the sisters live in a small family environment with three or four other sisters, share their space as appropriate with guests, and serve in whatever capacity is needed in response to their life of prayer in that place. The most recent branch house of the Sisterhood is in Victoria, British Columbia.

St. John's House, Victoria, B.C.

The lots are modest, the homes well-maintained in this leafy neighbourhood enclave. The road banks slightly to the left as you approach number 3937 St. Peter's Road. From the outside, the house looks like an ordinary suburban home: white stucco, brown asphalt shingled roof, a white door with a small covered porch, and three windows arranged along the top level like watching eyes. Attached to the side of the house is what looks to be a former garage at the end of the driveway; a railed patio sits atop this addition. Enclosing the property on three sides like a horseshoe are enormous mature trees. It doesn't look like a convent, but this is St. John's House. The house has three bedrooms for the three sisters who live there, and three additional rooms for guests or other sisters — as well as a beautiful chapel cleverly created from the carport.

In 2002, the sisters were invited by Bishop Barry Jenks to be a praying presence in the Diocese of British Columbia. In October of that year, Sisters Doreen and Valerie made the trek by car from Toronto to Vancouver Island. They were invited to share the home of the Roman Catholic Sisters of St. Anne, who had a beautiful retreat centre overlooking the Georgia Straight, complete with swimming pool. Sisters Doreen and Valerie were warmly welcomed and a creative ecumenical friendship developed. Unfortunately, within the year the Sisters of St. Anne had decided to sell their property and so the two St. John's sisters began looking for their own place, with the help of Bishop Jenks and his wife, Barbara. The sisters discovered just how strongly supported they were in the diocese. As Sister Doreen recalls, "we moved into this house the following May with nothing but our clothes. And it was amazing because from everywhere we got everything. We scrubbed the house and made curtains; the diocese provided furniture. People kept arriving with food. It was wonderful and uplifting."

The sisters' presence reignited interest in the religious life, and the number of associates in the province grew steadily. There are also now a number of oblates on the West Coast.

The sisters' ministry has been supported in part by the diocese, who provide their accommodation (the house is the former rectory of St. Peter's Church, which is next door), and contribute toward their food. The sisters receive honoraria for the mission work they do within the diocese, and derive financial support (the major part of their income) in the form of donations from parishes, associates and oblates, and all those who value the religious life within the church.

The work of the sisters is not much different than the work the sisters do at the convent in Toronto but it is influenced by the needs of the diocese. The sisters at St. John's House pray for the people and churches of the Diocese of British Columbia (constituting Vancouver Island and the Gulf Islands). They visit and worship with congregations throughout the diocese, choosing a different church to attend each week. They lead retreats and quiet days and workshops (on the mainland as well, in the Diocese of New Westminster); they provide spiritual direction and mentor those discerning a vocation to the religious life. They also work as volunteers in a number of inner-city and community ministries.

The sisters in Victoria have been a visible and steady presence at the province's Truth and Reconciliation hearings, being a prayerful support for First Nations people who are giving painful testimony of the abuse they suffered under the residential schools program, learning from them, and honouring their ancestral lands on which the sisters' home and much of Vancouver Island is situated. In the summer of 2014, the sisters joined ten thousand other people in the Walk for Reconciliation in Vancouver after the conclusion of the hearings. They have helped serve at feasts at the request of local nations. Their ministry is a powerful witness to the way in which each branch house of the Sisterhood over 130 years has responded to the needs of specific communities where the sisters live and work.

The sisters at St. John's House have made a commitment to be part of the change that is needed in relationships between First Nations, the Church, and the government. Sister Brenda, who has been the sister in charge at the house in Victoria for the past several years, has described the sisters' participation in this process using the image of the Hoop Dance — a dance that relates the story of a community's life and how to bring healing and harmony to the life of all peoples. The hoop, like the medicine wheel, is a sacred symbol of wholeness in First Nations culture. Each dancer interprets his or her community's story by spinning a series of hoops around the body, up to fifty hoops at a time. Each hoop is flipped up to the arm with a motion of the foot without missing a beat, and moves about the body. At times the hoops are interlocked to create images of the community's story.

As you visualize the hoop dancer telling the Sisterhood's story, you see that there are now two hoops spinning on the trunk of the body, two hoops on each arm, with the hoops spinning in opposite directions, and other hoops now in the dancer's hands. As the dancer takes the community hoop from the head down the body, the hoops begin interlocking, resulting in the dancer connecting the hoops in the shape of a dove — the Dove who brings the gifts of innocence and hope, warmth and generosity, introspection, perseverance, and wisdom — which in turn become the power to live a wholly integrated life. It is the story of the Holy Spirit's presence in our life.

Together with all the other Sisters of St. John the Divine, who are committed to pray regularly for the peace and reconciliation among all people, the sisters in Victoria are a witness in the twenty-first century to the power of love in mending and transforming broken relationships and lives in order that the seeds of positive change can germinate for the betterment of all God's people.

AFTERWORD

Why Be a Sister?

Why would a twenty-first century woman feel called to the religious life? And what can religious life offer a twenty-first century woman?

Those questions percolated within me while I discerned my own religious vocation several years ago.

Prior to entering the community, I had what most people would consider what it takes to be happy in this society: a family, a good job, a car, a home, food on the table, and enough money left over to travel occasionally. I loved being a mother; I enjoyed meeting up with friends for coffee; I liked (and still enjoy!) rock music. I could come and go as I pleased and did not have to answer to anyone. I was a faithful member of a parish community. As a medical secretary, I made a conscious commitment to treat all patients with care, respect, compassion, and genuine concern. All these gifts were generously poured out for me, and yet something was missing. As time went on, I found myself wanting to listen more carefully for the will of God in my life; to embrace that life of love to which all God's people are called.

Becoming a sister is not so much a life choice as it is a life calling. And that call can come at various points in a woman's life. Like many women, I began to feel a deep unease at how society assumes we must acquiesce to the corporate and consumerist ethos: we are expected to participate in the agenda of satisfying all our needs and wants with things we can buy, and only those things we can buy, because those are the only satisfactions which improve the corporate bottom-line. However, such things do not satisfy the human heart. A sense of alienation sets in — alienation from God and from our sisters and brothers.

As I considered what God was asking of me, I began to think about the monastic life, but I was unsure whether I would be accepted. I was divorced; I had children; I had only recently become an Anglican; I was, as they say, "a mature woman." And yet a yearning for this life — a very counter-cultural life — would not go away.

As I got to know the Sisterhood of St. John the Divine, I found my tribe, as it were: women who were on the same journey as I; women who wanted to live an intentional life in a Christian community. And I discovered that my own children (and eventually grandchildren) were welcomed with open arms by the sisters.

The religious life lived in community is a microcosm of society at large. It consists of women of diverse origins, faith traditions, upbringing, personalities, temperaments, and outlook on life. We're all different, and yet at our core we have the same strong desire to devote our time, energy, and our very being to God.

We long to share what we have been given by the grace of God. We offer an oasis of peace to a troubled post-modern, post-Christian world — a place of spiritual refreshment where people can be reconnected to the divine life-force. We witness to the power of prayer in all we do as nothing is possible without our relationship with God. For someone called to the religious life, the offering of our whole self is as close to God as we can possibly imagine in this life.

Being part of this life of prayer and service has allowed me to relate to myself and to others in a much more authentic way. It has given me much peace and contentment. Every day, I make a real contribution to the community and to the world through my prayer; and in return I feel valued and a part of something much greater than I could have imagined.

Does God call us through our desires? I believe so. Many of our desires are surface desires. However, even these may be the catalyst of the Holy Spirit and are worth exploring when discerning God's will in our life. They will take us to our deepest self, our deepest desire.

A woman in this century has many options and it takes courage to explore where God may be leading her. And certainly, it can be confusing to discern whether a prompting is of God, of this world, or even of our own ego. The religious life is only one path that leads to Christ, but it is one that demands the whole self. In response to the love shown me by God in so many of the circumstances of my own life, both positive and negative, I came to a point where nothing compared to my yearning to walk more intentionally *with* Christ and *for* Christ, with others. What the secular world proclaims as necessary for a whole and vibrant life leaves me, quite frankly, empty. It is through this emptiness that God continues to draw me into a relationship of total unconditional love so that I might show that love to others.

In 130 years of the Sisterhood's existence, women have been drawn by that desire. As we go forward into the future, more than ever, there will be people searching for "something more" in their lives. Some of them may feel called, as I was and as Mother Hannah and the early sisters were, to join a community like The Sisterhood of St. John the Divine — a place where their gifts and talents can be used in the service of others, and where they can join other women on an amazing journey just begun.

The Rule of Life
of the Sisterhood of St. John the Divine

A copy of The Rule of Life *is presented to each new member of the community.*

"Whatever he says to you, do it."

(John 2.5)

I INTENTION

The Sisters of Saint John the Divine, in the spirit of their patron, are called to live to the glory of God in fulfillment of the two-fold law of love. Each sister will seek to do everything as one who has been baptized into Christ's death, and has entered into the new life of his resurrection, by the power of the Holy Spirit.

We are committed to lifelong conversion and to growth in union with God through the life of prayer and the undivided service of Jesus Christ. In Christ we are both called and sent to be open and responsive to the needs of the church and of the world, and to pray and work for peace, justice, unity, and the integrity of creation.

II OUR COMMON LIFE

A strong community life, hospitality, and lifelong learning are the principles that undergird our call. Through prayer, mutual love, respect, and forgiveness we grow in understanding of one another and the life of the whole community is enriched.

Through openness to the guidance of the Holy Spirit and responsible participation in the common life, we move toward the fulfilment of our calling in Christ.

1. THE VOWS

The vows of poverty, chastity, and obedience are the means by which we live out our baptismal promises. Our vows are an expression of the Gospel values which shape and focus our religious life. Through them, we redirect to God our natural human life in its ownership of things, in the exercise of all creative powers, and in its responsibility and freedom of choice.

i)   Poverty

The vow of poverty is grounded in the simplicity of life which Jesus lived and taught. Poverty as expressed in community of life and goods is a single-minded response to God, who invites our love to show itself through the gift of our whole self.

The spirit of poverty manifests itself in contentment, simplicity of living, and joyful dependence on God. It requires us to use with reverence, responsibility, and generosity all that God entrusts to us — resources, energy, talents, industry, and time.

To be poor in spirit is to claim nothing as ours by right, but to reconcile to God, at all levels, the demands of self-seeking, self-preservation, and self-security. In poverty we bear witness that God is our whole support.

ii)   Chastity

The vow of chastity is grounded in the wholeness of love with which Jesus embraced humanity and all creation. For us, chastity is expressed in the celibate state. It is a way of releasing all our energies for total commitment to Christ, a wholeness in love which is creative and generative, demanding integrity and purity of life.

Friendship is a gift of God, to be developed responsibly and thankfully, for the enrichment of the whole community.

It is through loving and responding to love that we grow in likeness to Christ. Our powers of human love find fulfillment in a living relationship with him; an ever deepening commitment and more generous self-giving to the spiritual family in which God has placed us; and a constant reaching out to embrace humanity and all creation. In chastity we bear witness that God is our whole love.

iii)   Obedience

The vow of obedience is grounded in the singleness of purpose with which Jesus lived in order to accomplish the will of the One who sent him. Obedience as promised in the religious life is the offering of our gift of free will to God, that we may contribute to the restoration of all things in Christ. It is the loving and voluntary response of the mature and free creature, making us available to God for God's glory.

In fulfillment of the baptismal covenant, we are called to give obedience to God in the context of our vocation. Obedience in the religious life is the fulfillment of the will of God as discerned through respectful listening and discussion; through the Chapter and other formal decision-making processes provided in the Constitution; through the Community leadership as provided for in the Statutes; and through living together and sharing the fruits of our individual and common prayer. By our obedience we bear witness that God is our whole life.

2. Balance of Life

A balanced life is necessary for health of mind, body, and spirit.

The Divine Office and celebration of the Eucharist, offered daily to the glory of God and for the needs of the whole creation, form the framework for the day.

Each house of the community will establish a timetable which provides for a stable and balanced rhythm of life.

Each sister will have regular times for prayer, work, rest, leisure, communal recreation, study, and retreats. Each sister will do her best to maintain her health by regular exercise, adequate rest, and good eating habits.

3. Solitude, Silence, and Conversation

Silent waiting on God is essential to the nurture of our individual and community life in Christ.

Silence and speech, both gifts of God, carry a special privilege and responsibility in the building up of our common life.

Solitude, silence, and conversation are means by which we bring healing and wholeness to each other and to the world in which we live. Each sister will cultivate both the interior peace and the receptiveness to God which gives meaning to silence, and the loving and thankful heart from which right conversation proceeds.

We observe the silence carefully among ourselves, but for charity and hospitality's sake, we are not required to do so in our contacts with others or when absent from any house of the community. Each sister will observe the times and places of silence and will respect each other's need for quiet and space.

4. Work

As life is one, all our work is an extension of prayer and a way of growing in our relationship with God and our neighbour.

All work is of equal value in nurturing the common life and the witness of the community.

We accept all assignments as God's will for us, remembering that each of us is a representative of the community in the work entrusted to us.

We aim to be generous in response to work assigned and ready to help in any way consistent with obedience. We try to resist the temptation to identify with our work. We seek to be detached when work is changed, and to be faithful and to persevere when it remains unchanged.

5. COMMUNITY LIFE

i)   The Sisters

As sisters of St. John the Divine, we are responsible for giving ourselves generously to maintain joy and unity within the family. Each sister is responsible for fulfilling her part in the Daily Office, in prayer, in all duties assigned to her, and in faithfulness to the Constitutions of the Sisterhood.

In each stage of life, we offer our health, energy, sickness, and pain for God's creative and redemptive purposes. We accept with thankfulness, patience, and joy each circumstance that life brings, together with its privileges, responsibilities, and blessings.

We seek to follow the leading of the Holy Spirit in all events and circumstances in our lives and to find our stability in God.

All sisters bear a responsibility for the nurture and development of postulants, novices, and the first-professed, through their example of intentional community living, by faithfulness to their own life in Christ, and by their prayers for the members in formation.

As each sister grows in the Holy Spirit, the fruit of the Spirit (love, joy, peace, patience, kindness, goodness, fidelity, gentleness, self-control) will become increasingly manifest in her life.

ii)   The Reverend Mother

As we elect a Sister as Reverend Mother, we trust in the guidance of the Holy Spirit, to discern the gifts of leadership needed by our community. She in turn calls us to continual growth in Christian living through her loving concern, pastoral care, nurture, and guidance. She challenges each sister to respond generously and faithfully to God's will. She shares her vision and inspiration with the community and helps to facilitate the community's decision-making processes. She is our main contact with the leadership of the wider church. She helps to foster vocations to the Sisterhood, and she will set an example of faithfulness to the *Rule of Life* in the fullness of its spirit within the life and discipline of the Church .

iii)   The Members of the Novitiate

The counsels of our life, although not binding upon the members of the Novitiate by Vow, are of obligation both in letter and in spirit, in preparation for the life to which they aspire. They will be ready to share their thoughts and gifts in the community family, as well as to listen and to learn from the views of others. They should exercise confidence in the Novitiate Director and endeavour to practise frankness and openness.

iv)   The Novitiate Director

The Novitiate Director will exercise her responsibility with gentleness and love. She will be careful to show no favouritism.

She will endeavour to lead each member of the Novitiate to the mature acceptance of God's will for her life. To this end she will guide them in their prayer and reading, give individual care and counsel, and instruct them in the principles of the religious life, especially as that life is set forth in the Constitutions of the Sisterhood.

III THE MEANS OF GRACE

Our community life and prayer provide the spiritual resources through which we make ourselves available to one another and to those whom we serve.

1. Prayer

Prayer is God's gift, enabling growth in our relationship with Christ in every aspect of life, and releasing creative power into the world for the glory of God.

We have at least two hours each day set aside for the renewal of our life in Christ, through prayer including meditation, spiritual reading, and *lectio divina*.

The corporate life of our community finds its chief expression in the Eucharist and the Daily Office.

We commit ourselves to be faithful and attentive in daily prayer, both personal and liturgical, as it is our joy, responsibility, and privilege.

2. Retreats, Spiritual Direction, Reconciliation, and Healing

Regular times of retreat provide opportunities to deepen our union with God in prayer and the living out of our religious vocation.

Opportunities will be provided monthly for spiritual direction and the sacrament of reconciliation. Sisters are encouraged to make regular use of these means of grace.

The ministry of healing will be available in our houses on a regular basis.

3. Conference, Refectory, Recreation, and Enclosure

Our life together is enriched through meeting, common meals, recreation, and solitude. We make ourselves available to others in the strength of our community life and prayer.

Regular conference will be held, allowing the sisters opportunity to be accountable in living the common life, to hear the Rule of Life, to review the activities of the day, and to share general information. Sisters inform the other members of the household at conference when they intend to go out or to invite guests in, and are sensitive to potential conflict with community obligations.

As an extension of the Eucharistic celebration, eating together deepens our life in community.

Regular times of recreation afford a common social gathering for leisure and companionship. Each sister will have daily rest time, a weekly grace day, and an annual holiday of four weeks to ensure adequate free time for her development and enrichment.

An enclosure for the sisters in each of the houses provides a place apart for the sisters for silence, prayer, and the privacy and quiet necessary for the stability and development of our common life in Christ. The enclosure enables us to recollect the presence of God and to respond to God's will in our lives.

Each sister has a separate room where she may have privacy and silence for rest, prayer, and study. Sisters do not visit one another in their rooms except in special circumstances.

IV MISSION AND MINISTRY

Our community is called to be a stable and radiating centre of the presence and power of Christ, within the church and society. Our apostolate is the outflowing of our union with God and with one another in God.

1. OUR MISSION AND MINISTRY

We are called to be a sign of Christ, and by our lives of prayer and service to witness to the power of his reconciling and forgiving love. Our lives are shaped by the gospel imperatives of prayer, hospitality, spiritual guidance, ministering to those in need, work for justice and peace, and reverence for the whole creation.

As we minister to others in loving service, we minister to Christ himself.

2. EDUCATION AND TRAINING

Effective action must be informed by awareness of the world's need. Opportunities for ongoing education, study and training will be provided for the adequate fulfilment of the community's ministry, and for the creative enrichment of each Sister's life.

The risen Christ said to his disciples: "As God has sent me, so I send you."
(John 20:21)

ACKNOWLEDGEMENTS

In August 2010, when the sisters gathered for our annual General Chapter meetings, we talked about producing a new history to commemorate the 130th anniversary of the founding of the Sisterhood of St. John the Divine. The previous history, published in 1984 for our centennial, was a booklet of fewer than eighty pages, with black-and-white photos. This time we were inspired by a beautiful book published by the Sisters of St. Anne in Bethany, Massachusetts, entitled *Catch the Vision*. It captured many voices and presented a colourful portrait of that community.

The sisters agreed that we wanted our book also to be lively and interesting: well-researched, with a mix of good text and lots of photographs. We discussed several possibilities of writers from outside the community who could help us. Sister Elizabeth was asked to contact Jane Christmas, an author well known to our community and sympathetic to our way of life, to see if she would consider undertaking this project herself or advise us on other possibilities. We were delighted when she agreed to take on this challenge.

The sisters wish to express their deep gratitude to Jane — friend, associate, and artist of words — who accepted the challenge of undertaking a history of the Sisterhood. Jane worked closely with Sister Constance Joanna in the writing and editing of the text, she encouraged all the sisters to participate in writing about the many aspects of community life in Part II, and her light touch and delightful sense of humour have greatly enhanced the text as a whole.

Interesting words become even more meaningful with beautiful illustrations. We are grateful to Michael Hudson and Tom Arban for allowing us to use their professional photographs. We celebrate their artistry and the way they capture the sisters' buildings and life. Our own Sister Elizabeth took many of the photographs herself, scanned dozens of historical photos, and brought them all together in a creative marriage with the text.

The sisters express their profound thanks to the many other people who have helped with the production of this book in honour of the Sisterhood's 130th anniversary year:

To Mervat Iskander, oblate of the Sisterhood and assistant in the Sisterhood's Archives, for her skillful and dedicated assistance to our archivist Sister Margaret Mary and to the sisters who spent long and fascinating hours of research there.

To Janet Read for generously allowing us to use her beautiful painting, *From the East*, as our cover image.

To Bishop Gordon Light, for permission to print his wonderful hymn "She Comes Sailing on the Wind," and for the words of the title.

To our Primate, Archbishop Fred Hiltz, whose quoting of Bishop Light's hymn in the foreword gave us the idea for the title.

To Archbishop Colin Johnson, Episcopal Visitor of the Sisterhood, for his support of the community and this project.

To the Reverend David Harrison, whose blog, "Lost Anglican Churches of Toronto," provided much useful information and unravelled several mysteries.

To Mark Smith of Chrismar Mapping Services for the splendid maps of the Sisterhood's locations and the creative time line.

To Terry Montgomery and the staff at Montgomery Sisam Architects for providing a drawing of the new convent.

To William O'Neill, Executive Director of Kensington Health Centre, for sharing plans of the renovated Major Street Chapel (now the Kensington Hospice) and for the hospitality and tours offered to the sisters.

To the creative and skilled professionals at Dundurn for their part in the production of this book: Carrie Gleason, Laura Harris, Jennifer McKnight, Courtney Horner, Caitlyn Stewart, and all the others who have worked behind the scenes to make the production of this book a creative and enjoyable experience. We are also grateful for their patience in adapting to changed deadlines caused by the sisters' circumstances, and the way in which they brought the book to completion in time for the anniversary of Mother Hannah on February 9, 2015.

We offer profound thanks to all the sisters, associates, and benefactors who have gone before us. And most important of all, we give thanks to God our Creator, who called this Sisterhood into existence; to Jesus our Redeemer, who has walked the journey with us; and to the Holy Spirit who inspires and directs our future.

The Sisters of St. John the Divine, November 1, 2014

LIST OF CONTRIBUTORS

Notes

Foreword

1. Gordon Light, "She Flies On," *Common Praise* (Toronto: Anglican Book Centre, 1998), Hymn # 656. Reproduced with permission.

Introduction

1. Susan Mumm, *Stolen Daughters, Virgin Mothers: Anglican Sisterhoods in Victorian Britain* (Leicester, U.K.: Leicester University Press, 1999), 15.

2. Ibid., 19.

Chapter 1

1. St. George the Martyr Anglican Church opened a school for children in the parish neighbourhood in 1875. After the church was burned down in 1955, the old schoolhouse was converted for use as the new church and stands in the Grange Park directly behind the Art Gallery of Ontario.

2. Sister Eleanora, SSJD, *Hannah Grier Coome: A Memoir of the Life and Work of Hannah Grier Coome* (London: Oxford University Press, 1933), 32.

3. Ibid., 34–35.

4. Ibid., 28. See 30–31 in the *Memoir* for a list of names and residence of the committee members.

5. Ibid., 57.

6. Ibid., 59.

7. Ibid., 127.

8. February 8, 1883.

9. June 12, 1884.

10. The Orangemen were spiritual (and often literal) descendants of Irish Protestants who were defenders of the Protestant faith in the face of perceived threats from the "green" Roman Catholics. This struggle had begun with the Reformation and spread beyond Ireland to Scotland, Canada, and even the United States.

11. Sister Eleanora, *Memoir*, 86.

12. Ibid., 91.

13. Ibid., 98.

14. Ibid.

15. An agreed daily and annual rhythm that set out the sisters' common commitment to prayer, work, study, rest, recreation, and community life.

16. Sister Eleanora, *Memoir*, 128.

17. Ibid., 144.

18. Sister Eleanora's memory was not quite accurate. According to the Sisterhood's register of admissions and

professions, Mary Alice and Eleanora were admitted in April 1888 and so would have been postulants, not novices; and neither Mary nor Kate was in the community at that time. In 1889, at the Sisterhood's first chapter meeting, there were eight sisters and a novice present.

19. Sister Eleanora, *Memoir*, 114.

20. Ibid., 156–57.

21. Ibid., 156.

22. Ibid., 219.

23. Ibid., 162.

24. Ibid., 154.

25. Ibid., 215.

26. Ibid., 291.

Chapter 2

1. Linda Reid and Helga Elliott, "A Brief History of the Associates of SSJD" (unpublished paper), 1.

2. Eva Hasell's remarkable venture is chronicled in her book *Across the Prairies in a Motor Caravan* (London: SPCK Press, 1922). See also Vera Fast, *Missionary on Wheels: Eva Hasell and the Sunday School Caravan Mission* (Toronto: Anglican Book Centre, 1979).

3. The Kilgours had a much larger property on Bayview which Alice Kilgour gave to the City of Toronto in 1928 when her husband died. It was named Sunnybrook Park. Later, in the 1940s, the City of Toronto donated that property to the Province of Ontario to establish a veterans' hospital, which became the core of Sunnybrook Hospital, later Sunnybrook Health Sciences Centre.

4. *St. John's Messenger*, May 1923.

5. From a report in the Sisterhood's Archives.

Chapter 3

1. Archival interview with Noreen Spencer-Nimmons, 1999.

Chapter 4

1. *The Eagle*, Michaelmas issue, 1989, 2.

2. Doug Saunders, email to Sister Constance Joanna, August 15, 2014.

Chapter 6

1. Henri Nouwen, *The Spirituality of Fundraising* (Nashville: Upper Room Ministries, 2004), 3.

Chapter 7

1. Sisterhood of St. John the Divine, *Rule of Life* (2003), 8.

2. Sister Eleonora, *Memoir*, 127.

3. Ibid., 33.

4. *Gregorian Canticles* (Brown, 1877) was in use in the sisters' chapel in 1896, and *The Hymnal Noted* (Cambridge Camden Society, 1851) was also used around this time. Copies of *The English Hymnal* were acquired in 1919. In 1924–25, the newly published Sarum plainsong for the Ordinary of the Mass — *Introits, Graduals, Alleluyas and Tracts* — was well used, and *Psalms and Canticles at Mattins and Evensong* (edited by G.H. Palmer and published by the Wantage Sisters) was adopted for use in the Chapel. These were followed later by *The Order of Tenebrae* (1933) and *The Order of Vespers* (1951). Other resources used were *The Convent Psalter* (S.S.J.E., Bracebridge, 1936), *The Book of Common Praise* (Anglican Church of Canada, 1938), and *Songs of Praise* (Oxford, 1926).

5. Sisterhood of St. John the Divine, *Songs for Celebration (1984)*, #1

6. Ibid., #16

7. Ibid., #24

Chapter 8

1. The title "Angelus" comes from the Latin word for "angel," which begins the ancient prayer in remembrance of the Angel Gabriel's visit to Mary when he announced that she would become the mother of Jesus: "Greetings, favoured one! The Lord is with you" (Luke 2.28).

2. Brian Stanfield, ed., *The Art of Focused Conversation: 100 Ways to Access Group Wisdom in the Workplace* (Toronto: New Society Publishers, 2000).

3. Nouwen, *The Spirituality of Fundraising*, 4.

Chapter 9

1. SSJD, *Rule of Life*, 2.

2. For instance, Joan Chittister, OSB, *St. Benedict: Insights for the Ages* (New York: Crossroad, 1992); Charles Cummings, OCSO, *Monastic Practices* (Collegeville, MN: Cistercian Publications, 1986); Monks of New Skete, *In the Spirit of Happiness* (New York: Back Bay Books, 2001).

3. While they are complementary in many ways, the Enneagram is a tool for encouraging individual spiritual growth, enabling one to grow away from the points of weakness and temptation into the points of strength and perseverance. The Myers-Briggs on the other hand focuses more on group interaction, understanding why others behave the way they do, and helping people not expect others to conform to one's own behavioural preferences.

4. SSJD, *Rule of Life*, 3.

5. Ibid., 3–4.

6. Ibid., 3.

7. Ibid., 4.

Chapter 10

1. SSJD, *Rule of Life*, 9.

2. Thomas à Kempis, *The Imitation of Christ* (Charlotte, NC: Ignatius Press, 2005), 57.

3. Rowan Williams, *Resurrection* (Cleveland: The Pilgrim Press, 2003), 36.

Chapter 13

1. *Rule of St. Benedict*, Chapter 53.

Chapter 15

1. Anne Lamott, *Bird by Bird: Some Instructions on Writing and Life* (New York: Knopf Doubleday, 1995).

2. SSJD, *Rule of Life*, 2, 10.

Chapter 16

1. Dom David Knowles, *The Monastic Order in England*, 2nd ed. (Cambridge, U.K.: Cambridge University Press, 1963), 522.

2. Sisterhood of St. John the Divine, *Wings* (1984), 20–21.

3. Ibid., 27.

4. Ibid., 35.

5. Ibid., 43.

6. Ibid., 58.

7. Ibid., 61.

8. Ibid., 70–71.

Chapter 17

1. Helen Bradfield, Joan Pringle, and Judy Ridout, *Art of the Spirit: Contemporary Canadian Fabric Art* (Toronto: Dundurn Press, 1992).

Chapter 18

1. Brother Lawrence, *The Practice of the Presence of God* (Orleans, MA: Paraclete Press, 2011), 95.

A JOURNEY JUST BEGUN

Refrain:
She comes sailing on the wind, her wings flashing in the sun,
on a journey just begun, she flies on.
And in the passage of her flight, her song rings out through the night,
full of laughter, full of light, she flies on.

1. Silent waters rocking on the morning of our birth,
like an empty cradle waiting to be filled,
And from the heart of God the Spirit moved upon the earth,
like a mother breathing life into her child.

2. Many were the dreamers whose eyes were given sight
when the Spirit filled their dreams with life and form.
Deserts turned to gardens, broken hearts found new delight,
And then down the ages still she flew on.

3. To a gentle girl in Galilee a gentle breeze she came,
a whisper softly calling in the dark;
the promise of a child of peace whose reign would never end,
Mary sang the Spirit song within her heart.

4. Flying to the river, she waited circling high
above the child now grown so full of grace.
As he rose up from the water, she swept down from the sky,
and she carried him away in her embrace.

5. Long after the deep darkness that fell upon the world,
after dawn returned in flame of rising sun,
The Spirit touched the earth again, again her wings unfurled,
Bringing life in wind and fire as she flew on.

She comes sailing on the wind, her wings flashing in the sun,
on a journey just begun, she flies on.
And in the passage of her flight, her song rings out through the night,
full of laughter, full of light, she flies on.

Gordon Light
Used with permission